Norman Marsh's
TROUTFISHING

Published by
The Halcyon Press
C P O Box 360
Auckland 1

First published 1990

© Norman Marsh

ISBN   0 908685 60 2

Typesetting: Typeset Graphics Ltd.
Printed in Hong Kong through Colorcraft Ltd.

Norman Marsh's
TROUTFISHING

Dedicated

TO JEAN

Acknowledgements

My sincere thanks expressed to the following.
Brendan Coe of 'Rod and Rifle' who has nourished my writing over the past decade.
Joan Marsh of Invercargill for past and present encouragement.
Norman Nelson Marsh of Wanganui who can always be relied on to 'tune me up'.
Len Prentice of Southland, great fishing cobber and fellow tester of numerous brands of whiskys'.
Vern Williams, talented flyfisherman, a lovely man with a great sense of humour, for his excellent photographs.
John Craze and members of the Motueka Freshwater Angling Club for happy associations.
Members, past and present, of the Southland Flyfishing Club who keep the flag flying.
My young friend Dion Maclean, of Motueka Valley, wise beyond his years and a great guy to share a rod.
John Goddard of Surrey, England, for his unstinting advice and that terribly infectious chuckle.
Finally, to all my fishing friends throughout New Zealand and overseas who, in one way or another, have added to my store of angling knowledge and shared the delights of the troutstream.

Contents

Introduction

Early Days

Most of us cut our teeth fishing for small fish — either spotties from a sea jetty or bullies from a backwater. To a wide-eyed boy, gazing in admiration at his first fish not much bigger than the bait, size is secondary. Nor are the method or the equipment important. A reel of cotton, bent pin and a worm are a passport to Paradise. Even when the rest of the gang has gone home, the young angler is still there, waiting patiently. Such dedication is always a source of wonder to both parents and teachers who fervently wish such singlemindedness could apply to keeping a room tidy and to schoolwork. Often it is the grandparents who seem to recognise that the need for solitude, peace and tranquility is not confined to grown-ups.

But there is more to it than that. For the tyro angler, there is the uncertainty, the suspense, the element of the chase and, sooner or later, the baptism of a fish well and truly hooked. All praise to the bully, that hungry little fish that has committed thousands of young people to a lifetime of angling.

There comes a time in a young angler's life when small fry are banished forever and trout become the centre of interest. My apprenticeship started early, around the age of six, when, during weekends and school holidays I stayed with my grandmother. She lived alone in a small cottage within a stone's throw of a small stream, a tributary of the River Aire in Lancashire. Feet dangling over the side of an ancient Roman bridge, we would gaze down on the occasional angler plying his rod and call excitedly if he hooked a fish. During those balmy days of fresh cream, home-made bread, and penny ice creams, I was well satisfied with my jam jar and net. No big game hunter stalked his prey with greater care. A swift scoop would capture a silver minnow which, enlarged by the bottle glass, would be carried proudly back to Grandmother. How she eventually disposed of this daily procession of little fish I can only guess. Down the old privy after bed-time I fear. It was during one of those halcyon holidays that the unbelievable happened, an event, still clear in my memory. While pursuing a frightened bully under a rock overhang, a small trout dashed into my tiny net. To my young eyes it looked enormous, the most splendid creature I had ever seen. And it was MINE! Into the jam jar it went, its tail sticking out the top and, with a chest like a pouter pigeon, I presented it to my long-suffering, ever-loving grandmother. In the morning it had gone. She said "Back home", but I fear it followed the minnows.

By the time long-trouser days arrived we were living not far from the Leeds and Liverpool Canal. There I fished frequently for 'coarse' fish — roach and perch — the former plentiful but shy, the latter voracious but in small scarce shoals. At weekends, along the bank sides, scores of 'match' fishermen at evenly spaced 'pegs' would compete for prizes, around £100, a princely sum in those days. Skilled they were, eagle eyes intent on watching a porcupine quill float, at the same time lobbing small knobs of 'cloud' bait (a powdery confection of crushed bread crust and custard powder) near the cocked indicator. The object was not to feed the fish but to hold the shoal near the tiny suspended maggot. For the New Zealand trout angler, using a #22 gilt hook on 7x nylon may seem strange but then the roach record was, and probably still is less than two kilograms, with perch weighing a little more. The canal, being still water, contained very few trout.

My father, who often wished I would put my angling energy into mathematics or science, arranged permission for me to fish a small stream no more than a long jump across. But it did contain small trout and to a young boy, it was like being given the keys to the tuckshop. Every Friday after school my heels had wings as I tramped the eight kilometres from town, over the whaleback hill and into that lovely Pendleside valley, once notorious for its witches' covens. A friendly farmer's haybarn provided shelter, and with a few provisions, following a breakfast of ham and eggs, the days would pass as though they were hours. My only company, wild duck, curlew, rabbits and hares, and wonder of wonders, in the purple evening shadows, Mr Fox himself. Such happy times spent searching for trout — normally three to the pound, although occasionally there was a brightly spotted half pounder (225 grams), which meant pleasant dreams for many a night.

I remember the patriarch of the stream. He lay alongside a high stone wall in a pool below the bridge. In the shadow it was almost impossible to see him but a cautious peep over the edge of the wall would reveal him in all his portly glory. Today a two-pound (900-gram) brown, while not to be scorned, hardly raises the eyebrows but to my young eyes that bridge fish seemed enormous and the thought of hooking him made me tremble. But in clear water, despite many attempts, he was far too cunning. That is until it rained.

For once I was in the right place at the right time. There he was, bang in the middle of the pool away from the safety of his hidey hole. His broad olive-green back was almost out of the water as he fed in the flooded stream. After shaking at the prospect, I had no difficulty in hooking him but now, in hindsight, I realise the fish was playing me. After giving me some encouragement to hold him tight, he decided he'd had enough and with one great pull, plunged back into his hole in the wall. I was shattered. One day, during a summer drought, I reached my little stream to find the pools full of trout but most of them either dead or dying. Some were lying on the bottom, others were just able to swim or hold their own against a gentle current. Those still alive were blind, their eyes covered with a grey film and many had body sores. What a heartbreaking sight that was. A farm worker came along and together we picked up dying fish and placed them away from the river. What had struck was known locally as the 'ghost' disease — in the text books it is 'furunculosis', brought about when rivers are low, and the water lacking in oxygen this allowing a concentration of minute parasites.

It was a boy named Jack Groggins who led me into evil ways. Not that I needed much urging. When he told me of a stream over the Border that was absolutely jampacked with trout I became a willing partner. Jack was the only other boy at school who took fishing seriously. His father, a champion coarse fisherman, also owned the local tackle shop, something at that time I believed to be the highest status a man could achieve. How I loved to stand in his small backyard workshop, with its smell of rod varnish, reel oil, and the toasty aroma of maggots in the large Huntley and Palmer biscuit tins.

While I much preferred to fish for trout, Jack and I would occasionally set off in the local bus to a small lake containing a fair stock of roach and perch and a fish we were almost afraid to catch, the sharp-toothed pike. Apart from worms, which we needed for the perch, we carried a small, covered bucket containing a few unfortunate dace, small coarse fish, destined, we hoped, for the pike's dinner. For the roach we had a fair-sized tin full of maggots. Somewhere along the journey the tarsealed road gave way to a bumpy, gravelled country lane and it was there that, after we hit a pothole, the bucket tipped over and sent our live bait slithering beneath the feet of the other passengers. With some hilarity they entered into the spirit of the chase. But the real fun started when, in trying to put them back into the can, a friendly helper knocked over the tin of maggots. Unfortunately, with the heat of the past few days, they had "matured" and had changed into very lively bluebottles. A few flapping fish were one thing but a few hundred buzzing, evil-looking insects were another matter and, after a good tune-up from the bus driver, we were put down with a half hour's walk to the lake.

I wonder where Jack is today? I hope he remembers the bluebottles! He may even remember the time we fished the forbidden stream. This was the one where he said the trout almost begged to be caught. Unfortunately it was private water, stocked by some wealthy landlord for his fishing guests and kept under guard by a vigilant keeper. We had been creeping around the stream for some time when Jack pushed me under an overhanging bank and whispered to keep quiet. I heard the sound of approaching footsteps and someone settling overhead. Then a rod poked out over the bank and during frequent intervals we were showered with handfuls of maggots. We stood knee-deep in the stream until a poke in the ribs from Jack indicated we should move off and, with some very quiet wading, we slunk out of the firing range.

It took only an odd episode like that to convince me that fishing for trout in my little stream was much healthier. Sometimes I would be invited by a member of an upstream fishing club to fish two well-stocked mill dams and it was there that I was introduced to fly-fishing. The mill manager soon weaned me away from worming by landing two fat trout on a dry fly. And so simply. He just stood on the dividing wall between the twin ponds, let the wind blow a fine dapping line out onto the surface and, by dipping his rod tip, he made the fly dance on the water. When a swirl appeared and the fly disappeared I could hardly believe my youthful eyes. It was magic. From that day on anything but fly fishing seemed pedestrian, and before too long, for the pricely sum of eight shillings, I became the proud owner of a second-hand split cane fly rod — an Alcock's 'Golden Guinea' which, in today's currency, cost me about two dollars.

It was about that time I heard of another small stream which, according to legend, held monster trout. It was not privately owned so at cock crow I walked the 11 kilometres over hill and dale to fish a very small moorland 'beck' which, after a long hot spell, was really a series of shrunken troutless pools. By lunchtime, after scrambling through bracken and many rocky gorges, I was very, very hot, and so thirsty that I drank from the stream. It was in the upper reaches that I saw the trout, a very long fish but no thicker than my youthful wrist. It must have been starving because, despite my clumsy casting, it grabbed the fly and, far too quickly, allowed itself to be dragged onto the tiny gravel beach. Thin it may have been but having been caught on a fly, in my eyes, it was my trophy. Unfortunately the trout wasn't the only thing I caught. That thirst-quenching drink had disastrous results when I contracted hepatitis or, as it was known in those days, 'yellow jaundice'. That put paid to my fishing activities for quite some time but in due course a wiser young angler returned to his own little stream at the food of Pendle Hill.

Years later, I returned to live in that community, not only enjoying an extended fishing area, but also having the opportunity to lease a rough shoot. In those days, pheasants, partridge, pigeon and hares were plentiful as were rabbits taken by net and ferret. During that time I also learned to poach, a confession now, at my age, made freely. My tutor was Tommy, a semi-professional poacher who, despite having only one arm, was extremely successful at his nefarious trade. His method of taking pheasants was classic, if not unique. Long before the first songster of the day burst forth, Tommy would be busy placing his brown paper cones along the edge of the wood. Inside, at the point of the cones, he put black syrup, or treacle, with a handful of wheat, barley, or whatever he could find. Dawn, and the pheasants would drop from low perches and strut into the pasture, find the paper hats and don them. Tommy couldn't wait long. The keepers were also early birds and even dull-witted pheasants soon kick off dunces' caps. But some were slow in learning, got a whack for their trouble, and were quickly bundled into his bottomless poacher's pocket.

Of all the game birds in the district, one of the most difficult to shoot was the wood pigeon, a fast-flying, hard-winged bird whose keen eyesight made an approach in open country practically impossible. Tom taught me how to catch them. Late in the evening the birds would settle on the topmost branches of young pine plantations. Thick underbranches made it difficult to see the birds from the ground, but from the hills overlooking the tight packed pines, the blue-grey pigeons stood out like candles on a Christmas tree.

Tommy's method was fiendishly clever. Why bother with the old birds when you could crop the young! At nesting time the soft cooing would betray a nesting bird, whereupon Tommy would climb the tree to the nest and tie a short piece of twine to the leg of one of the two or three chicks. Then, using a wooden needle, he would thread the twine through the bottom of the nest and tie it to a twig. After a few weeks, when the chicks had grown to the right size, he would go around the marked trees and collect his feathered booty. Hardly cricket, but he never killed to excess, always making sure there was at least one bird free in any one nest. Nor would he take rabbits or hares in milk, out of season, or undersize trout. But poach trout he did. During the summer months, when the scythes were back in the barn and the sun not long down over the spinney, his thickset, crouched figure in hobnail boots could be seen slowly wading up the river's edge, searching under boulders and bank. His arm would swing and a trout would describe a silver arc onto the bank. The handicap of one hand was overcome by the ingenious use of a rubber glove pierced with drawing pins at the thumb and forefinger. You would know Tommy in the dark. There was the ever-present smell of ferrets, sometimes nestling in his shirt and occasionally showing a cherry-red, whiskered nose between the buttons. This may have accounted for his being a bachelor, intended or otherwise, and also for most of his winter evenings being spent in a warm corner of the village pub.

Back in the then sooty town of Nelson, Lancashire, I learned the art of fly tying. I can still hear Arthur Hargreaves's voice booming out, as if it was yesterday, and see him reaching for the dreaded, pruning, razor blade. 'Nay, lad, wings are too long and tails are too short!'. It would be a winter's evening with snow on the garden shed roof and an icy wind trying its best to get through the wall cracks and a tiny paraffin stove fighting bravely to keep it out. With fingers like gherkins, but with a touch as delicate as fern fronds, from the gorgeous array of fur, feather and tinsel sparkling in the glint of the 60-watt bulb, Arthur taught me the art. He was a lovely tier.

Under his deft fingers the fly would take shape, wing slope, hackle beard and precisely spiralled body, until, after a final critical gaze, he would pronounce solemnly, 'That'll catch fish'. And catch fish they did. Along the weedy edge of a beer coloured mountain tarn, silvery-flanked, or dark, heavily spotted trout, would fall victim to his skill. Super-tier Arthur may have been, but he was as odd as the rest of us. Despite his having a fly box bulging at the seams with dozens of patterns, he persistently tied on the same team — Snipe and Purple end, Partridge and Orange first dropper and Waterhen Bloa top fly. His only compromise was to alternate the droppers occasionally. Looking back I feel Arthur may have done just as well with other patterns for he was a master of trout tactics, searching out trout wherever he went and fishless days were rare. It was on the rivers that his long hackle spiders and brilliant spinners got a well-deserved airing, the former being fished directly upsteam on short line with long leader and recovered in short, smooth pulls.

He was a good fishing mentor too. He taught by example and, as I now realise, he left many an easy trout for me. 'Na then, Norm, tha can doo' better than that,' he would chastise as my fly fell below, or too wide of a rising fish, or a badly judged cast made a dragging fly. It would be nice to report that Arthur died tying on one of his favourites, but, sad to say, on a fishing expedition on his motor bike, he fell foul of a passing car, suffered severe injuries, and never recovered. It would also be good to record that some of his excellence and polish had taken root, but now, having lived longer than Arthur, I have long succumbed to fly tying short cuts, settling on something less than perfection in the belief that the prime requirements of a trout fly are that it should be strong and consistently catch fish.

The years that followed, wandering the hills and dales, spending wonderful hours trouting, are still rosy in memory. But dark clouds were gathering then in Europe and those halcyon times were soon to end. For the next few years, at sea, on active service, I had time enough to ponder, look back on my early years, and realise how lucky I had been. Later, whatever my expectations of a post-war England, I was restless, disturbed by reading Zane Grey's fabulous stories of trout fishing 'down under'. By chance a friend declined the opportunity to emigrate to New Zealand and, with visions of marvellous rivers and lakes full of very big trout, I took his place. A month or so later, gazing down at my first four-pound (two kilogram) rainbow I found I had indeed arrived in Paradise. During the next 36 years wherever I could find trout I fished for them and during that time learned a great deal about New Zealand trout and how best to catch them. If I can pass some of this experience on to others and still entertain, I rest happy.

Part 1

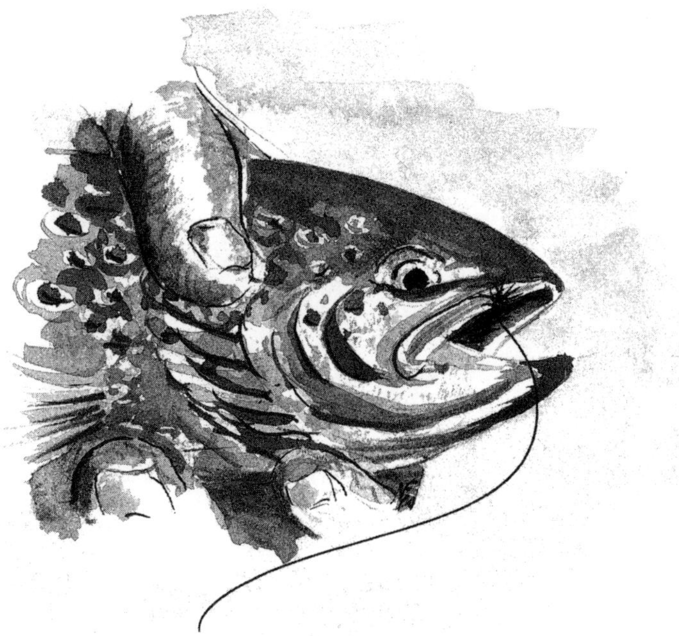

All About Trout

1

Any New Zealand angler with the surname of Youl has every reason to be proud of it. It was a Mr J.A. Youl who, in 1864, arranged and supervised the packing of 2700 trout ova on the *Norfolk* bound from London to Melbourne and Hobart. They were the gift of Frank Buckland, a colourful character of his day, and Francis Francis, the then editor of the English sporting journal, *The Field*. Brown trout from English chalk streams, namely the Itchen, Wycombe, and Wey, provided the ova source. Without modern refrigeration (very low temperatures were necessary to retard hatching), the only solution was to place the ova in moss-lined trays which were packed inside tons of ice.

Earlier attempts had failed but this time, thanks to Youl's perseverance, some living ova did arrive in Australia and were successfully reared. In turn ova from this stock was sent to Tasmania and, in due course, to New Zealand. Despite some early setbacks, the raising of ova and the liberations of trout fry in New Zealand are now a legendary success story, but it is interesting to note that this first small consignment of trout ova was almost an afterthought and that they nestled between 18,000 unlucky Atlantic salmon eggs which perished. Thanks to the efforts of these determined men we now enjoy some of the best trout fishing in the world. Perhaps one way of giving thanks is to record briefly how painstaking these efforts were. Here is an extract from an 1873 issue of the *Lyttelton Times*:

The first of the consignment for Otago proved to be entirely bad when opened, and the second was very little better. But very few fish indeed were hatched out in Otago, and after being liberated in the rivers nothing more was heard of them, whilst Mr Johnson failed to bring any of the five of six thousand presented to this province to life. The ova on this occasion were obtained to the order of the General Government, from the Stormontfield hatching establishment on the Tay, Scotland. Having been placed in boxes containing a few hundred each, they were conveyed to London; each parcel was supported the whole distance by hand in order to prevent jar.

An icehouse for the reception of the ova had been constructed in the forehold of the vessel, and about twenty tons of ice were used in packing around the boxes. The voyage occupied a hundred days. The curators of the Canterbury and Invercargill Society lost no time in going on board, where they succeeded in making arrangements for getting the ova out on the following day. The Invercargill ova were placed in a large case and covered with ice and straw, whilst cases about four feet by three feet, and three feet deep, had been made for the Canterbury portion of the shipment, each case being lined with zinc, over which was a coating of flannel to prevent the ice melting.

The ova boxes were fixed in tight with horse-hair and ice, added to which the cases containing the boxes were covered on the outside with matting, so as to resist the power of the sun, Mr Johnson also took care to do his packing as near the ice-house as possible. The Southland ova were despatched by a steamer specially chartered, while the cases containing the Canterbury boxes of ova were placed on board the s.s. Alhambra, suspended by indiarubber slings in order to prevent jar of any kind. The Alhambra sailed from Port Chalmers at four p.m. on Monday, May 5th, and arrived at Lyttelton about the same hour on Tuesday, May 6th. Mr Johnson had the ova conveyed to the Lyttelton station, where a special train was waiting, and the boxes were suspended by indiarubber slings. The train was only driven through to Christchurch at a slow walking pace, and the boxes were left at the station during the night.

When the ova boxes were opened there was found to be a great difference in the condition of the contents, the whole of the ova in some being entirely bad, while in others there was a large percentage with a healthy appearance. The first layer of moss having been removed from these boxes, the ova were emptied into a stream of running water, which had been previously iced, and subsequently all ova shewing the slightest signs of life were taken out of the stream, and placed in the hatching boxes in the fish house. It may be said there were from one thousand to two thousand placed in the boxes, and that there are several hundreds of these which have a very promising appearance.

Catching trout is easy, as any poacher (providing he is in his cups) will tell you, but we have better things to do than mention his methods. Long gone are the day's when the capture of a trout meant the difference between a feast and hunger. Today, sportsmen have surrounded the trout with a legion of rules — and if you are troubled with sleepless nights, there is no better cure than to read the *Freshwater Fishing Regulations*. Keeping to these rules makes catching trout a sometimes frustrating experience and yet at other times it is as easy as licking stamps.

We cannot enter the mind of the trout but we can at least examine some of his ways and by doing so increase our chances of duping him. Let us start by asking a few questions. Just what has the trout going for him in the survival stakes? Certainly not his brain. Scientists agree that in 'brain for mass' proportions the trout rates pretty low, some experts awarding the bee laurels for intelligence. But when it comes to survival instincts the trout,

Jean Marsh helps a river brown back home. Note distinct marking.

Sea run brown. Peculiar yellow gill spot occurs on some trout.

'Pocket water' where it pays to search every nook and cranny. Trout could be anywhere in this delightful stretch of river.

especially the brown, must come near the top of the list. Successfully stalking brown trout, whether in river or lake, is an art and, like all other artforms, is learnt mostly through experience. The angler who can wade in upstream shallows within three or four metres of a trout and not disturb him is indeed a master of the craft. This is achieved by wading or moving along the bank very slowly, quietly. You can sing *The Bells of St Mary's* for all the trout cares — by quietly I mean being careful not to send out any stream bed or bank vibrations. You should make as small a target as possible.

An important factor when stalking trout is to note the depth at which the fish is lying. All things being equal it is easier to stalk a fish in the shallows than in deeper water because of the refraction of light rays. The trout's circular view, popularly known as his 'window', shrinks as he rises towards the surface while the reflection of the stream bed on the undersurface expands. They say a picture is worth a thousand words and this is never so true as when trying to explain the trout's underwater vision. A glance at the appropriate sketch shows that light rays are so bent by the water that the trout may see terrestial objects up to 20 metres from the centre of his 'window'. The taller the object the easier to see. If the same object is moving, his alarm bell will ring all the sooner. The lesson is soon learnt. What is the point in carefully stalking a trout and then swishing a three-metre rod vertically? Why keep a low profile then clank the stones with your boot? Trout should be courted not bustled!

The Trouts Window

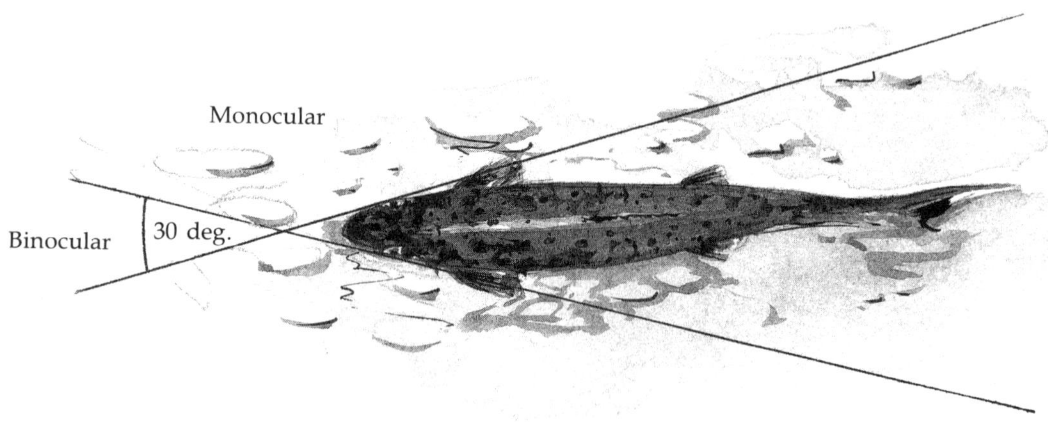

The Trout Zones of Vision

The Effect of Light Refraction

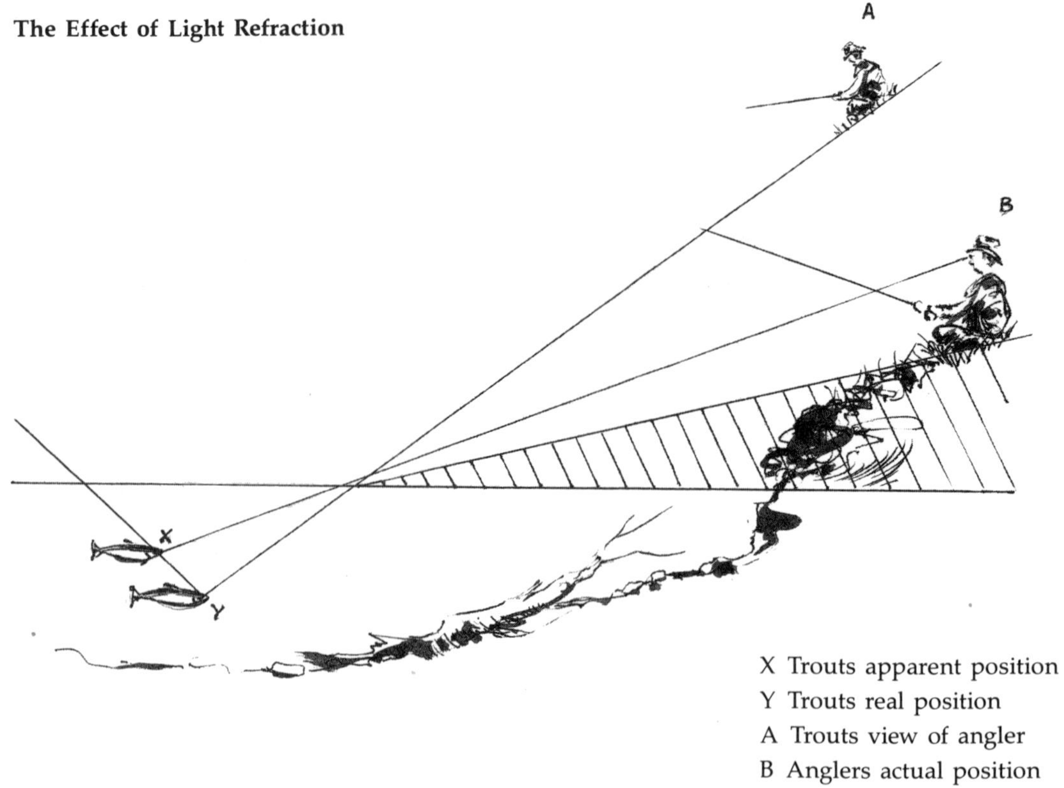

X Trouts apparent position
Y Trouts real position
A Trouts view of angler
B Anglers actual position

After stalking trout for more years than I care to remember I can still be taught lessons by them. Only the other day, after moving up the river bank, slowly and in good cover, I spotted a very nice brown, just under the surface, obviously waiting for a passing morsel. The fact that he took one now and again showed he wasn't alarmed. Creeping (the angler who deems this below his station desperately needs this book), I approached the fish. Confident. Then he was gone. Why? Obviously he had seen something untoward, some slight mistake on my part, but enough to save his bacon. My point is that even taking extreme precautions doesn't mean you are home free. The trout is indeed a worthy adversary.

How on earth (or in water) does the trout in all sort of currents and rapids manage to keep his balance? And how, if he is heavier than water, does he manage to stay in position without wearing himself out? The answer is in the silvery tube we sometimes see when cleaning a fish. More often it is deflated but occasionally we see the air bladder lying close to the backbone and above the kidney, that dark red smear lengthwise below the backbone. The air bladder is perhaps the most important piece of equipment the trout possesses. By using it he maintains an equilibrium between water pressures which allows the graceful manoeuvres we have come to expect from him.

This ability to delicately adjust buoyancy is also the source of some conjecture as to why trout at times refuse to feed, even when ample food is available. One theory goes that when barometric pressure falls the trout's stomach is uncomfortably pressuring the air bladder and to relieve this condition the trout gets as far as he can from the surface. Certainly we have all experienced those days when trout hug the bottom and when even a nymph drifted deep is scorned. Whatever the truth, a great number of us do 'tap the glass' before setting forth and, if on that day we are not up to catching trout, then at least we have an excuse.

A well-known angling maxim is that when thunder is about you won't catch trout but that almost as soon as the weather brightens trout come 'on the feed'. I experienced a striking example of this when fishing at the mouth of the

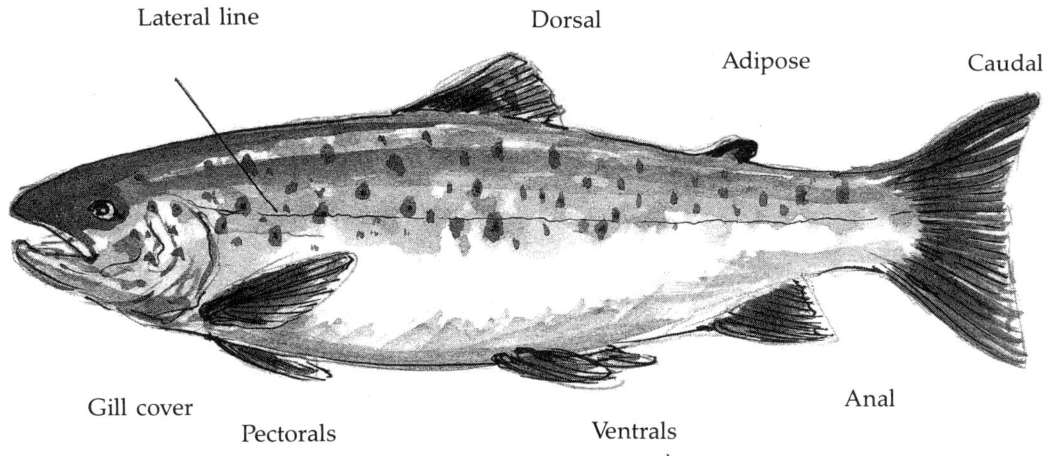

Brown Trout

Worsley River at the head of Lake Te Anau. That night, as Len and I huddled up in the bow of his little boat, we were witness to one of Fiordland's violent thunderstorms with lightning so bright every flash could be seen through closed eyes. But, by the following morning, it was all over with the sun peeping through the cumulus clouds and, although the river was running high, it was clear along the edges. In the newly-created backwaters trout were lined up like Aunt Sallys at the fairground.

One needed only to float a bushy dry fly over them for a guaranteed take and even Len, a novice, managed a fish or two. Perhaps he thought fly fishing was too easy because, despite every encouragement, he never did take it up. Since then I have been dubious of the thunder theory but I have also had enough blank days to keep me guessing. Some days, with plenty of food drifting downstream and no apparent reason why the trout were sulking, I have returned home, tapped the glass and found it going anti-clockwise. Whatever the truth of all this, I think the pressure must be very low to really affect the trout. The best advice I can give you is to always look at the barometer then go fishing anyway.

Can trout 'hear'? They certainly can but not in the sense that we do. Trout are extremely sensitive to vibrations and feel these through tiny pores along a fluid-filled canal running along their flanks and known as the lateral line. Airborne sound waves are ignored. Recently I fished over an unsuspecting trout and nearly jumped out of my skin at a nearby road blasting explosion whereas the trout showed not the least sign of alarm. But the snap of a bankside branch, the stomp of a heavy footstep, or a dislodged boulder or stone will put a trout on full alert. He may dash off instantly or be put "on alert" depending on the degree of alarm. Just

because he fails to run for cover doesn't necessarily mean he is unaware of danger. The angler who fails to recognise subtle signs can spend many unproductive and frustrating hours.

It is important to realise that trout fall into two classes — some are in a feeding mode and others, for whatever reason, are not. A trout that has been thoroughly disturbed will sometimes settle within sight of the angler and, to the uninitiated, appear to be still available. Now is the time to observe the trout and notice the extent of his activity and, more importantly, to assess the situation. If the trout, when first observed, is in a feeding mode, moving laterally or lifting and then becoming stationary, it is a fair bet that he is disturbed and waiting for any further indication of danger. He may return to feeding but he will certainly be harder to catch. Pestering a bothered trout is poor fare. Far better to pass by and seek a better quarry.

The Quarry. One can only admire the sleek form of the wild brown trout.

We humans, supposedly the supreme beings in the animal kingdom, often ignore things unseen. We are deaf to sounds a dog can hear very distinctly. We are blind to colours a bee can find attractive. Many animals' senses other than ours are so finely honed it seems we humans are only on the edge of possible sensations. What of the trout? Does he have a so-called 'sixth sense'? Many anglers will swear that an observed trout, even after some time without apparent cause, will gently drift away to deeper water. I have seen this happen many times — a trout stalked, cast to, and apparently unalarmed, suddenly stop moving and after a minute or so, slip away. Starting from the premise that if the trout had never been approached there would be no reason for him to move from his feeding station it is reasonable to assume that the approach has disturbed him. That disturbance can be measured in degrees. The sudden appearance of a large unfamiliar and threatening form on his 'window's edge' will surely put him into top gear and far away.

But what if the angler approaches from good cover, keeps a low profile and is vibration quiet? Then perhaps, even if he is visible on the 'window's edge', the image is so small as to be of little consequence to a feeding trout. So between the massive invasion and the gentle intrusion there is quite a range. Think of an angler with good scrub or tree cover behind him and standing and one who is almost on hands and knees. Both are to a degree visible to a trout but the one nearest to the trout's level and is camouflaged stands the best chance of being undetected. Then why do some trout disappear before the first cast and others delay their departure? We come back to the 'sixth sense'. Is it possible that the trout, by some instinctive mechanism, can measure the amount of light entering his eye through the window? Can it be that a reduction in light energy blocked by the angler is automatically registered and that, even if small and not immediately acted upon, an impulse is slowly ticking away in some primitive remote alarm system? Whatever the answer it comes to this — the angler will always be at a disadvantage in stalking trout but by understanding the 'window' he can certainly narrow the odds.

Frequent observation of trout behaviour is almost certainly the best shot in the angler's arsenal. Time so spent will pay handsome dividends. Recently I fished the middle reaches of the Motueka River with my occasional angling companion, Vern. Characteristic of this river are the lovely rock formations at the head of many of the long pools and it was from a cluster of these that we watched at least six large trout feeding with gusto. The pool head was very deep and the stream bed not visible. Rock terraces are great insect-collecting agencies spilling the contents into the pools below almost at a drip-feed rate. They also create those creamy suds which, after passing through major rock clefts, form, from the trout's viewpoint, a sizable carpet of insect cake. Back to the pool, each fish seemed to have a defined territory although occasionally their paths would cross and three or four trout would move up the sud feed line together. When a trout reached the top of his short beat he would turn quickly, race down to his starting point, and repeat the process.

As the fish were sometimes breaking the surface my friend decided to try a small dry fly. After a few casts it was obviously a wrong choice. Next he tried an equally small Pheasant Tail nymph but even that usually reliable imitation suffered the same fate. At this stage we settled down to think it out. What were the facts? The trout were very active,

The silvery sheen and star burst spots betray this sea-run brown.

obviously feeding. The food source was spread, making the trout erratic in their upstream course and, although there was the odd rise, it seemed they were taking insects from just under or in the surface film. It was reasonable to assume that, with such a bounty of natural insects available, a single dry fly was unlikely to attract attention. Nor would one artificial nymph among scores, perhaps hundreds, of naturals. We agreed that two things were necessary. One, that any artificial would have to be sitting right in the suds, and two, that it would have to advertise its presence.

Vern chose one of his specials, a near black emerger pattern with dark fur body, a tiny starling hackle and that marvellous innovation, a tiny polystyrene ball wrapped in an equally small piece of panty hose, this being tied behind the hackle. The trout were practically underneath us and only a short cast necessary to place the fly in the feed line. A fish of around 1.5 kilograms swam underneath it then erupted in a mighty splash. But he did not grab the emerger! Exciting stuff though. After five unrewarding minutes we decided on our next strategy. The next time one of the zigzagging trout came near the fly Vern would lift the rod tip and induce movement into the emerger. On the next attempt a trout took a quick sidestep, and without hesitation took the fly.

Down to the depths he went and, with the reel on light check, he took the fly line and some of the backing with it. The fish reappeared on the far side of the pool leaping to rid himself of the hook but the fly held and five minutes later I slipped the net under him, a splendid Motueka brown. Meanwhile, throughout the tussle, his friends continued to scour the suds and, after releasing the fish, it was my turn to win a prize, a smaller fish but still a great fighter. Having seemingly solved the problem it looked as though we were in for a treat but the upstream breeze that had very kindly kept the suds within our casting distance suddenly dropped, and the feed line moved out of reach and the trout with it. This experience shows that reasoned observation of the trout's behaviour, together with the ability to adapt to a situation, is as important to the angler as tying a secure knot or good casting skills.

After this incident we decided to move downstream but the bank was extremely difficult to negotiate — steep, with rafts of driftwood and layered willows over deep water. Eventually we made it, and enjoyed sport along the shallow edge of the riffles. But, on the return journey, things went sour. While traversing a steep bank edge my foot caught in a root tendril tipping me forward into the river and I fell heavily onto a submerged, razor-

sharp rock pinnacle. The point pierced my kneecap and I knew I was in trouble. It turned out to be septicaemea which kept me out of action for quite some time. I live close to the river and from my sickbed, on calm evenings, I swear I could hear the trout chuckling.

I love trout, not so much to eat, although a fresh golden-fleshed fish in breadcrumbs is sometimes on the menu, but in a very caring way. Perhaps love is too strong a word but if caring for and protecting a fellow creature is meant then so be it. I think that the love affair between many anglers and the trout begins with an admiration of the trout's beauty. Then, after a long acquaintance, comes a deep respect for his exceptional qualities, not the least his ability to challenge us. When I watch the trout in his natural clean, fresh water habitat, with infinite grace, rise to a passing mayfly, I marvel at the beauty of this most efficient creature. He and I are locked together but I love it. We dance to each other's tune.

2

Searching for Trout

Unless the fly fisher learns the art of spotting trout he or she will forever be on the back foot. Trout are past masters at concealment, with speckled flanks and dark olive backs blending into any background. The exception are trout lying in quiet water over sand or silt beds. Easily seen trout can be regarded as a bonus especially if they are "available". By that I mean that they are not only within snag-free casting distance but also where they can be landed.

Recently, I sat on a large boulder (one of many used for bank protection) and watched five trout, none less than 1.4 kilograms and the best nearly two, all fossicking in the feed line suds. From my high vantage point it was impossible to miss them, playing musical chairs for the best feeding position and with tantalising regularity. They were swirling for

nymphs in the surface film and, by standing on the bankside boulder and casting over a battery of large bone dry willow branches, I had the nearest fish just within reach. But a tangle of submerged logs in the very deep water below the boulders made the chances of landing a fish from that position extremely difficult if not impossible. But I own a small chainsaw and I have plans!

Generally speaking, trout living in gravel bed rivers are much lighter in colour than those living in bush streams where the water is usually stained or ale-coloured. In streams with multi-coloured gravels, dark cobblestone, and with perhaps stretches of sand bed, trout colour will vary, and even appear to change, depending on the depth and the angle of viewing. A trout lying below the surface appears dark olive or grey but as

24

soon as he nears or breaks surface it is obvious why he is called the brown trout. The trout owes its remarkable ability to camouflage itself to dominant light values reacting on the eyes. This in turn controls skin pigments and varies the colour. The exception is a blind or near-blind trout which will invariably appear almost black showing that trout do indeed need eyesight to tune into the background habitat. These are usually old, emanciated fish with large heads and eel-thin bodies. It really is a kindness to remove them and kill them as quickly as possible. Not a very inspiring end for a once spendid adversary but it is a compassionate, not a cruel, act.

Whereas trout in clear smooth water are relatively easy to see, those in rippled or choppy water really take some spotting, and this special skill comes only with experience. In disturbed water it is better not to look for the trout's complete shape but scan the area for something that appears at odds with the stream bed pattern. In fast water with swirly currents trout can be detected by carefully watching the water pattern for any unusual movement. In slower but deep water, especially over sand, the darker moving tail is sometimes a giveaway, but dozens of submerged objects look suspiciously like trout especially when the current shimmers the river bottom. On and around a river, nature favours rounded objects. Straight lines are rare. Any shape of troutsize length in line with the river flow should be carefully scrutinized.

Only the other day, on the Motueka,

Typical trout lies in a pool. Current runs left to right.

with the water higher than normal, I stalked up a gravel beach watching the shallows and dropped quickly when I saw a familiar dark shape on the bottom. It didn't seem to be moving but I have had too many 'stones' suddenly shoot away to risk scaring a candidate for the fly. After five minutes of covering the object with both dry and nymph I moved nearer, looked hard, and was still convinced it was a trout, even to a pectoral fin. But was it? I moved a metre closer, still keeping low. Now within five metres I was now not quite so sure and moved just a little closer. I leaned over to get just that much better view and found I was looking through the flickering water at three dark stones, so lying in the shape of a trout. In other than smooth clear water these little fiascos are always on the cards and it is from such incidents of trial and error that the beginner learns the craft.

The best advice I can give any budding fly fisher is to stand still. Because of the angle of refraction the trout has a much keener eyesight than any angler and even if we cannot see the trout it is quite possible he can see us. The best thing the angler can do is to keep off the skyline and use whatever cover is available. At 20 metres he or she is within the trout's range of vision and there is the chance of being spotted. In fact, the angler's image, including his surroundings may well be three metres up in the air!

Obviously we have to move sometime, but this should be done with great caution. The trout, unless in still water where he has to do the moving, must face the current so we should approach from behind trying to keep within that 30-degree sector known as his 'blind spot'. Anyone can spot a trout under their feet but to spy a trout some distance away, some knowledge of stalking is required. A basic rule is to always try to keep below the skyline using whatever cover is available. A stark silhouette warns every trout within 20 metres to head for cover. As you approach the tail of the pool one of the best positions is behind a bush or tree and some way above stream level. Looking down onto a pool from a hidden position, especially in strong sunlight, is like being dealt four aces and with trout unaware of your presence, you can leisurely work out your tactics. At stream level facing reflected glare, and especially in broken water, the advantage is with the trout.

From experience I believe that if a trout can be spotted without being alarmed a competent angler has a 70 percent chance of hooking him. Without seeing him and fishing blind, although in likely water, that percentage is much reduced. Is there a trout there at all? What depth is he? Is he feeding? What special little currents and eddies can be used to get the fly to him? All problems when fishing for unseen trout. To see or not to see a trout is the difference between reading by eyesight and trying to read braille with gloves on.

From an approach along a gravel beach it is nearly always possible to reach trout in pool tails. Traditionally this is from below, trying to keep inside the blind sector, keeping body, and in particular the rod, low. Even in shallow water where the trout's outside field of vision is much reduced it takes skill not only to see him but to approach to within casting distance without alarming him. If possible, move from a hidden vantage point, or if there is only a clear grass bank top, then by careful knee and belly approach, mark your target using a prominent stone, rock or weed patch in relation to the trout's position. Then when at the trout's level, where he will certainly be more difficult to spot, scan the stream bed carefully for your marker and the trout's relative position. If the river is running above normal, trout

An almost certain prospect for trout between the bank and the deeper water.

Typical backwater during high summer where many of the river's best trout find a home.

feeding on the shallows may be more easily approached than under low water conditions but even then a cast which places the nylon directly over the fish's back stands a good chance of spooking him. This is where being able to curve cast can pay dividends.

By far and away the best method of catching trout on the shallows during low water conditions is to stalk low, keeping well away from the water until directly opposite the fish. Then, keeping even lower, and finally crouching, move across the beach and make a low horizontal cast to a point no more than a metre upstream and a little to your side of him. When you use this technique, the first object the trout sees is the fly drifting towards him without any telltale nylon . This humble little crab crawl may well generate a bit of hilarity from an onlooker but if the reward is a nice trout — what price dignity?

Fortunately, trout do rise to surface insects from time to time and reveal their position but hatches of mayfly, caddis and stonefly can be somewhat irregular which makes it important for the fly fisher to be able to recognise typical trout lies or feeding stations. As I pointed out in a previous chapter, to survive, a trout must make a profit on the energy used to obtain food and to achieve this he must find the best feeding station possible. This is commonly known as the 'feed line' and in most pools one is usually dominant. In summer conditions it can be recognised by a convoy of surface suds but in spring it may be difficult to find. The feed line brings with it a multitude of of aquatic insects and a surprising amount of fine river debris — twigs, leaves, bark, weed and other small objects. How simple it would be if the whole course of a river was contained in a narrow channel with the trout bow to stern. But how uninteresting! With obstructions such as large boulders, logs and rock bed, the water flow is bounced from one side of the river to the other creating alternating beach and high bank. The resulting currents contain more variations than Grieg's Piano Concerto and to get the best out of his sport the fly fisher must learn to read them.

Take for instance a typical long pool, say half a football pitch in length, with a broad gravel shallow riffle at the top, a 'stretch' where the water is of fairly uniform depth, the pool proper with a smooth 'glide', one bank deep but shallowing to the other side and the tail of the pool, broad with fast water over cobblestones. The pool tail, although not usually the most profitable can, if properly approached, produce good trout. Trout can be found in any part of the river or stream but some parts are more productive than others. You may be lucky enough to spot a fish in the pool tail in broken water or behind a large boulder forming a nice back eddy, but if the water is shallow, great caution in approach is required. Generally unproductive is the thin water (or shallow rapids) between pools, but the pool tail edge is a different matter, especially if the water runs close to willows in small coves of respectable depth. By stalking very slowly up the edge, using the cover of the overhanging branches and by wading out sufficiently to take advantage of the dark reflection of the willows or bank, it is possible to overcome the bugbear of 'glare'. An undisturbed trout feeding in broken water, and within casting distance, is a fly fisher's delight. In riffles, a poor cast is forgiven and given an eager

Oreti River. John Goddard fishes prime area. Trout lie hard against the gravel edge in the left foreground.

trout, sooner or later it needs only a reflex strike to hook him. But fly fishing pleasure is by no means measured by the number of trout landed. Perhaps on a favourite river, it is a delight to stalk up a pool tail edge and simply enjoy watching active feeding trout.

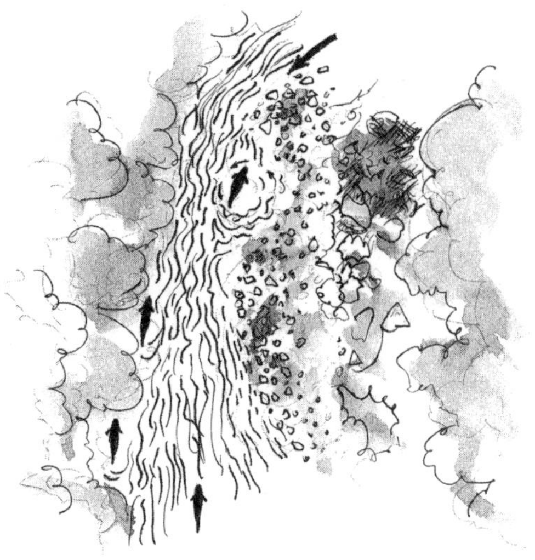

In the pool proper and in the smoother water, the chances of spotting trout are much improved, but being visible to the trout, one should proceed very carefully. I am long past the stage of being surprised when I see a fly fisher stalking slowly up the stream edge, keeping a low profile but with rod held erect! If no cover is available it is vital to present the trout with a very low profile. The widest part of the pool tends to be featureless and of uniform depth but trout food is certain to be concentrated more in some parts than others. The quickening of currents along the shallow beach edge, caused by a larger than usual stone or some captive driftwood, is a good sign. If glare makes it impossible to see the stream bed, the wise angler treats every swirling eddy

behind one of these obstructions as a potential trout-holding spot. Recognising such places is the next best thing to actually spotting a trout. The area to place the dry fly or nymph is predetermined, for the trout will be lying no more than a metre behind the obstacle with perhaps another companion just downstream. Place the first offering at the bottom of the eddy and then work carefully to the top.

On a large pool it is not uncommon for the beach to give way to a gradually rising pebble bank, but if this is devoid of cover the angler has a problem. Under these circumstances walking along on top of the bank edge is near suicidal. The trout will be long gone before you are in sighting distance. The solution here is to use your viewing height to spot trout but keep the rest of the body hidden except for the upper part of the head. Creep if necessary unless the bank is infested with broom, gorse or blackberry.

Recently I hosted an American fly fisherman, complete with his two-gallon stetson, and our first trip found us on a fast boulder-studded bush stream. My experience is that overseas visitors tend to shy off the creepy crawly stuff, opting for long casting. This may be in order on home waters but here in New Zealand our trout give short shift to this upstanding approach. I pointed out the first fish and when he was near casting distance, and knelt in the stream; I knew I had a real angler on my hands. In some situations it is impossible to even creep, crawl, or sidle along the bank edge and, providing the water is not too deep, wading is the alternative. At this low level, unless in very still sunlit water, spotting a trout can be very difficult but, providing the angler wades very slowly with frequent pauses and if the fish is active, there is still a good chance. By noting bank projections or any obstruction forcing the current to quicken and form quiet eddies, one can anticipate trout lies. Any area that is sheltered from the main flow yet handy for a trout to slip out and collect any drifting insect can be regarded as a likely holding station.

River banks collapse from time to time leaving large clods of earth along the edge, mounds that create lovely little backwaters which are favoured feeding stations for trout. A dry fly dropped just upstream of these barriers and left to swirl behind for a few seconds often produces a quiet rise and an exciting sequel. I recall coming across such a trout on a wilderness river. He was lying directly behind a large earth clod near the head of the pool. The edge was gravel and between that and the fierce centre current ran a relatively calm narrow tongue of water. It was just as I prepared to cast for him that I was surprised to see him turn downstream towards me, reverse, and settle a short distance above. Then, to my amazement, he swam upstream, herded bullies up against the beach and, with sudden dashes, seized them. Not altogether unique, though. In Lancashire, many years ago I once witnessed something similar when a large trout in a very still pool full of minnows suddenly charged at the shoal, forced some of them flapping up onto the sandy edge, and snapped up the little silvery fish as they floundered. We often think of the trout as one of natures most graceful and beautiful of fishes but they also seem to be most efficient killers.

Trout lying mid-pool and deep are not a beginners' delight. In fact they are the most difficult of trout to catch. From ground level they are also very difficult trout to see. Where surface glare makes it impossible to see the stream bed the angler should move to a position where trees or high bank on the opposite side provide a dark reflective background. It is quite surprising how this change can reveal otherwise unseen trout. Mid-pool trout on the stream bed are also noted for

inactivity and if weed beds are in evidence they are extremely difficult to detect. This is where the previous advice — to remain still and wait for the trout to move — can be most profitable for sooner or later he must move and reveal his presence. Further upstream we come to the most potentially rewarding area of the pool, the 'eye', that area of water eddying back from the pool 'throat' current and providing trout with the ideal situation. This is relatively calm water to rest in, yet very handy to move out from and intercept any passing food.

The first area to inspect is the calmer centre of the eye where trout may cross and recross any sandy strips or fine gravels in search of insects. Following this a search along the beach edge where reverse currents bring a constant food supply is sometimes rewarding. In these areas trout are sometimes difficult to approach because, facing downstream against the current, they can easily spot the approaching angler. After many years with the trout rod one tends to think there is nothing new but last season, on the Upper Oreti River in Southland, I came across a very big trout, which did surprise me. He was lying against the opposite beach in fast reversed current and the only reason I spotted him was because he actually forced his head and shoulders onto the gravel edge to catch what I presumed to be bullies. His next effort proved even more spectacular and he had to flap his side against the stones to regain the river. Fortunately my companion, J.G., also witnessed the trout's strange behaviour so it wasn't a case of a tall tale!

In situations where reflected light is a nuisance it sometimes pays to defy tradition, move upstream of a potential trout lie and search the stream bed looking downstream. Obviously great care should be taken to offer a small target and if a trout is seen then his position

Trout will be lying along the shadow edge of the willows with at least one good fish resting on the lower stones.

should be noted and approached either from the side or behind. Another prime trout lie is against the 'drop off', that angled underwater shingle bank or apron leading into the pool head. An odd fish may be found lying over on the apron but the main contingent will be nose up to it taking advantage of the back eddies and being first in line for the drifting goodies. Fortunately the clean gravel background makes fish spotting much easier, particularly as trout in this area are usually active. But where the water deepens the trout are hard to see and, as this is where the big fellows hide out, it is well worth considering climbing to a high vantage point to look down into the pool or even crossing to the top of the far bank for a closer look.

One of my favourite haunts is a backwater where no matter what time of day there is at least one trout cruising around. These quiet hideouts offer food for little effort, so it is little wonder the trout find them so attractive. These big dining areas are jealously guarded by the portly connoisseurs and rarely do you find small trout in them. In these productive areas time spent still and watching even for five minutes or more will nearly always prove worthwhile. Reflected light and dark weed backgrounds sometimes cause a problem but backwaters usually have plenty of bank cover and from a hidden position it is usually not too long before a slow-moving, dark shape appears, probably picking up disturbed waterboatmen or bloodworms. In high summer pay particular attention to the shade under any overhanging trees where trout are always on the lookout for falling insects.

While I am reasonably competent at hooking cruising backwater trout I got my comeuppance last season on the Mataura. My good fishing friend, Len Prentice, brother of the well-known singer, Suzanne, with his usual generosity had kindly allowed us the use of his fishing cottage only a few minutes from the backwater. It was a midsummer evening, with the sun still highlighting the pool bed and four lovely trout cruising around it. Quietly rubbing my hands I crept to casting distance and placed a tiny Pheasant Tail nymph in the path of the nearest fish. He passed on. Never mind, the next one was coming so I wasn't too fussy which one I hooked. He passed on too. Turning to a third I gave him my best and got the same result. Every now and again, one would stir up the silt, circle and feed on whatever he'd disturbed. Bloodworms I suspected but even my imitation of these tiny creatures proved useless. An hour later I was still trying, by then reduced to chasing them on my knees. Eventually they tired of the amusement and moved into deeper parts where the river brushed the pool. Occasionally one would surface, a bad move, because waiting at the top was a very small Coch-y-bondhu and the bonny fish took it with relish and proceeded to imitate a Hamilton jet. When a second fish made the same mistake I couldn't help tasting sweet revenge. Both were returned to the water, so no harm done. When I next went to that backwater it was with J.G., a very talented angler, so I stood back to watch the performance and to learn something. I might have been watching myself the season before. My friend spent well over an hour before giving up and his only consolation was in watching me give a similar performance. History didn't repeat itself on that occasion!

If the fishing for the day proves dour,

it's often worthwhile to move to the junction of the main river and a tributary. Small side streams during high summer bring aerated water into the main river and, during normal flow, an extra food supply. Both conditions attract trout and the place to search is on the inside edge of the common current tongue. No matter whether you can see trout or not, a dry fly presented at an angle upstream and bobbed down this riffly edge makes not only for very easy casting but gives the best of all chances of a take. It is such a good trout area that, after resting the stretch for ten minutes, I usually fish it a second time.

The most effective way of spotting trout is to let them show you where they are. This may mean a little patience but it will pay dividends. Never look for a specific trout in a broad stretch of water but remain well back and scan the pool

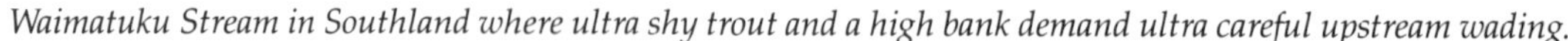

Waimatuku Stream in Southland where ultra shy trout and a high bank demand ultra careful upstream wading.

Perfect example of a 'feedline'. While hungry, trout will rarely stray from this food zone.

Tranquil pool on the Rai, Marlborough, where cruising browns (and rainbows) test the angler. Author hooked one while straddling the tree trunk on left.

overall. Register the general pattern of the river bed and note anything incongruous, particularly something of the right length that looks darker than the gravel. Check for any movement or quick change in water patterns. Mark the spot by some other feature. Scan the remainder of the pool and return to the original suspect. If it still looks promising do not move in for a closer look but send out a dry fly or a nymph well upstream to cover the spot. Only then, if there is no result, move in and inspect again. Be prepared to spend some unfruitful time on suspects but be confident that sooner or later a 'sitter' will present itself. Wherever a change in water velocity occurs there is a good chance of finding trout.

Downstream, and sometimes upstream of large sheltering boulders, are prime lies. Fish the eyes of the pool carefully but do not disregard the gravel edge especially where any bank projection creates a trailing current.

Searching for trout is the essence of fly fishing on most waters. It is a skill to be learned and success comes only with long practice. Trout are masters of disguise, so at every opportunity I make sure they teach me something. So far I have learned that if I keep very still and use whatever cover is available I can sometimes, not always, beat them at their own game. And with trout, you can't do better than that.

3

Troutstream Insects

Joe Bloggs, from long experience, knows that during some time of the season, when the river is at a certain level and in a particular run, one type of artificial will produce results. It did last month and he can bet on it producing again. Well nearly always! Must admit to the odd blank day! Mind you he's been fishing that stretch for the past 10 years and knows every cobble, boulder, sunken log, and rusty back axle. Whether it is a Purple Grouse, a Coch-y-bondhu, or a Dad's Favourite it's the regular old mate that does the trick. Well, nearly always!

Enter Fred Globbs. Ever since he was knee high to his Dad's landing net (folded) he wants to know what makes things tick. Why do trout feed more on some days than others? Why, when there are many mayflies floating downstream do the trout ignore them? Why, during a

fantastic evening rise, is it impossible to hook a trout? He can't resist the urge to find out more of the trout's world and, on the premise that it revolves around trout stream insects, he finds out a little bit more about them. Does this give him an edge on Joe Bloggs? Does this bit of enterprise earn him more trout? No doubt, each is happy in his own world. It is not a contest.

But some knowledge of trout stream insects, regardless of whether you will catch more trout as a result, is a fascinating business, and is just a matter of sparing the time to discover what kinds of aquatic insects inhabit a particular type of water, in what season they are prevalent, and at what time of day they are available to the trout. An occasional autopsy will soon determine if your guess is a good one. The list of aquatic and

34

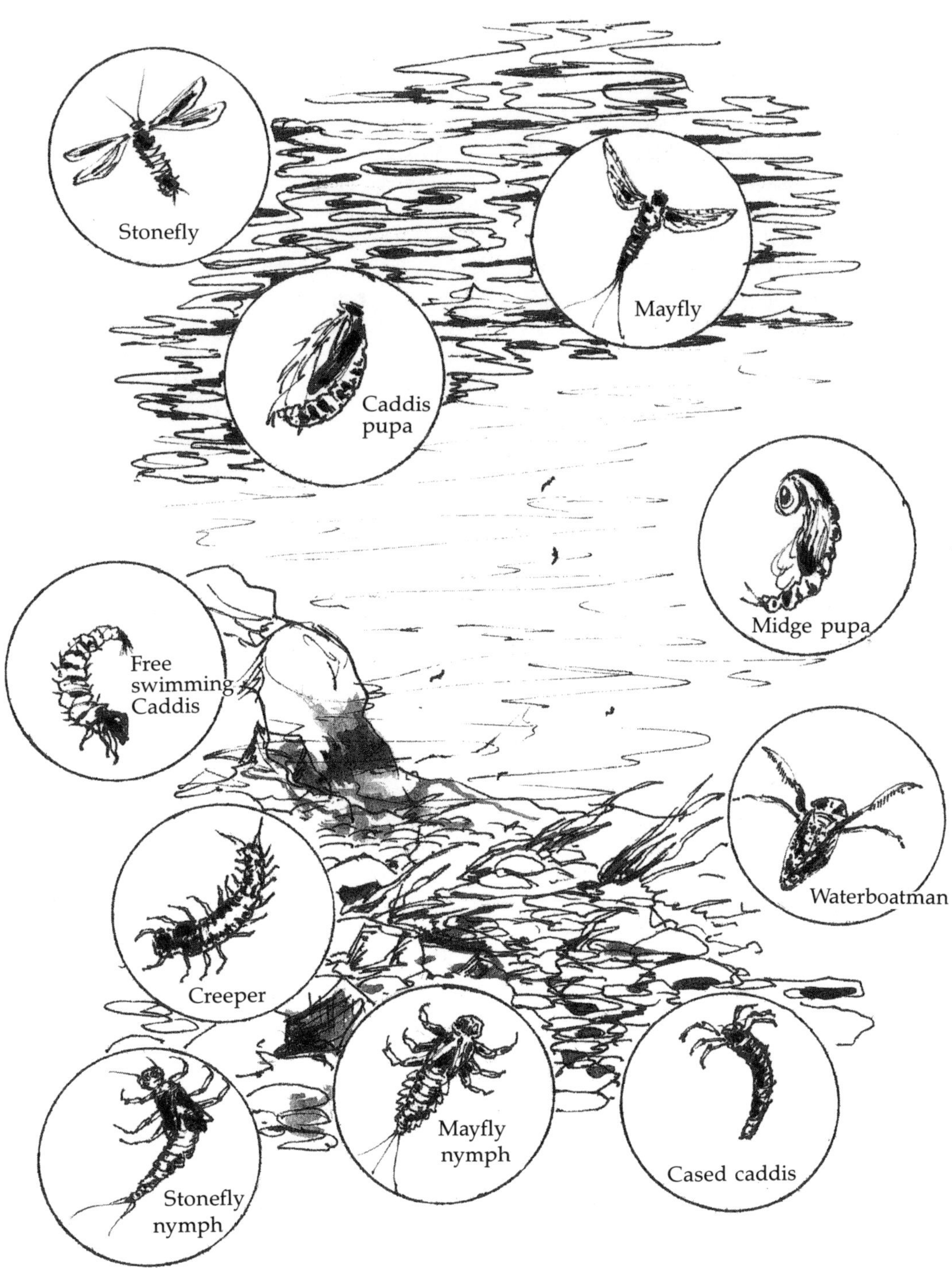

Principal Trout Food Insects

terrestrial insects is long, but fortunately for the fly fisherman, not all fall prey to the trout. If they did we would need a suitcase instead of a fly box.

Let's have a look at some of these small but wonderful creatures:

MAYFLIES

The name was given by anglers to a well-known U.K. insect, but there has been confusion ever since. You see, there are many species of this beautiful insect and having labelled one, they didn't know what to call the others. The problem was, and still is to some extent, that different species have different cycles so that they hatch in general from February to October in England, and from August to April in New Zealand. Confused? Some anglers now call the group 'upwinged flies' but this title, not having caught on universally, only makes things worse. A case of the devil you know I'll stick to 'mayflies'.

Mayflies have a four-part development cycle and, as they spend most of their time under water, they are a common trout food. They start life as eggs dropped into the water by adult females. Then, as nymphs, they go through many changes, or instars, until the mature nymph rises to the surface, and transforms into a winged pre-adult or dun, finally changing into an adult or spinner. This double adult trick is unique to mayflies.

Depending on the species, mayfly nymphs come in all shapes and sizes but common species are easily distinguished from other aquatic insects. The most plentiful are the little brown *Deleatidium* mayfly nymphs, wiggly fellows with three, long, nicely spread tails, while another is *Coloburiscus*, chocolate-coloured, spiny-gilled hunchbacks with short tails, very plump and very sluggish. A third common group are *Nesameletus*, little torpedos, mottled, with feathery tails. They are rapid swimmers. My

popular nymph, the Grey Darter, is a good imitation and, even better is the Blue Darter with its blue Mallard wing case. Full dressings of these are given in the chapter on fly tying.

Mayfly nymph habitats, depending on the species, vary greatly from clean gravel to weed beds, from silty sand beds to moss-covered debris. But a river contains all these features so at some time or other the trout can expect different types of mayfly nymphs to be washed down. I emphasise "wash" because apart from lake, pond, or backwater cruisers, trout do not normally search. They find a comfortable feeding station behind a boulder or log and wait for any passing insect. Trout food is nearly always borne by the current and generally tends to concentrate into 'feed lines'. The angler who learns to recognise these 'hot spots' will be well rewarded. Mayfly nymphs, having tiny claws, hang on tight to the stream bed features, and are pretty secure against even fast currents. But some do migrate in search of a better stone or underwater niches and then, at the mercy of the current, inevitably finish up in the trout's stomach. It is during high water, when the nymph's world is turned topsy-turvy, that the trout can look forward to a banquet.

The transformation to sub imago or dun occurs when the nymph, after forcing its way through the surface film, floats a short distance before shedding its nymphal coat or shuck. The emerging insect is then quite different ' it's a frog to princess story. Delicate wings over a slim tubular body and two or three whispy tails confirm their generic title of *Ephememera*. The trout, of course, have no such romantic notions and few insects escape their waiting jaws. In the process the trout produce the angler's delight — the 'rise'. But trout do not occupy every nook and cranny of the river and enough duns do escape to ensure the survival of the species. Ascending duns can be recognised by their deliberate direct-line flight, as compared to the fluttering flight of caddis and stonefly adults. In the shelter of streamside shrubs and trees, duns settle for a day or so, then change form again, this time into a more brilliant insect with intense body colour and rainbow-tinted gauzy wings.

It is these imago or spinners that spiral into the evening sky, dancing and mating, a brief encounter, leaving the male spent and the female a short, egg-laying finale. Once again the trout gets his chance. After the eggs are dropped or dipped into the water, her mission completed, the female falls almost lifeless to the surface. The numbers are often so great as to trigger a trout-feeding frenzy. A mixed blessing for, with such a surfeit of natural insect targets available, the chances of the angler's artificial being taken becomes a lottery. You may well be advised under these conditions to offer the fish something very different, such as a small Black Gnat or Coch-y-bondhu. When you are driven to desperation, with trout are rising all about you and ignoring a spinner pattern, I recommend changing to a small nymph such as the Pheasant Tail, or my Evening Emerger drawn very smoothly through the rise form. But more of that later.

CADDIS FLIES

Quite the equal of mayflies in the trout food stakes, caddis flies are one of the most adaptable of aquatic insects and come in a great variety of forms. They enjoy a three-stage cycle — egg, larva, and finally the adult. It is almost certain that, if you carry out a stomach autopsy on your next trout, caddis will be in evidence. Most likely the horn-cased caddis, made up of tiny crescent-shaped tubes, constructed, depending on local habitat, from a marvellous variety of materials, ranging from fine gravel fragments to bits of lignite and from sand to small leaf particles. Inside the case is the larva, a soft-bodied insect with strong foreclaws and a tenacious hook on his backside. This makes separating him from his case extremely difficult but the trout solves this by eating and digesting the lot! It is by no means uncommon to find between 500 and 1000 horncased caddis in a single trout stomach. On more than one occasion I have counted over 3000! Uncased caddis are larger and although more vunerable to predators are much more mobile. One of these is the net-building caddis, a dull grey, woolly looking larva with a prominent black head, also frequently found in trout stomachs. Caddis nets are not easily seen but, if submerged twig debris is carefully searched, they can be found. Another uncased sort is the green or olive caddis, recognised by the strong colours, the black and orange head markings and the formidable foreclaws. Predators on juvenile mayfly nymphs, these caddis also become a juicy morsel to the ever-waiting trout.

All caddis larvae pupate. Horncased caddis simply seal the end of the case, leaving tiny apertures at both ends for oxygenated current flow. Uncased caddis spin a nice little cocoon and decorate the outside with tiny gravel fragments which can be seen attached to the underside of many a stone. After varying periods of pupation the caddis fly bites through its temporary tomb and floats quickly to the surface where, without ceremony, it bursts through into the air. Transformation is quick so it is during the trip from stream bed to surface that the trout must make the most of his opportunity.

The main caddis hatches occur during the evening and frequently carry on into near dark and for the angler it is a most exciting period with large trout, normally shy during daylight, becoming almost cavalier as they gorge on the helpless caddis. Different from the usually quiet rise of the trout to a mayfly, the rise to caddis is easily recognised. It takes the form of a splash and during dusk these little white flashes against the dark far bank are a sure signal for the angler to tie on a small wet fly such as a Turkey Caddis, or Grouse and Purple patterns (described in Chapter Seven).

One needs only to shake any streamside bush to observe the adult caddis. They sport wings that are tented over the abdomen, appear almost mothlike in fluttery flight and quickly settle when disturbed. A prominent feature is the long antenna and they are tailless. Adult caddis are well worth imitating with dry sedge patterns during the height of summer when large trout lie close to or under the bank. A small deerhair hopper pattern is deadly stuff if cast onto the overhanging grasses and gently let fall in front of an unsuspecting fish.

STONEFLIES

The name itself makes the habitat obvious. These oxygen-loving insects are a very important trout food and therefore of interest to the fly fisher. While low country streams host some species of stonefly it is in the upcountry and mountain streams that they are almost dominant. Stoneflies, have a three-stage cycle, — egg, nymph and adult. These extremely sluggish nymphs are easily recognised by the double wing pads and the outrigger-held legs. Their colour varies between black and brown and they have small antennae and invariably two rather stout tails. One exception is the Large Green Stonefly nymph, which is olive green with a salmon pink abdomen. A mature numph measures up to 40 millimetres. An imitation of this unique New Zealand stonefly nymph is very

popular with back country anglers and a good pattern for this insect is given in Chapter Seven.

All aquatic insects are tenacious — they have to be to survive periodic floods — but the stonefly stands head and thorax above them all. One literally has to drag a specimen from a sampling net, with a force, in proportion, to pulling a bogged ewe out of the creek. Still water and slow-moving reaches of a river contain few stoneflies but in the middle reaches, even if they are not common, trout regard them with relish. Where they are plentiful, especially in riffles, a stonefly nymph imitation is fairly sure of a response. A word of warning here. In streams where stoneflies are not common, trout, when faced with a large stonefly artificial, will not only refuse but flee to the nearest cover. Stonefly nymphs, after a period from 12 months to two years, depending on the species, shed their nymphal shuck, crawl to the stream edge and emerge as winged adults and, after laying their eggs onto and into the stream, the females spent, also become available to the trout.

OTHER TROUT STREAM INSECTS

While the three classes described above form a greater part of the trout's diet, there are many other insects that, in season, are well worth the angler's attention. One that appears regularly, if not in large numbers, is the dobsonfly, a creature known to most anglers as the 'toe-biter' although it would take a mighty big dobsonfly to nip a digit. They may seem a bit of a Frankenstein to us but trout greet them with open jaws. And no wonder — one average-sized dobsonfly larva must be the equal of a days feeding on mayfly nymphs. This formidable-looking insect can be recognised by its very large black head, soft, putty grey body flanked with what appear to be little tentacles and prominent strong foreclaws or 'nippers'. These unlovely creatures are voracious and carnivorous to boot and woe betide any unfortunate, immature nymph or larva that crosses their path. They are found in most streams and rivers and in spring and early summer or after heavy rain many larva are dislodged from the stream bed.

Fishing the Rai River in Marlborough, my young companion Dion and I found good-sized rainbows lying deep but feeding avidly. In such circumstances, some knowledge of trout stream insects can pay off. Using a suitable imitation we enjoyed the thrill only rainbows can give when hooked. Autopsies on the two we kept for smoking showed our choice had been the correct one. The stomachs were packed with 'toe-biters'. I have seen some ingenious and ingenuous imitations of the dobsonfly larva, one being made simply out of black and brown cotton, but have yet to find a successful one. My pattern of the uncased caddis, the grey woolly caddis larva, is a reasonable imitation (see Chapter 7 for the pattern). I can vouch for its usefulness during the early season when the rivers and streams are running above normal or with colour. Adult dobsonflies, one of the largest of our aquatic insect adults, grey with lacy wings, while interesting in a general sense, are unlikely trout food and of little consequence to the angler.

Wherever the angler encounters quiet bankside stretches or backwaters or weedy lake edges, he should think of the waterboatman. A walk up the shallow stream edge on a summer's day disturbing the myriads of boatmen should be enough to convince the fly fisher that here is a prime trout food. Watch a large trout cruising over silt beds, notice the little puffs of mud as he

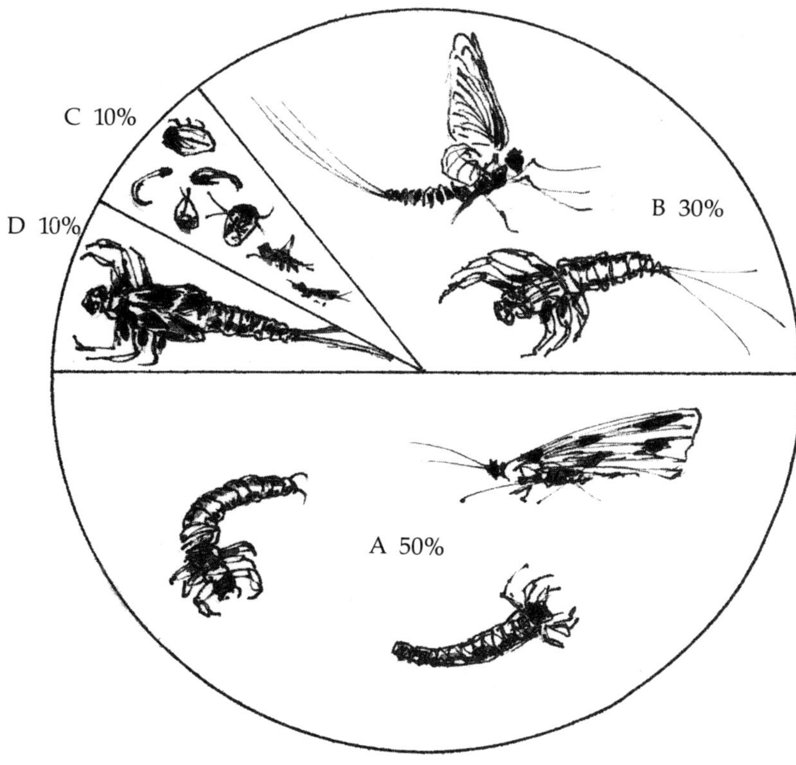

The Trouts Menu

A Caddis
B Mayfly
C Various
D Stonefly

furrows, circles back, and browses through the cloud for disturbed insects including waterboatmen. Forced to rise to the surface periodically for air, these little paddlers are easy prey to the trout but they can be his Achilles heel when an artificial boatman is skilfully cast in his path. In clear shallow water, ambushing these big cruising trout is regarded by many fly fishers as the ultimate in angling excitement.

One season, while fishing a West Coast stream with John Goddard and John Morton (an explosive mixture) I left them to fish the main river while I followed a tiny side stream. Less than 100 metres through the flax and toi-toi it opened up into a sizable pond, mostly weed but with some irregular sand beds. It was like finding Aladdin's cave. There, patrolling the perimeter, were two large trout with another two inspecting the sand beds and none of them less than two kilograms. With little cover it meant my crawling to casting distance over the semi-swamp but the rewards were worth it. All but one made a temporary exit before being returned and even that one felt the hook. All fooled by a No. 16 Waterboatman (the pattern described in Chapter Seven).

Overseas, on the hallowed waters of the English chalk streams, during May and June, there is a period known as the 'duffer's fortnight' when trout, big and small, gorge themselves on large mayflies. We in New Zealand have no comparable occasion, apart from sporadic and local 'mad rises' which can occur any time during the summer and autumn, but we do enjoy one period when hooking big trout, becomes, if not child's play, then something akin to receiving a tax rebate. Not mayfly but beetle time, when droves of both brown and green beetles take to the air and, bless them, often end up falling into our rivers, streams and lakes.

It must seem like Christmas to the trout to encounter literally thousands of these juicy insects floating above them and they make the most ot it. I have seen trout with stomachs distended and beetles dropping out their jaws, still trying to cram in more. Large trout, normally secretive, move out from their safe holes to join in the feast and it must be a sad angler indeed that arrives on the river just after the frantic activity. Some time ago, for a lark, an angling friend and I gave the trout a free feed. We were staying in a fishing hut and during the evening, from below the windows, we collected a handful of brown beetles. The next day, after positioning ourselves above a nice run on the river, we proceeded to drop in the beetles. What had seemed a troutless stretch now became a hurly-burly 'free-for-all' with fish showing everywhere. We were tempted to throw in a hooked beetle for good measure but this seemed too much like underarm bowling so we passed them by with our haloes still intact. One of the easiest artificials to tie, green and brown beetle imitations are a must for the fly box. One or two patterns are given in Chapter Seven.

Surely, one of the angler's most exasperating experiences is when the trout are feeding on little sawfly larvae. Commonly known as the willow grub these tiny insects can be found tucked up inside those ruddy red galls or blisters on the willow leaves. After pupation the larvae bite through the husk and lower themselves to the ground or stream by spinning a fine thread. The larvae, yellow with tiny black heads seem especially attractive to the trout who, once establishing a lie below or alongside willows, feed exclusively on them and generally disdain the angler's artificial. The problem is that the willow grub is so small, equating to an 18 or 20 hook size and, unless one uses something like 6x or less than one kilogram breaking strain nylon, the artificial must appear too unnatural. Fishing with such lightweight tackle near handy willow roots may be sportsman-like but a good fish will break your heart as well as the nylon. The best chance, and it needs a delicate touch, is to cast a little dry fly well up the feedline and hold your breath. Trout can be caught on a willow grub imitation.

Back country anglers know the cicada well. From time immemorial small boys have searched grass and tussock for these noisy but elusive insects and sold them to fishers at the going rate. Some kilted anglers catch their own and others make up weird creations ot imitate these distant relations of the waterboatman. Happy the angler, lying on the banks of a mountain stream listening to the chirp and clickings of the cicada, to the slurping accompaniment of big hog-backed trout. A floating cicada imitation should be fairly sure of a response. These insects present a large and inviting target to the trout and during the flight season a big trout makes the best of it and so should the angler. A large deerhair Humpy or a large straw-coloured artificial dry is good medicine when the cicada is about. For the fly tier a good imitation is described in Chapter Seven.

More than 300 years ago, Izaak Walton, our great angling forbear, included the hawthorn fly in his now famous list of artificial trout flies. A close relation of the midge and the daddy-longlegs this fly with its black spotted wings is known in New Zealand as the blossom fly. Naturally the trout couldn't care less what they are called but he knows a mouthful when he sees one and on windy days in the summer months, it is not uncommon to find blossom flies taken. I imagine only one in 500 fly anglers knowingly carries an imitation of the blossom fly but if the

fly box holds a black palmered-type fly he could be in business. Wherever hawthorn trees are in evidence, a change to large black gnat or to the blossom fly imitation, fished in the surface film, can often turn a blank day into one to remember.

I recall fishing the Mataura with an American friend some years ago. Fish were moving but with those peculiar whorl rises which often indicate aborted nymphs or subduns in the feed line. Try as we might, and using various nymphs and other wicked creations, we couldn't connect. It took my friend, Max Horowitz, to point out a little black insect sneaking silently along the willow edge. It didn't travel far before it disappeared in an underwater gulp. After the penny dropped, and with some of his Black Gnats, we finally came to grips with some splendid Southland browns. Since then I always carry a couple of Black Gnats in the fly box ready for that special day.

One of the smallest of the trout stream insects is the midge. These important little chaps, often mistaken for sandflies, appear on the river in countless thousands especially in the late afternoon and evenings. They also cause much head-scratching by the fly fisher because they are so small and difficult to see in the gathering gloom that the scores of rising trout seem be to taking 'nothing'! No wonder, because the the trout are not rising in the true sense but feeding on the ascending midge pupae, tiny curved insects with conspicuous, dark wing cases and bulbous heads. Many anglers with an empty bag after fishing for ravenously feeding trout, feel humiliated. I still do, but I have learnt that the trout, with so much natural food to choose from, is not deliberately ignoring my offering. I make sure they see my 16 Goddard Midge Pupa by drawing it smoothly in front of their snouts. While

I would rather see a trout rise to a dry fly in clear conditions I take great satisfaction in hooking a late evening mystery fish and enjoying the rip, tear, and bust antics of a big brown in the dark.

For those who often fish lake edges, ponds, or backwaters, the damselfly is an important trout food insect and well worth imitating. While they are usually more available to the trout as nymphs, when adults are flitting around the edge of a lake, or anywhere in quiet water, trout will leap quite some distance to take them. Some time ago my friend Brian Moyse, from Christchurch, presented me with a most realistic imitation of a red damselfly which has proved its worth on more than one occasion.

Mention must be made of the familiar daddy-longlegs or cranefly. While the spider-like adult is rarely taken by the trout, the grub-like larvae is a most welcome addition to his fare and appears often in trout stomach autopsies. It is a common trout food, and for the amateur fly tier well worth imitating when streams are running full or better still, falling after rain. An outstanding memory I have is of deceiving a very big brown trout in a Fiordland river. What made this fish special was that he took a cranefly larva imitation without the slightest hesitation, obviously fooled by the piece of rubber band wrapped around a caddis hook. Now you can't get a more simple dressing than that!

Since settling in this trout-laden corner of New Zealand I have had another problem to tackle. In fruit-growing areas trout have become used to taking the passion fruit hopper, a small delta-winged insect. This little pest, while being good trout tucker, has the reputation for being difficult to imitate and it took me quite some time before I came up with the answer. Since then my imitation has proved reliable in consistently fooling the sophisticated Motueka browns and, if further proof is needed, duping those diabolically shy Riwaka trout. This simple but effective pattern is described in Chapter Seven.

It remains only for me to urge you, by means of a small, fine mesh net, and a pocket magnifying glass, to examine the wonderful world of the stream bed. You may well find as you marvel at nature's art in miniature that becoming familiar with trout stream insects, is well worthwhile.

4

The Artificial Fly

Dry, Wet, Nymph, or What?

Fly fishing is a complete mystery to outsiders and the mystique surrounding trout flies must seem somewhat akin to Druids' rites. I mean, take for instance, Greenwell's Glory. Mention the name to any fly angler and he or she may well picture the olive-coloured trout fly with the blackbird wings tied for Canon Greenwell in 1854 by Arnold Wright, a well-known fly dresser of the day. To the newcomer it could well mean a new brand of pumpkin soup. Red Tipped Governor hardly bears thinking about, whereas Twilight Beauty, could well raise the eyebrows. What a plethora of trout fishing lore for the beginner to absorb!

Only the other week at the local fly fishing club, during a fly tying session, I tried to imagine I was a disinterested party, sampling the conversation. 'What's the wing case made from?' 'Blue mallard specula.' 'Mustad.' 'No, Patridge.' 'Remember a slack loop when tying in!' 'Pinch of blue rabbit for the thorax.' 'Three turns only for the ribbing.'

Perhaps the more experienced angler will be patient if I start with a little background. Trout flies are no recent phenonema. Evidence exists, in the form of Grecian drawings, that a feathered lure was used to catch fish as far back as 504 BC. When one thinks of the gigantic strides in technology since then, it is a humbling thought that as far as sport fishing is concerned, we haven't moved very far for the past 2000 years! To be sure we have more sophisticated equipment, but basically our little bits of hook, fur and feather, are very similar to the ones our forbears used.

Born in 1599, Walton, our famous

forbear although primarily a fisher for coarse fish such as the roach, perch, pike, carp (no wonder he was known as the Compleat Angler), did fly fish for trout. So we go back a long way. Walton's claim to fame lay in offering a list of imitation trout flies that were copies of natural insects. These are described in his well known *The Compleat Angler* first published in 1653, when Elizabeth I and Sir Walter Raleigh were front page news. In those days, rods were usually made from wood — hazel, ash, willow or lancewood. Fly fishing lines were of braided horsehair, the plaits diminishing to a two or three hair twisted tippet. Imagine fishing upstream in a strong downstream wind with such a lightweight line. On windy days, using rods of more than 4.5 metres, those buckle-shoed baggybreeched anglers let the wind do the work and lowered the rod tip to let the fly settle or dance over the stream. And, of course, such an outfit was ideal for downstream wet fly fishing, the current catching the line and swinging the fly over the trout. No different from today.

Over the following 200 years there was no remarkable change in the materials or design of trout flies, but then an inspiration occurred to an enterprising fly fisher and the modern floating fly was born. Many have been credited with its creation but with the passage of time and the truism that 'there is nothing new under the sun', he or she is anonymous. However in *A Book of Angling*, written by Francis Francis and published in 1867, the author refers specifically to the dry fly and entreats the anglers of his time to use both wet and dry depending on the river fished and the water conditions.

In that era, Frederick Halford, a talented fly fisher of the English chalk streams and an amateur entomologist, gave a new dimension to the dry fly by tying what he termed exact copies of the natural insects. So superior did he regard floating flies that in his book *Dry Fly Fishing in Theory and Practice*, published in 1889, he went so far as to condemn the use of other than floating flies on chalk streams. In those days hooks were tied to gut, a product of the silkworm and very variable in quality, but in the late 1890s the development of eyed hooks turned the world of angling upside down. It was now possible to imitate the smallest of flies, neatly and with the advantage of being able to change the fly with comparative ease. The difference between old newspaper and a soft toilet roll, between a battery and A.C., it revolutionised fly fishing as did nylon fishing lines in our time. Since then, apart from one or two embellishments, the dry fly has changed little — the construction of Halford's flies and our own is practically the same. What has changed is the present-day fly angler's conception of how a trout fly appears to the trout.

Up to the turn of the century it was a choice between wet fly and dry fly, with nymph fishing, as we know it, practically unknown. We have to thank George MacKenzie Skues, a London solicitor and fisher of the Itchen, a small but famous English chalk stream, for popularising

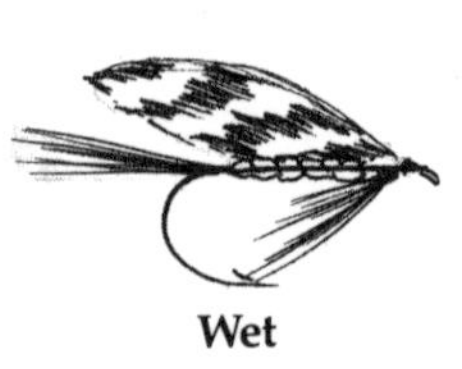

Wet

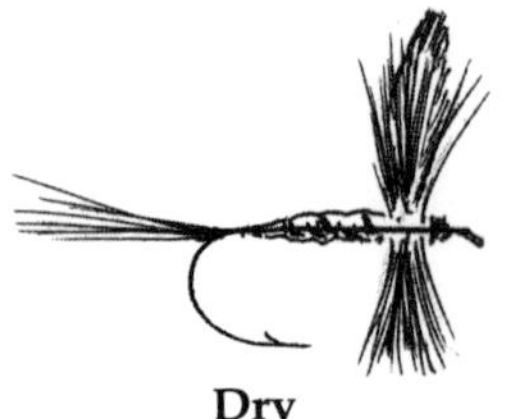

Dry

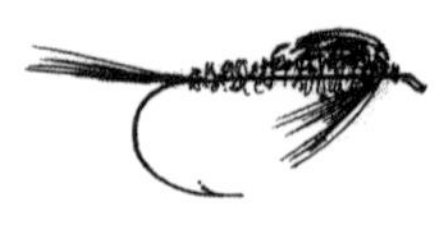

Nymph

nymph fishing. His many books, including *Minor Tactics of the Chalk Stream*, published in 1910, have become classics not only for the wealth of information but also for the most enjoyable style of writing. While it must have been obvious to a great number of fly fishers that 90 percent of the trout's food is taken below the surface, it took Skues to persevere in fishing for trout with an imitation of particular mayfly nymphs. On an English chalk stream this type of nymph fishing requires all the delicacy of fishing with a dry fly and I wonder what Skues's reaction would be today if he could watch a Buller fly fisher, pitching a #10 Buller Caddis into white water with red wool for a sighter. Times change, of course, but I'm not sure he would approve.

Closer to home, after the introduction of trout and salmon to New Zealand in 1878, bait fishing, spinning, lure and wet fly fishing were the recognised means of taking trout. Dry fly was practically unheard of. Nymph fishing too is a comparatively recent phenomena, popularised by Tony Orman in his book *Trout with Nymph*. In the great North Island lakes, mainly Taupo, Rotorua and Tarawera, there are still thousands of anglers during the season quite content to either spin or trail a lure behind a boat, not the most interesting method but one suited to fishing a large lake where the main source of trout food is the smelt. On the famous Tongariro, up until recent years, downstream lures such as Parsons Glory or Tamati, were the standard techniques, but today, many anglers fling all sorts of popeyed things at the large, unseen rainbows. Not all of them, mind you — some do fish with a heavy orthodox nymph or a brightly coloured lure and such exponents are a pleasure to watch. But many locals now give this crowded river a wide berth during the height of the season.

From the foregoing you can see that what constitutes a fly to one fisherman means something entirely different to another and that throughout the ages fishing flies have always been a controversial subject. Providing it is lawful and does nothing to detract from other anglers' sport, then the type of fly used should be entirely up to the individual: Let's face it — we go to a great deal of trouble and expense to catch the trout and in waters in no danger of being overfished it makes sense not only to harvest them but to have some fun in the process.

But anglers are just as unpredictable as their prey. For some, the simplest and quickest method of extracting trout is to throw a worm into the river and wait for results. Others, relying on the trout's natural aggressiveness, entice him to clamp onto a flashing hooked spinner. The second angler may not like the method of the first, and a third type of angler may dislike both. The fly angler often regarded as a snob by the others, has the distinction of trying, in a sense, not to catch the fish. He or she uses a fine nylon and fine hooks and, because the trout may reject the artificial fly quickly, the fly fisher stands only a fair chance of hooking tne trout. He or she may spin when the occasion and the water makes it sensible to do so and may still be considered a fly fisher but the gulf between bait and fly is wide. The fly fisher is sometimes branded with the name of 'purist', implying that he or she looks down on other forms of trout fishing, but it is rare to find a fly fisher so bigoted as to want to deny other legal methods. What may be taken for a superior attitude may be that, after all the apprentice years, the fly fisher simply doesn't want to fish by any other means.

It is difficult to explain the fascination of fly fishing. Perhaps one who has fished for the gigantic salmon of Norway or for the elusive bonefish of the Bahamas may argue the point but I for one think fly fishing is the most delightful way of confusing not only the trout but the caster. Of one thing I am sure — from the moment a novice experiences the almost unbelievable when a trout takes his offering, nothing more than a concoction of hook and feather, there is no turning back. The one sole ambition then is to repeat the performance as often as possible. The trick is to know where and when to do so. The dry fly fisher enjoys the ultimate in trout fishing experience, that thrilling moment when, in full view, in clear water, a portly trout, spying an oncoming dry fly in his little window, rises to it. But all trout are not that obliging. Trout are no different from any other wild creature. To survive they must weigh up the value of the presented food against the effort needed to secure it.

Regardless of whatever we choose to call the fly, or what we think it imitates, it is the trout's conception that matters. If the fly is presented over him so that the imitation appears natural and if he regards it as food and he is not in a 'selective feeding mode' then he will take it. If he is feeding selectively, that is taking one particular insect to the exclusion of others, then we arrive at what is probably the true attraction of dry fly fishing — picking the right fly for the right occasion. On rain-fed rivers with rock-studded pools and attendant riffles and rapids, a dry fly riding cockily down the current stands a good chance of being taken. Standing in such a river, with the current swirling gently around his or her legs, casting a supple fly line upstream and dropping the dry fly at the top of a ripple, is to the fly fisher the ultimate angling pleasure.

But perhaps a drift of migrating mayfly nymphs is in full swing, carried under the surface by the current and taken avidly by the trout. What then the dry fly? In fact, slim pickings indeed. Enter the nympher, the tackle the same as the dry fly angler's but with a small imitation of the natural nymph on the tippet end. With similar skill he or she pitches the nymph upstream above the active trout, letting it drift down the feed column just under or in the surface film. If the angler can see the trout, he or she watches intently for any suggestion that it has moved to take the artificial nymph. If lucky the angler will see the white flash of jaw at the right moment or perhaps the glint of a gold or silver flank. In many cases nothing at all will be seen but instinctively the hook is set at some undefinable movement. This, the mark of the talented angler. He or she will fish the same type of water as the dry fly angler and, if there is a hatch of mayfly or some other insect, may change to a dry fly and win both ways. But here's the rub. It is all too easy for the nymph angler to become addicted to the nymph and when an active trout is spotted that could well take a dry, the temptation to use the ever appealing nymph is very great. In this case perhaps the fish has become more important than the fishing?

What of the wet fly angler? What type of water is he or she at home on? Why use this most ancient of fly fishing methods? As we know, stream and river vary not only by the day but by the hour and trout food is not always drifting downstream. Sometimes the cupboard is temporarily bare and it is often under these conditions that the wet fly fisher scores. Trout are normally hungry blighters, aggressive and very much territorially minded. Even fingerlings will try and oust a smaller competitor, a trout in the path of a wet fly fished downstream reminds me of a spaniel ambling up a woodland trail when a rabbit suddenly dashes across his path. No question about the reaction. He instinctively chases it. So with the trout and the fly, but bear in mind the tiny lure (tradition ensures it being called a wet fly) is travelling at approximately 30 kmh when it sweeps across the trout's vision and he has little time to inspect it. He may chase it but there is no guarantee he will take it. Conditions have to be just right. The fly may appear too big, the nylon too obvious, or the fly may suddenly drop in speed as the current weakens. Apart from skill in casting and anticipating where trout are likely to be lying, hooking a trout on a wet fly is a matter of luck. Even then, with the trout begging the fly upstream, he is still easily lost. But to the wet fly fisher, this method, with its gentle methodical casting, the smooth swing of the line, the anticipation as the line finally bends into the critical taking position, allows for ample contemplation. And isn't that just what Izaak recommended!

There is one type of water that not only encourages an all-round approach but on occasions positively demands it. I refer to lake fishing where, faced with a vast expanse of apparently troutless water, even the veteran trouter experiences a flutter of doubt. Here, no one method can claim superiority and it is a wise angler who is prepared to dance to the trout's tune. Big lake trout, along a calm lake shore are the easiest to spot — you keep still, the trout moves. Lake trout need to patrol to survive. They generally swim a regular distance between certain points and repeat the performance almost as a ritual. It is not difficult to move ahead of them and lay out a small dry fly in ambush. Keeping the fish in sight is vital to success and here comes the bugbear. Without a shore or bank background the slightest breeze riffling the surface effectively renders the angler blind and he may wait forever if the trout has spurned his offering, or even worse, missed seeing the fly. So, apart from the first few hours of calm during the morning, the dry fly angler will have the rest of the day off, unless he or she wants to chuck and chance it.

For the wet fly fisher the wind becomes an ally, hiding not only the angler but the telltale nylon now submerged and difficult for the trout to see. If the wind is onshore so much the better. While the wind makes casting a little more difficult it is drifting trout food inshore and the trout are well aware of this. Here the traditional wet fly, perhaps a Red Tipped Governor or a Twilight Beauty, comes into its own, the subtle retrieving movement drawing the attention of the cruising fish. As on the river, patience is necessary but sooner or later the fly must encounter a trout, with the chance of a sudden pull.

One of the most prolific lake trout foods is the midge pupa not yet so well recognised in this country. In the U.K. where trout stream fishing is even more at a premium than in the past, manmade trout-stocked reservoirs are the mecca of the vast majority of fly fishers. On these distant waters, attractors, chompers and buzzers, trout fly creations which have yet to reach our shores, are used. The effectiveness of midge pupae imitations was brought home to me by one of the doyens of English stillwater fly fishing, John Goddard. Fishing Lake Wanaka and using his Suspender Midge creation, he duped more sophisticated kiwi trout than I care to recall. This very simple artificial emulates the surface-film, floating pupa by using a tiny ball of ethafoam in fine, white, nylon mesh. More details of this successful imitation are given in the later chapter on fly tying. It seems that although we have the bigger trout, we can still learn a lot about catching them. Writing of J.G. and Wanaka reminds me of a little miracle. After our usual three-hour blessing of calm during which we duped one or two cruisers on the dry fly, a sou'west breeze soon turned into a stout wind. Now I have seen some pretty good casters — enough to know I'll never be one of them — but, not satisfied with throwing the fly line out towards the middle of the lake, this genial Englishman, for good measure, threw half the backing after it! Then came the crunch, literally! His carbon fibre threw in the towel and splintered near the butt. Sadly we wandered back along the lake edge. A good fish showed near the shore and John insisted I try for it while he continued back to the car. But the trout gave me short shift and I was at the car to greet him. He was carrying his shattered rod and someone's cast-off, a broken, half-metre piece, from a fibre glass rod. Surely it couldn't be the exact taper to slide over the broken ends of the carbon fibre? It was, and by scoring and breaking off the found tube, it proved to be a perfect splint. Together with some plastic glue it made an excellent repair!

From what I have said the reader may think that it is the all-round fly fisher who receives the most enjoyment from the sport. Not so. He receives no more than those who use the dry fly, the wet fly, the nymph, the lure or bait. As long as anglers continue to pursue trout we will always employ a variety of methods and who is to say that one is better than the other. But for the fly fisher, the satisfaction comes with deceiving trout by whatever titbit he chooses. Dry, wet, nymph, or what? Your choice!

All green, brown, chuckling water and trout.

Wintery weather on the Eglinton.

A good example of stalking very wary trout.

An Oreti backwater trout meets his match.

Fly Tying Materials

5

Invariably, when visiting a sports shop, my first objective is to inspect the fly tying material. Bright coloured feathers and shiny tinsels draw the fly tyier like a fly to a jampot and, despite having accumulated enough feathers to stuff a mattress and more than enough fly tying bits and pieces to decorate a Thailand Temple, I still leave the store with a much lighter wallet. All fly tiers are the same — squirrels, addicted, doomed forever to collect everything from canary cast-offs to combings from the cat. The great unwashed may well laugh at such idiosyncrasies but the typical fly tier lives in dread of being caught without the right material and it takes only a magazine article describing a new super-duper trout fly to send him or her ransacking through mothballed feather boxes. Whether it is a tail feather from the

Argentinian crow or rump fur from a Tibetian musk ox, he or she stands a good chance of finding it in the motley collection. Fly tiers can be easily recognised by their propensity to stroke blue-furred cats and, at weddings and race meetings, stand with glazed eyes observing the feathered millinery of female guests. Acquiring fly tying materials can almost become a sport in itself especially when it means trying to catch a mean rooster in a muddy farmyard, picking the best out of the family sewing box without being caught or making yourself scarce after forgetting to take those Mallard wings out of the back of the refrigerator.

My feather collecting days go back a long time to when I tied my first trout fly. On my schoolboy allowance a real vice was out of the question but a fly tying article in the *Fishing Gazette* caught my attention. It mentioned, for the poor, and the likes of me, a fly vice substitute in the form of an engineers' pin vice, inexpensive and obtainable from the hardware store or as they were then known, the 'Ironmongers'. It cost two shillings, which seemed like a small fortune, but having just won a schoolboy's snooker championship and collected a £1 prize, I splashed out and bought one. A pin vice is a short steel rod with a tiny drill chuck on the end, ideal for holding small hooks and, after my father cajoled an engineer friend to weld it to an old table tennis net clamp, I was off in search of feathers. This proved most enjoyable as the little beck I fished was four miles (6.4 kilometres) from the town and, even though traffic was nowhere near as heavy as today, casualties lay all along that lovely twisty road. Magpies, crows, the odd grouse, blackbirds and thrushes galore, rabbits, hares, weasels, stoats, were all taken home for skinning, much to my mother's dismay. They were cured with rock salt and the feathers mothproofed and for days after the house would reek of mothballs. My father, with his dry sense of humour, swore this kept not only the moths away but also his friends! Doting and amused relatives became used to my begging visits for embroidery or knitting scraps and an hour's work after school, scrubbing the backyard of the local poulterer, earned choice partridge, pheasant and duck feathers.

My early attempts at imitating shop-bought flies raised only affectionate smiles from my parents and schoolboy friends but to the local trout they were a source of ribald humour. Perhaps if I had persisted, success would have come my way but young anglers have an aversion to being laughed at and I quickly reverted to the shop-bought articles. What saved the day was my avid appetite for angling

books. I haunted the local library, soaking in as much angling lore as possible much to the detriment of school work. At the time, had there been a trout fishing examination I would have been a certainty for either Oxford or Cambridge. It was when I was visiting the library, nose into a book on fly tying, that a voice over my shoulder enquired if I tied flies, to which I replied, 'No, but I'd like to'. And so began a friendship with Arthur Hargreaves, an ex-weaver, but through an accident, partially disabled. And, lucky for me, an expert fly tier.

A fast bike ride after school would see me watching Arthur tying the delicate, soft-hackled flies that are so successful on North of England waters. Partridge and Orange, one of his favourites, tied not with ordinary orange floss silk but with hot orange, a deeper shade that turned mahogany when wet. Another, the Waterhen Bloa, a slim spidery fly tied with the delicate Payne's Grey, a spoon-shaped feather from the underside of a waterhen. Watching his nimble fingers made fly tying look so easy, and, under his tuition, my crude efforts blossomed.

Up he comes.

What joy, when, on a later visit to my favourite stream, one of those chuckling trout couldn't tell my homemade fly from the real thing and ended up with the smile on the other side of its face.

At the time I was so enraptured with learning the little skills and methods of fly tying that Arthur's real legacy didn't become apparent until many years later. This was to appreciate that a trout caught on a fly of one's own creation means a double pleasure. Now 50 years on, I try to pass on Arthur's philosophy. Fishing and fly tying should be FUN. And, so saying, let's have some with fur and feather.

FLY TYING TOOLS

Fly vice: Many years ago I bought a Sunrise Tyemaster, a vertical split jaw vice, screw type closing. I must have collected some back pay at the time because I purchased an extra one, thinking that it would come in handy when the first one wore out. After 20 years I am still trying to wear it out. Then it cost about ten dollars, now near trebled. But what is the interest on that ten dollars over 20 years? About the cost of a new Sunrise Tyemaster I reckon! Actually any moderately priced vice will give good service.

Hackle pliers: These ingenious clamps are essential for the modern tier. In the past, it was not uncommon for flies to be tied with fingers only from start to finish. How they managed this has always been a mystery to me but I suspect they had seamstress's or surgeon's fingers. One can only hope the trout appreciated the subtle difference. The important requirements for hackle pliers are that they be strong in the grip and that the jaws clamp perfectly flat and, if possible, are serrated. Make sure there is plenty of room for your finger in the ring.

Bobbin holders: Two kinds are normally available — short and long spigot. The short will give you a better grip of the bobbin but not such a nice control of the winding thread. The long spigot gives excellent winding control.

Scissors: Buy the best you can afford. The need here is for fine delicate sharp points that can sneak into awkward feathery places. A cheaper, larger pair is useful for snipping wire or tinsel or cutting thick quills. Again, make sure the finger and thumb rings are large enough.

Scalpel: A good scalpel is a joy forever. The complete item can be bought from the chemist — handle, dear, replaceable, fine-pointed blades, cheap. A one-off buy and well worth it. Or you can buy the

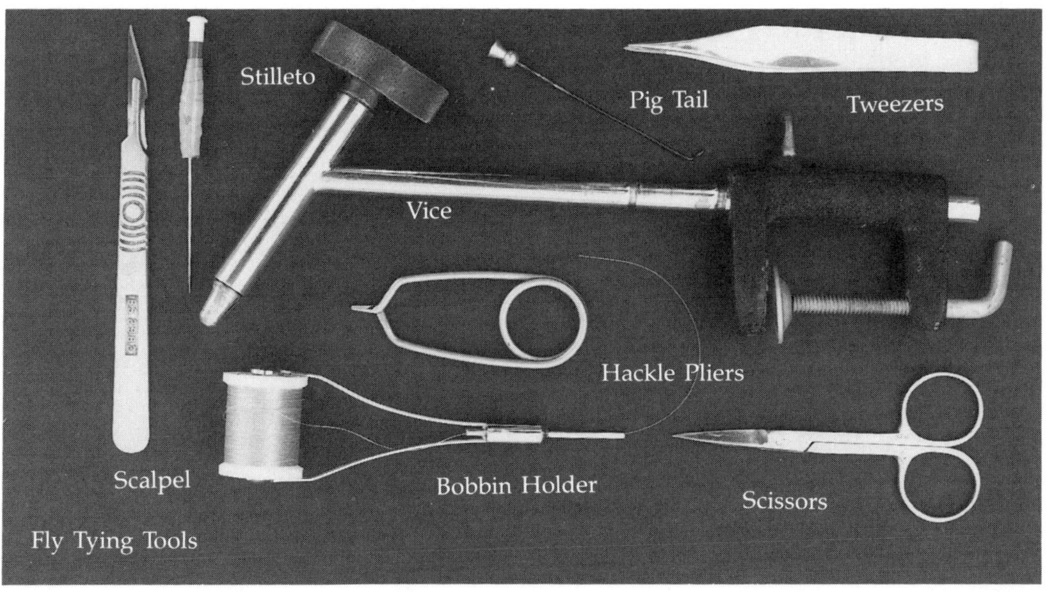

Fly Tying Tools

blades and fit them into a pencil-type homemade wooden holder. But take care. Fingers are non-replaceable!

Stiletto: These are real workhorses — for picking out fur dubbing on nymphs, splitting wing segments for winged flies, anointing fly heads with varnish. And they're a godsend for little splinters.

Pigtail: My contribution to the fly tying world! Simply a bodkin with a pig tail curl on one end. This, with a rubber band attached to a spare stand, can quickly pluck any hanging material away from the work area and can be released just as easily.

The above basic equipment will enable the beginner to tie most trout flies and lures. Other items such as winging tools, whip finish tools, hackle guards and gallows for tying parachute flies can be added later if required.

FLY TYING MATERIALS

Hooks: We can usually get away with some imperfections in fly fishing items but not when it comes to hooks. If you must economise with some material then make sure it isn't hooks. From the hundreds of sports fishing hooks there are only a few of interest to the fly fisher. They must be needle-sharp to penetrate the trout's jaw without excessive force; fine, yet strong enough to take severe side strain without bending; and not over-tempered to the point of snapping. Other features such as shape and thickness depend on the type of fishing and the preference of the angler. Because of ready availability Mustad hooks are detailed here but other makes such as Partridge are equally suitable.

Dry fly: #94840 Standard. Sizes 10, 12, 14, 16, 18

Wet fly: #3666, #3904A. Sizes as for dry fly.

Nymphs: As for wet fly but include #9672 Long shank.

Lures: #3666, #9672. Sizes 6 and 8.

This is a good time to raise the matter of barbless v. barbed hooks. After using them for years, most fly anglers (and all other types of anglers) are addicted to barbed hooks. It seems that what was good for our ancestors should be good enough for us and in any case why should we give the trout a good chance of escape? The fact is that providing we keep a tight line, barbless hooks hang onto trout equally as well, the great advantage being that a fish can be released quickly and with the least damage. There are also two nice side effects — on striking, the barbless hook penetrates easier and should one latch onto your finger or face, the possibility of a doctor's fee is much reduced.

Among angling incidents those that involve hooking yourself usually stand out in the memory, no doubt because of the pain involved and the dread of having the hook cut out. It wasn't pain that dismayed me when I saw the #12 Kakahi Queen embedded in my finger whilst fishing the north branch of the Clinton. It was the sight of big rainbows, rising in a long turquoise green pool on a summer evening. With only an unhygienic knife (and a long trail back to camp) and the rainbows going berserk it took only a minute to decide what to do. Grasping the hook and looking skywards I yanked it out in one swift movement. But it is not an action to be recommended. Had I been using barbless hooks it would have been a much nicer memory.

My friend, John Goddard, angler of repute, uses nothing but barbless hooks and increases the trout's chances of survival by bringing the fish to the bank with the nose right up to the rod top. Then, with a quick stab, he removes the hook. With 90 percent of trout hooked in the edge of the jaw, the fly or nymph is visible and can easily be released by this very efficient method.

Feathers: There must be very few people who are not in some way or other fascinated by feathers. In this age of scientific marvels we can imitate fur, crocodile and snake skin and many other natural materials but I have yet to see a fair job made of feathers. To a fashion model, or a New Guinea native, or a person stuffing sleeping bags, bird feathers are most desirable. To the fly tier they are indispensable, not only for their lightness but because they are virtually indestructible.

Despite the relatively few feathers needed for a great range of trout flies, the budding fly tier is doomed to collect feathers of all shades and hues for the rest of his tying life. Feather fetish is not too strong a label. I know — I am among the leading lights. Put a group of people in a farmyard and the fly tier is easily recognised, loitering behind, eyeing the ancient rooster with the sparkling neck feathers and picturing them in his treasured flybox. Such birds are rare and even when they are found it takes some persuasion and a touch of guile to obtain them, such as mentioning the high cost of feeding old birds or the offer of an occasional trout.

If from a rooster, the hackles are long, pointed and springy; if from a hen bird they will be soft with rounded edges. Cock hackles are used for dry flies and hen hackles for wet flies and nymphs. Dry flies especially require stiff, fibred hackles that stand proudly on the tensioned water surface and you need enough length to create a collar or ruff of fibres near the head of the fly. Wet flies and nymphs need to be fished below the surface which makes the soft hen feather more suitable. Whether bought or acquired, the hackles will vary greatly in quality. Loose hackles are a nuisance and poor economy. Far better to secure the whole neck or cape, inspecting it for quality by bending the cape skin and frilling the hackles. They should spring positively from the skin, have little or no down or 'flue' at the base, not be 'chalky' on the concave side, and, as mentioned, be long in proportion to width. Also make sure there are plenty of small to medium sized hackles on the cape. An average cape should supply at least 200 usable hackles.

Roosters especially bred for fly tying feathers are guaranteed but they are rather expensive. Wild Asian game

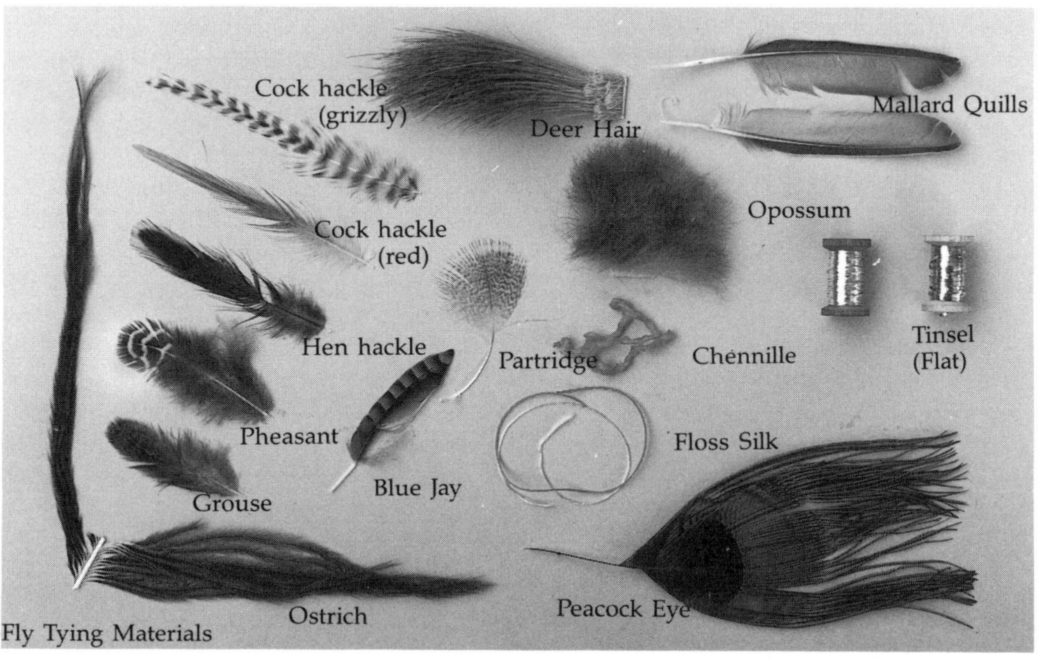

rooster crossbreds are cheaper but the quality in some leaves much to be desired. Whether it be to imitate a specific insect or tie whatever he or she fancies, the fly tier uses many different colours of hackles, some plain, others of varied hues and patterns but most of our standard fly dressing can be tied from a black, brown, and ginger, or a mixture of them. For the uninitiated here are descriptions of some cape colour variations:

Grizzy: Black and white chequered, or white with black bars.
Furnace: Red/brown with central black stripe.
Cochy y bondhu: As for Furnace but with outer black frill.
Badger: White or cream with central black stripe.
Dun: Blue or smoky grey.

Any sort of feather that doesn't come from a rooster or hen is known as a plumage feather. The list is legion — from duck breast or wing, partridge or grouse neck, peacock herl, turkey or pheasant tails, blackbird wings, ostrich herl, goose quills, and so on. All provide the tier with a particular feather for a particular pattern. Many plumage feathers can be obtained from farming and shooting friends but some, such as grouse or partridge and others difficult to obtain, need to be bought from a reputable dealer

Fur: Many fly fishers regard fur as the ultimate fly dressing material. One has only to look at the profile of any hair, fur or wool bearing animal with strong sunlight behind. The halo effect is remarkable. A trout, of necessity, must nearly always view floating insects against strong light which makes the translucent quality of fur or hair most important. Imagine trying to find a lost wristlet watch in a blackberry thicket. Difficult if not impossible. But what if the sun is reflected from the glass watch face, creating a tiny but obvious twinkle from the nondescript background? Natural insects, especially the gauzy winged mayflies, when viewed from below, emit this glow to some degree and, if the fly fisher's imitation can do the same, the fact that the fly is more noticeable must increase the chances. Even when submerged, fur (or hair) has some light-reflecting properties which makes it very suitable for nymph bodies.

The most versatile of furs is a hare skin from which can be obtained the greys and sandy fur for Hare and Copper nymph or underfur and guard hair for Grey and Blue Darters. Opossum fur is also popular for nymphs and a great favourite for tying Taupo-style lures. Other useful furs are provided by seal, rabbit, squirrel and mole. Deer hair flies are becoming more popular with anglers and in this country patches of this versatile material should be fairly easy· to come by.

Thread, silk, tinsel: It is a fallacy that the fly tier is forever raiding the embroidery box. He or she soon realises that an inexpensive spool of thread, tying or floss silk, makes a lot of trout flies and increases the chance of domestic harmony into the bargain. Prewaxed silk, even if a little more expensive, is a decided advantage. For small flies, up to say #14, fur can be dubbed directly onto the thread without the use of additional wax. If only it were available in finer sizes. Two spools — one black, the other brown — will keep the beginner happy for many a moon. Depending on the variety of trout fly patterns tied, quite a range of floss silk colours will be needed but again, at less than 20 millimetres per fly body it won't break the bank. Just make sure the spools fit your bobbin holder.

Scores of trout fly patterns require the use of either gold or silver tinsel or fine wire. I have never bothered with either for small trout flies using instead

20-gauge fine gold thread which is much easier to wind and just as effective. A visit to an electric motor rewind specialist may see you with a lifetime's supply of fine, dark, varnished copper wire for wrapping nymph bodies. For bright wire, the varnish is easily removed with emery paper. A few turns of fine lead wire under the nymph body are useful for deep lying trout, so a spool of that is required.

Passing through Wellington one time I called into a well-known sports store. When they realised I wasn't going to buy a carbon fibre rod I was left to my own devices and soon spotted a tangled lead line on the shelf. After a bit of Calcutta bargaining I bought it for about $3. Ten years later and still using it, so I can't complain. Before leaving the metals I must mention Lurex, a flat gold or silver tinsel which is very flexible and can be obtained in the one-millimetre size. It even stretches and makes winding tags child's play.

Other bits and pieces: Not all trout fly bodies are tied with feather or fur. Wool, once popular, is now little used, apart from for lures, but of recent years many manmade materials have entered the field. Swannundaze is a trade name for a bevelled plastic material that, when wound on a bare hook or particularly over a floss silk underbody, makes a lovely imitation stonefly or caddis. An American product it can be purchased here and comes in a variety of colours. If too thick, simply hold it in a steam jet and stretch. Polywing, polyyarn and polydubbing are all synthetic yarns, the names being self-explanatory. Polywing I have used for many years but I admit I was surprised when, as guest of John Goddard in England, on the evening before we fished the Kennet, we tied up a few of his Mayfly patterns and he used cream polywing for the bodies. Those chalk stream trout thought highly of them and even this duffer managed to catch his share. Like wool, chenille is hardly used these days except for tying night flies or lures. Raffia is still used for some patterns. My good friend Dennis Pain ties a remarkable imitation of a grasshopper using a flax strand. This artificial can catch a trout when the rest of us have given up.

A final but important item is nail varnish or head cement used to secure the final turns of thread. I usually search for chemists' bargains in the nail varnish department being reluctant to pay fancy prices for something used so mundanely.

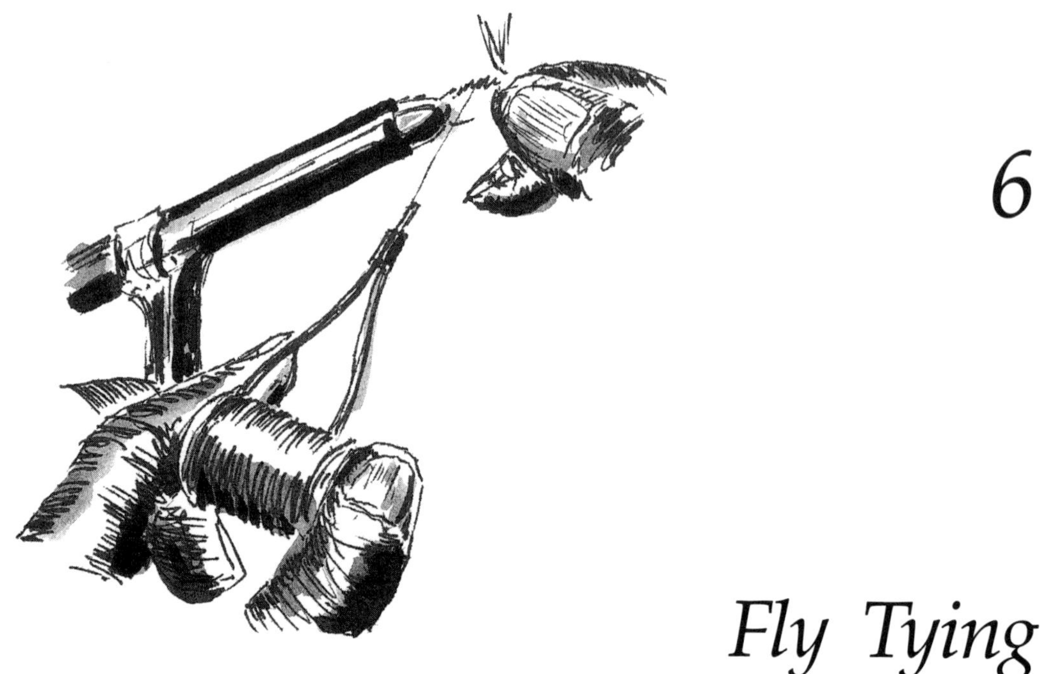

6

Fly Tying

Whether it is first or the five hundredth, a self-tied fly gives the tier a special satisfaction. It may not be perfect, it may lack form or balance, or have other shortcomings, but the homemade trout fly means independence. No more reading about that 'special' pattern and the frustrating search for shop-tied imitations. For a modest outlay, and with some patience and plenty of application, anyone can tie their own trout flies. Fly tying is often regarded as some mysterious art beyond most, but the truth is, that after even a few hours' practice with non-complicated instructions, a tyro can produce a trout fly that has every chance of fooling a trout. I've told you about the materials — now let's tie one.
A BASIC DRY TROUT FLY — RED SPINNER (Hackled)

Materials
Hook, #12-94840 Musted
Tail, Ginger Cock Hackle (large from rear of cape)
Body, Red Floss silk
Ribbing, Fine gold thread
Hackle, Ginger Cock Hackle (small from front of cape)

Select a hook from a box or packet of Mustad #12-94840, using tweezers, and place it firmly in the fly vice. Whether you embed the hook point or leave it protruding a little is a matter of choice. The former prevents pricked fingers and the latter gives you more scope in tying. By the way, these instructions are for righthanded people — lefthanders will have to work in reverse.

Take the bobbin holder loaded with black, waxed thread, and with the left hand draw out about 40 millimetres. With the taut thread held diagonally across the top of the hook shank near the hook eye take one turn to the fly head then three turns back to the hook bend, trapping the thread (Fig A). Let the bobbin take the weight and rest.

Continue to wind the thread smoothly down to the hook bend and rest. From the large hackle tear off a small bunch of stiff fibres, say ten. With the thread taut again and diagonal, the tips of the fibres to the rear and the butts underneath and in the 'v', take a slack turn around the fibres bringing them up and onto the upper side of the hook (Fig B). Remove fingers and examine for correct placement (Fig C). With practice no inspection will be necessary. Secure with another two turns and, similarly, tie in the gold thread. Take the tying thread back three turns to the hook eye and tie in the floss silk by previous method then continue with thread to behind hook eye, leaving at least two millimetres free space (Fig D).

Wet the fingers and dampen the floss silk to prevent fraying. Wrap even turns to the hook bend and, with a broad reverse turn, wind back in smooth turns to join the tying thread, slightly increasing the body taper as it approaches the hook eye. Secure the floss with two turns of thread, wind the gold thread in well-spaced diagonal turns to join the floss, four at the most. Secure again and, with the scalpel, cut away the surplus ends (Fig E). Take great care not to cut the tying thread. When using the scalpel never slice at material but place the blade edge in position first then gently pull the material against the cutting edge.

The body of the fly is now complete and the next and final stage is to tie in the hackle. This could have been tied in with the first turns on the bare hook but it is shown tied now to make the tying of the body easier for the beginner. Select

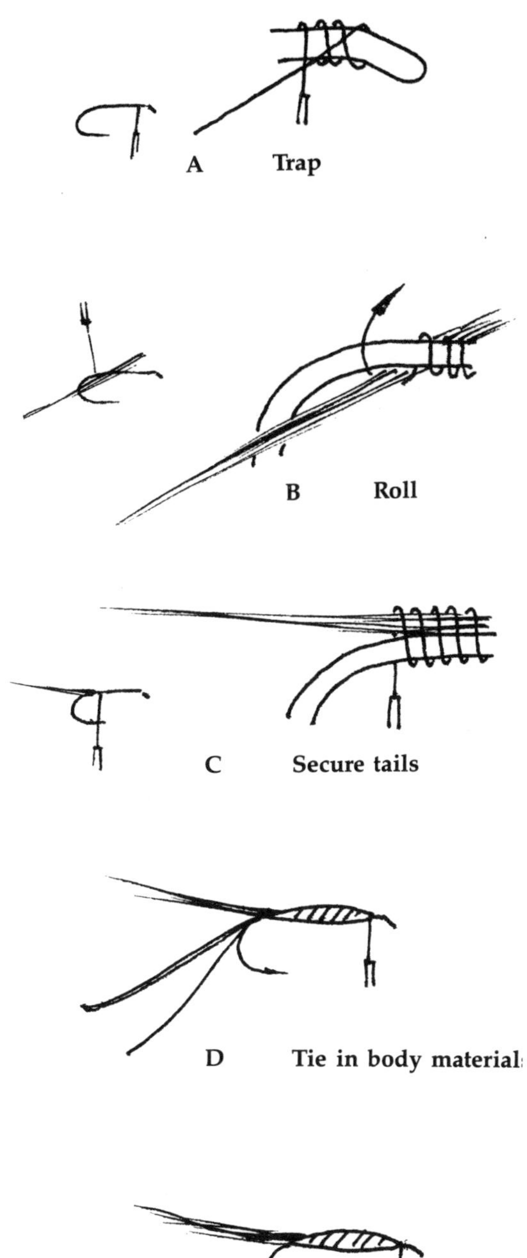

a hackle about 60 millimetres long with fibres slightly longer than the hook shank, strip off the down or 'flue' from the butt end and, with the diagonal technique, quill under the hook shank, tie in the butt with feather tip towards hook bend (Fig F).

Think of a cock hackle as an umbrella. It will have a concave and a convex side. The 'cave' side should face the hook eye so that when it is wound around the hook the fibres will point that way and help the fly to float better. Grip the hackle tip with hackle pliers, place a finger in the ring and wind three turns, four at the most, around the hook, keeping near but clear of the hook eye. The hackle, if compact, will now be spread like a ruff or collar so take the thread again and, keeping it very taut, wind it through the hackle to finish just behind the hook eye (Fig G). All that remains now is to cut away the surplus part of the hackle and secure the final turns of the thread using three half hitches or a whip finish. Although not essential with well-waxed thread, a drop of nail varnish transferred from the stiletto point to the knot, makes for a very durable trout fly.

The question of whether the addition of wings to an artificial trout fly improves the chances of catching trout has always been a matter of contention. It will never be properly addressed because of the many variables surrounding fly fishing. One school of fly fishers say they hook just as many fish using hackled flies only, while another maintains they would catch even more if they used flies with wings attached. No two anglers can fish for the same trout at the same time so we will never be sure. But one thing certain is that the natural mayfly has prominent wings. We fly tiers imitate all the other parts of the fly so why not imitate the wings as well! Whatever the truth, the appearance of a dry fly, providing the pattern calls for it, is much enhanced

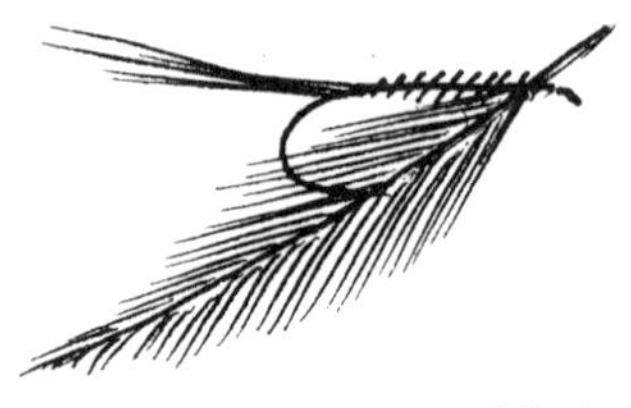

F   Hackle in

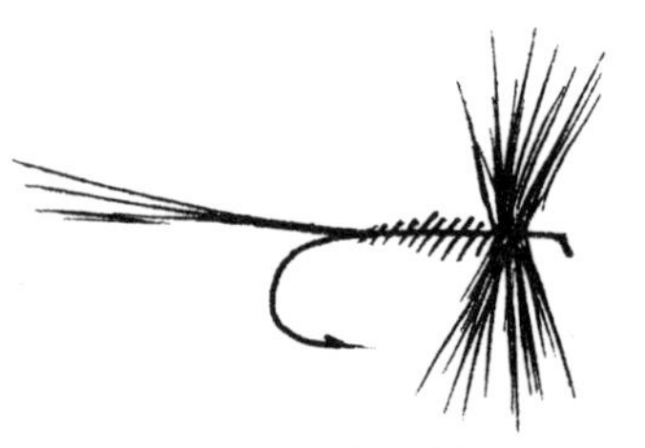

G   Hackle wound

with the addition of wings but I have a sneaking suspicion that it makes little difference to the trout.

Tying wings on a trout fly is generally regarded as a difficult operation, which it isn't, but it may be why many tiers adhere to the hackled dry fly. Many tiers have no hesitation in tying wings on wet flies but run for cover when it comes to tying split quill wings. Not that quill wing slips are all that durable. A good chew by a decent trout and the wings look like last year's dish cloth but what a delight they are when new. On the premise that you pays your money and takes your pick, the relatively painless method of tying in quill wing slips follows. There are other materials that simulate fly wings but once tying wing slips is mastered tying in any other material should be easy.

Before I describe tying in wings, a few hints on wing feathers should prove helpful. From the chapter on natural insects the reader will have gained some idea as to the shape and form of mayfly wings and although it is not the intention to imitate these slavishly it is possible to give the impression of wings. The wing feathers of many birds can be used but by far the most common are those from the mallard duck. They are easily obtainable and if the right feathers are chosen, are easily manipulated.

First you need a pair of matched wings from which the quills of the lower primaries and all the secondaries are selected (FigH). From a quill feather a small section known as a wing slip is chosen, the width depending on the size of fly being tied. From its counterpart on the other wing an identical slip is chosen and when placed back to back the two pieces are ready for tying onto the back of the hook (Fig I). It should be noted that all feathers, to a greater or lesser degree, have hundreds of tiny hooks and eyes along the fibre edges keeping the fibres interlocked in much the same fashion as a zip fastener (Fig J). It is essential not to disturb this feature so care should be taken in removing slips from the quills. Slips are so much easier to manage if, instead of being cut from the quill (a common practice), they are torn from the quill. First select the right slip width, grasp it very tightly between finger and thumb, and then tear it off with a quick positive twist. If this is done properly the fibres will not be disengaged.

After the initial tying thread turns have been wrapped, take the paired wing slips between the thumb and forefinger of the left hand with the tips pointing forward and the straight edge underneath. Obviously, once the slips are between the fingers, the butts are out of sight but the

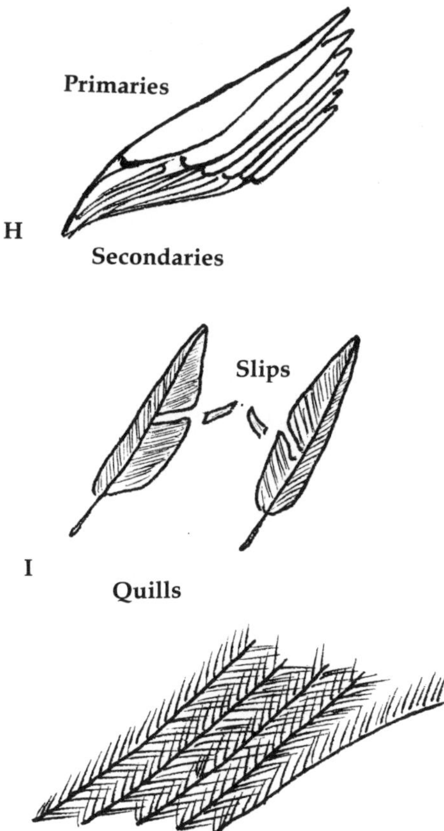

rest of the slip is visible. When eventually erect, the wings should be slightly longer than the wound hackle so the amount left protruding should be gauged accordingly. Holding the slips very tightly, position them on the hook at the 'shoulder' point. It is vital that the slips are held parallel to the hook shank before proceeding. Now take the bobbin in the right hand with about 100 millimetres of thread taut and pinch it upwards between the thumb and forefinger of the slip fingers. The bobbin will now be above the slips. Form a loop or inverted 'V' and stroke the bobbin spigot downwards, brushing it against the finger tips which can then once again pinch the thread. The bobbin is now below the slips.

We now have the slips held tightly in position, with the thread running up the near side of the slips and down the far side (Fig K). The object now is to draw the hidden far side thread down vertically, closing the upper loop down onto the slip fibres which, if done positively, will concertina them one on top of the other without twisting (Fig L). Do NOT let the slips move even a fraction. Bring the thread up again through the thumb and forefinger, repeat the loop and pull down. Do this four times then, still holding the slips firmly, gently raise them erect and take three turns of thread tightly up against the FORWARD edge of the slips. Then, and only then, can you gently SLIDE your finger and thumb from the slips. These should now be upright and secure (FigM), a good time for the tier to admire his handiwork and wipe the sweat from the brow. But we have a little more work ahead of us yet.

The back to back wing slips may stick together but the natural parting can be induced by the judicious use of the bodkin. The slips should spring apart making it easier to carry out the next and final stage, a figure of eight between the slips (Fig N). Lift the thread upright in front of the slips, take it between them and to the rear in a loose turn (not tight), then under the hook to appear at the rear of the slips, back through the upper cleft of the slips, still loose, and down the far side of the hook. Again take the slips between the thumb and fore-finger, not too firmly this time, then make a firm pull to tighten the thread. This will have secured the slips completely and it now remains only to position them properly by two or three turns to the front edge of the slips or the rear (Fig O). What were wing slips, if now cocked can rightly be termed wings. Very nice. No tier makes a perfect job on the first attempt but after some practice satisfaction is sure to follow.

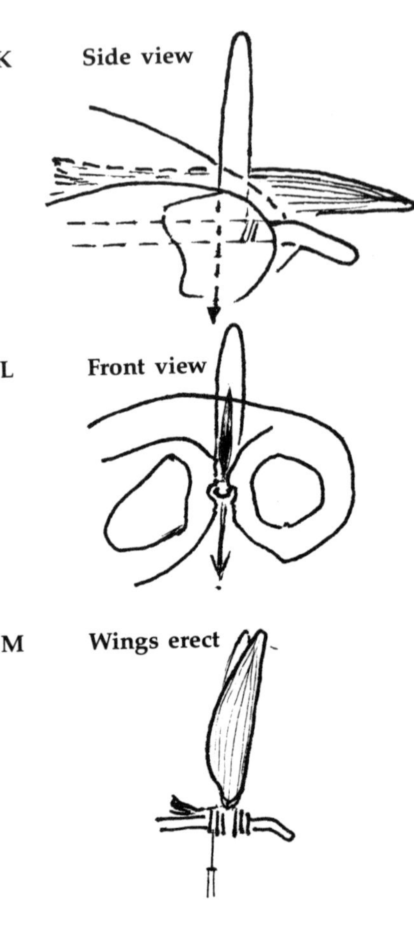

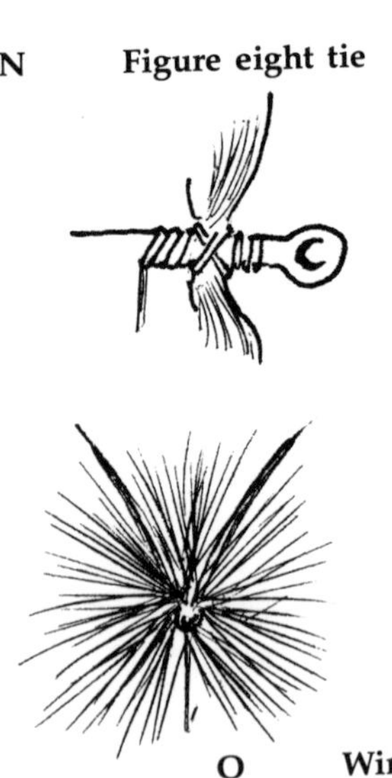

To complete the fly carry on with the thread to the hook bend, tie in and wrap other material, then follow the previous directions for tying in the hackle. Make sure the hackle stems are well secured with at least three tight thread turns. Take two hackle turns right behind and one last turn in front of the wings before cutting away the surplus. Secure the thread and, after tying a neat head, cement. After the skill of single wings has been mastered, tying more durable double wings can be achieved by pairing double slips. This dry fly pattern, an authentic Red Spinner, is a simple dressing but one that takes the beginner easily through basic tying techniques. Other patterns require slightly different techniques but basically, only the materials change.

Once familiar with the fundamentals the tyier can attempt other patterns, perhaps the traditional Red Tipped Governor. This effective trout fly requires a body of peacock herl, hen pheasant wing slips, ginger hackle, and a bright red floss silk tag. No ribbing. Pheasant wing slips are looser in the fibres than duck's so a little more care is necessary but the tying-in principle is the same. Two or three strands of peacock herl make for a nice plump body and the tag or butt needs only two or three turns of silk but these should be wrapped on the bend of the hook . Another well-known pattern is Dad's Favourite and although the same peacock herl is used, the 'flue' is rubbed off the thin quill strand before winding it for the body. By using an ordinary eraser and a final rub of the fingernail, on close inspection, you will see the quill is bicoloured or striped lengthwise. When tied in by the thin end and wound taking care to butt each turn to the preceding one), a distinctive striped effect appears very like the segmented body colouring of many natural mayflies .

Some patterns require a fur body which is attached to the tying thread by a method known as 'dubbing'. This means pinching a small quantity of say rabbit, hare or opossum fur from a skin and 'teasing' it onto the tying thread, a process made easier by applying a further coat of soft wax. Ski wax is ideal. The fur-loaded thread, taut at the hook bend, is then twirled with the thumb and forefinger until tapered, fine at the hook. This is now wound in very close turns to the fly 'shoulder', thickening as it approaches the hook eye (Fig P). A ribbing of fine thread or wire makes for a more durable body.

Having dealt with basic dry flies we can turn to the tying of wet flies which are really dry flies with a different type of wing. As with dry fly wings, quill wing slips are used but, instead of the slips being tied back to back, they are tied with the concave sides facing — in effect, not 'flared (Fig Q). Tips point to the hook bend with the wings held close to the fly body. This allows the fly to 'swim' smoothly across the stream, a necessity when fishing down and across. A problem area when tying in wet fly wings is getting them to sit low on the hook. This is achieved by not making the first winging turn too tight. The same procedure as in winging dry flies is followed, up one side of the wing slips and down the other, but the first pull down should be gentle and each succeeding turn tighter and always toward the fly head. Never tie back over the first turn. The wings lie close together and figure of eight turns are not required. The classic lines of the traditional wet fly are shown (Fig R).

Although a type of nymph fishing was practiced early this century, it used to be regarded as the Cinderella of the fly fishing world, a method looked down on by many English chalk stream anglers until relatively recently. Even now, on some famous overseas waters, some restrictions are placed on it. Not so in New Zealand where to wait for a 'dry fly' hatch could well mean a fishless day. For every mature mayfly there are hundreds of nymphs, the great majority doomed to a watery death either natural or via the jaws of a hungry trout. It makes sense then, when the conditions favour it, to use an artificial nymph, and fortunately these are very easy to tie.

The previous instructions on tying wet and dry fly bodies hold well for tying nymphs but there are one or two additional features. While most nymph artificials need no extra weight, when trout are found lying close to the stream bed the only solution is to get the nymph down to the fish. A few turns of fine lead wire helps to achieve this. Before the wire is wrapped a coat of nail varnish helps to secure the turns, which are then covered with spaced, tight, turns of tying thread (Fig S). As an example we can tie a Hare and Copper and a Pheasant Tail nymph. Materials for the Hare and Copper are obvious. After a few turns of fine lead wire we carry the thread to the hook bend and tie in a few guard hairs of hare fur for the tail. Then the fine varnished copper wire, say 20-gauge

On the well-waxed tying thread spin a fine cigar of sandy hare fur plucked from between the ears. Wind this in tight turns to the 'chest' or, in angling terms, the thorax area, forming a plump, tapered body. Secure with a half hitch and follow with the wire in well spaced turns, no more than four. This produces a rough, segmented effect, gives the nymph more durability, and adds a little extra weight. Unweighted this pattern becomes a very useful slow sinker. Cut away the surplus wire and, after perhaps adding a mix of longer speckled guard hair and a little blue underfur to the thread, wrap this to form a dark, plump thorax. On this pattern there is no wing case, often a

prominent nymphal character but, by tying in a tiny bunch of long hare fur over the thorax, I find a few more fish come to the net. It is a mistake to overuse lead wire because the great majority of nymphs are taken by trout either in or just under the surface film,· a situation where a deep sinking nymph can ruin your chances.

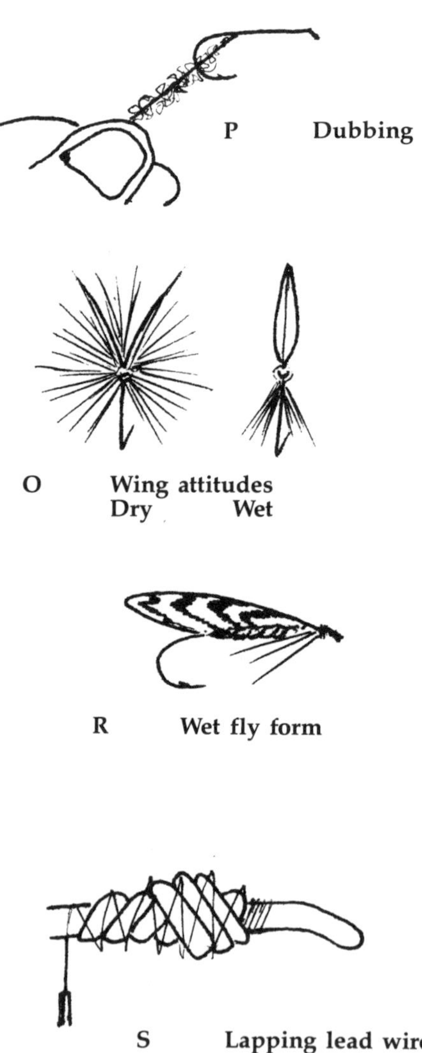

One of the most common nymph species in New Zealand is *Deleatidium vernale*, a small brown nymph maturing into a dun or mouse-coloured mayfly. It is the model for our next pattern, the Pheasant Tail. Banished to an island with a well-stocked trout stream, (take me tomorrow) and allowed one and one only nymph pattern it would without any doubt whatsoever be the Pheasant Tail. Created by the famous English river keeper, Frank Sawyer, it has become the darling of the nymphing fraternity, simply because it imitates many of the more common brown nymphs.

The materials are simple — a hook, a few rusty red pheasant tail herls and a strand of unvarnished copper wire from start to finish. After the wire is wound to the hook bend, the herl is tied in by the point ends leaving sufficient for short tails. Then twisted with the wire to form a feathery rope and wound back towards the hook eye. The herl and wire are untwisted, the herl wound to make a plump thorax with a couple of spaced turns of wire to secure it. And that's it! Simple but very effective. A nice variation is to form a body with the herl, and use the wire as a ribbing. Then tie in another bunch of herl in the thorax area leaving short points over the hook eye. Take a few turns to form a good thorax, tie the herls at the shoulder point, then take them over the thorax collar and tie in. The short herl points can now be doubled back and tie under the thorax to roughly simulate legs (Fig T).

Other fur-dressed nymphs are the Grey and Blue Darters, patterns I devised some years ago which have since proved effective in waters throughout New Zealand. Naturally one dotes on one's own child but once tried these imitations usually find a permanent place in many nymph boxes. Unlike the Pheasant Tail with its clearcut lines, the Darters are rough-bodied nymphs which, from a trout's viewpoint, probably look like Nesameletus nymphs, emerging mayfly nymphs or caddis fly. Whatever, they catch trout and that's good enough for me! After you've tied in a few hare fur guard hairs for a short tail, use mixed grey and sandy hare fur for the body, then ribbed with fine gold thread. The thorax is blue rabbit fur and the wing case that beautiful irridescent blue speculum feather from the mallard duck wing. When the fly is completed the blue fur thorax is picked out with the stiletto to simulate leg form (Fig U). I tie both weighted and unweighted, with, for identification, black tying thread for weighted, and brown for the reverse. The pattern for the Grey Darter is given in chapter seven.

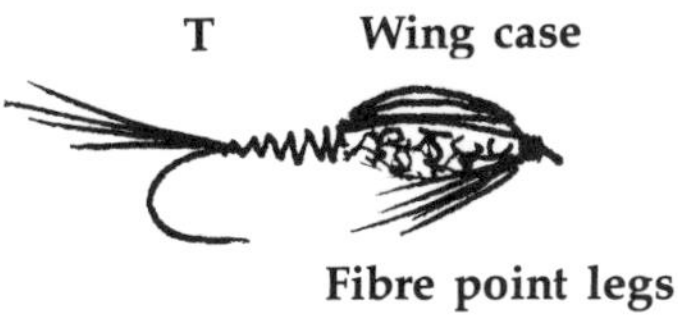

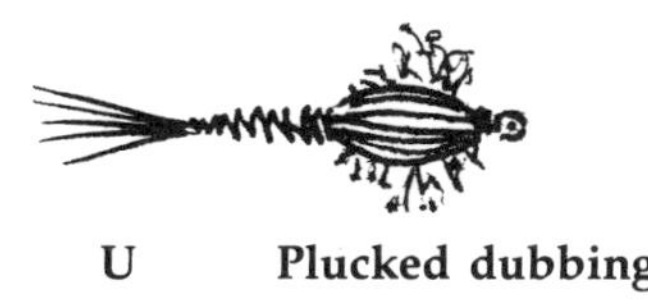

If fur is the premium material used in tying nymphs then peacock herl must run a close second. Some patterns use it as a body, others as a wing case. Wound with a ribbing of fine gold tinsel or crimson silk, peacock herl not only imitates plump insect bodies, but, with its countless reflective fibres, shines out like a beacon to the trout.

Unfortunately it's fragile, but this can be overcome by twisting the herl with the tying thread or ribbing before winding. For beetle bodies it is ideal but one needs at least three herl strands to form a plump body (Fig V). I usually form an underbody of crimson silk before winding the herl and, after some use, the herl takes on an attractive reddy glow. Another trick is to tie an underbody of gold Lurex which gives an even better effect.

Stonefly nymphs are tied in exactly the same way as mayfly nymph artificials but using long shank hooks. Some patterns use Swanundaze, a plastic body material which when tied over a coloured flass silk underbody base is very effective. Longer hooks can be used — Mustad 9671 or 9672, IXL or 2XL. Short tails are tied using a couple of goose biots (fibres from the short side of the wing quill feather usually dyed black or brown). Stoneflies have a double wing case but this feature can be covered by tying a very prominent overwing case of dark turkey or similar feather.

In the 'other trout food' category are two especially good imitations which, fished under the right conditions, will fool many a trout. These are the beetle and the waterboatman. During the summer months when swarms of the brown and green beetle are about, considerable numbers fall into the stream or lake, a welcome treat for the trout. Beetle artificials are the easiest of flies to tie and a good pattern for the beginner. All you need is a hook, say #14 or #16, some rough brown wool and a few strands of peacock herl. After taking the tying thread to the bend, tie in the peacock herl and the wool, in that order. Wind the wool to behind the head leaving plenty of space, then fold the herl over the back to behind the head and tie in with at least four turns of thread before cutting away the surplus. Acrylic wool,

which has a wonderful sparkle, is ideal for beetle bodies.

For brown beetle imitations, use bronze peacock herl and, for the green beetle, the brilliant green sword feather from the same bird.

Waterboatmen imitations are nearly as easy to tie using synthetic polywing yarn for the body, green kea wing quill feather or pheasant tail fibres for the wing case and two cock pheasant tail fibres for the legs, tied splayed to imitate the natural 'paddles' (Fig W). On completion the primrose yellow/green yarn is sliced lightly under the body with the scalpel to create a 'fuzzy' effect, which traps tiny air bubbles, imitating a feature of the natural insect.

V   **Dubbing or wool**

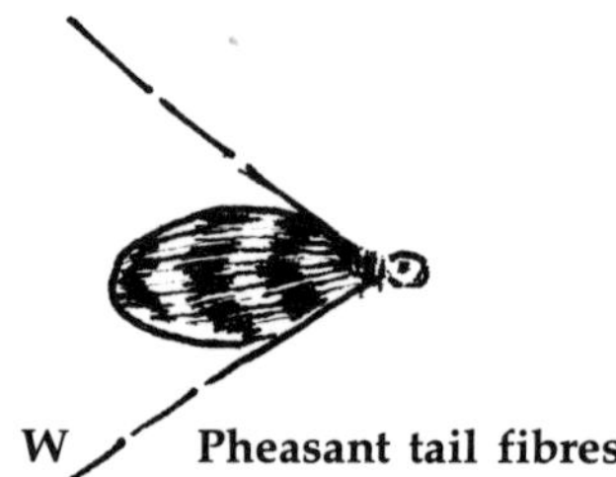

W   **Pheasant tail fibres**

If all the methods of tying trout flies were described here, not only would the budding fly tier be fast asleep but the element of original discovery would be gone. In this chapter there are enough instructions to start the tyro on a proper course. That he will never arrive at his destination is a foregone conclusion. Throughout his tying life he will never run short of things to learn. While there are some very talented fly tiers there are no so called 'masters'. The only real examiner is the trout and the tier who can say, without reservation, that he ties flies that fool the fish all the time is either a

Tight corners — best fish.

So near and yet?.

Bi Visible
Greenwells Glory
Brown Spinner
Twilight Beauty
Early Brown
Red Tipped Governor
Humpy
Houghton's Ruby
G.R. Hares Ear
Blue Darter
Damselfly N.
Kakahi Queen N.
Pheasant Tail
Brown Squirrel
Joe's Hopper
Purple Grouse
Invicta
Green Beetle
Woolly Caddis
Mot Marvel
Water Boatman
Suspender Midge
Horn Caddis
Red Setter
Muddler Minnow
Mrs Simpson

brave man or a fool. The true reward for the amateur fly tier is in creating a mixture of fur feather and steel that will, on some occasions, produce that eternal surprise when a most desirable trout opens his mouth and takes in your little creation. And after a little practice the amateur tier will have the satisfaction of knowing that a shop-bought fly will have no better chance of success than his own fair effort.

TEN TOP TYING TIPS

1. Be sure to leave plenty of space behind the eye. When you judge there is enough, allow a little more. This area of the hook shank is valuable. In most flies, wet, dry and nymphs, it is where most of the material is concentrated. A neat head is the mark of the competent tyer.

2. Don't get hung up on having to always tie a whip finish. Okay — if you can tie them without any problem, do so. But from many years in the business of flytying I can assure the reader that two or three half hitches, varnished afterwards, will be just as secure.

3. Work close to the fly. Nothing worse than working with a big thread loop. Four centimetres is as long a working thread as you normally need for wrapping. The exceptions are long overloops for wing tying.

4. Don't work with inferior materials. Flytying is material cheap and labour intensive. Buy the best you can afford, think of the big overall outlay on tackle and remember that the fly is what the trout inspects.

5. Learn to economise when applying thread turns and body materials. Bulky shop bought flies are also tied to attract the angler. Trout prefer them somewhat slimmer.

6. Although you should start by keeping as strictly to the original pattern as possible, when you are proficient don't be afraid to experiment and if your efforts are based on streamside observation perhaps one day your fly will join the hallowed ranks with Greenwell's and Twilight Beauty.

7. Work towards excellence but not slavishly. Decide on your best standard and if the trout agree with this make it your criteria. Rows of poorly tied fancy flies are best left in the bottom of the fishing bag. Better still, attacked with a scalpel and given a new lease of life.

8. Take your time. Many new tiers aim for professional speed. This will never be within reach of the amateur. No need for it. Five minutes to tie any fly well is better than rushing a dud.

9. Neatness in not only tying but in workspace and material storage should be the hallmark of every tier. A makeshift plastic wastebag placed strategically under the bench is a must. For storing hook boxes, silks, wires, threads and small bit and bats, a small plastic four drawer sewing cabinet is hard to beat.

10. Hooks. Probably the most important choice you have to make. Become familiar with hook sizes and their particular purposes. A personal choice but once you have decided on a brand and three or four styles, then always use them, confidently. And remember, it doesn't matter how well tied the fly is, or how much a trout may fancy it, if the hook is not razor sharp, the old adage may apply to you. 'A fly at one end and a fool at the other!'.

7

Trout fly Patterns

The following trout fly dressings are a small selection of the thousands of patterns available to the fly fisher. Space alone restricts the list to those which I have either devised myself or those which, over the years, have earned a regular home in my fly box. With the plethora of fly tying materials available it is easy to let the imagination run riot when sitting at the fly bench and some weird and wonderful creations emerge. Witness any fly tying book. You may, by good fortune, hit on a dressing that regularly dupes trout into thinking it is food but if the tier is familiar with trout food insects his chances improve immeasurably.

The following list is a fraction of what I term 'useful' trout flies. 'Useful' as against 'surefire' because despite all our skill at the bench, or use of the finest of materials, and all the knowledge gained or handed down, we will never create the 'perfect' trout fly. However I can recommend the following patterns. They work!

DRY FLIES

Adams

Invented in the 1920s by an American angler this fly has stood the test of time and in many parts of the world. Its success is no doubt due to the colour resemblance to many mayfly duns.

Hook:	#14/16 Mustad 94840
Thread:	Grey
Tail:	Grizzle cock hackle fibres
Body:	Grey poly dubbing
Wings:	Grizzle hackle tips
Hackle:	Grizzle/Red cock mixed

Blue Spinner

An evening trout fly which I devised when fishing the Mataura River, famous for its 'mad rise', a phenomena to be seen to be believed. Not all spinners sail downstream 'spent'. There is a phase where many female spinners, after egg laying, settle on the surface with wings erect or nearly so. The blue spinner is pretty successful during this phase. But not always — how often have I tried to solve the riddle of the rise. Here's hoping I never do!

Hook:	#14/16 Mustad 94840
Thread:	Black
Tails:	Grey cock
Body:	Peacock herl quill
Wings:	Grey cock hackle tips (well spread)
Hackle:	Grey cock

Brown Bi-Visible

Atttributed to the *Skues of America, E. R. Hewitt circa 1898,* the bi-visible is what it says, easy to see. This by reason of the bi-coloured hackle, part of which is very pale, making the fly easily visible on broken water. Not a still water fly.

Hook:	#10/12 Mustad 94840
Thread:	Black
Tail:	Brown cock hackle fibres
Body:	Brown cock (palmered)
Hackle:	Sandy or cream cock

Brown Spinner

A splendid summer dry fly which takes selective trout in still water conditions. Should be on hooks size max 14.

Thread:	Brown
Hackle:	Chocolate brown cock
Body:	Dark brown oppossum fur, ribbed russet red herl from cock pheasant tail feather
Ribbing:	Fine gold thread
Tail:	As for hackle

Cicada

Offer one of these to an English fly fisher and he may wonder whether to fish with it or use it as an ornament. Mainly used on back country rivers, an imitation of this seasonal insect is the scourge of wilderness trout. Apart from its attractiveness (it's partly constructed with deer hair), it floats extremely well and is ideal for bouncing down the rapids so well-loved by rainbows. To watch a big trout rise to a Cicada from the bottom of a deep blue/breen pool is to have sampled Paradise.

Hook:	#10/12 Mustad 94840
Thread:	Black
Tail:	Deer hair tips
Wings:	Badger hackle tips
Body:	Deer hair
Collar:	Peacock herl
Hackle:	Brown cock

Tying method: Tie in hair tails. Spin three or four deer hair collars, packing from the hook bend to the thorax area, and secure. Trim hair to form a plump body and secure. Tie in the hackle tips and split, sloping to the rear. tie in the brown hackle and peacock herl. Wind hackle at least three turns then wind the herl to form a thick collar. Finish with a well-formed head and cement.

Early Brown

Finding a satisfactory imitation of the dark brown mottled mayfly, *Deleatidium myzobrachia,* had always plagued me. The outcome was the Early Brown, a pattern that, when these lovely mayflies are evident, takes more than its share of trout.

Hook:	#14/16 Mustad 94840
Thread:	Brown
Tail:	Dark Furnace cock
Body:	Chestnut or Burgundy floss silk

Ribbing: Fine gold wire
Wings: Speckled brown hen
Hackle: Dark furnace cock

Gold Ribbed Hare's Ear

An old English pattern dating back to Halford's days when chalk stream fishing could be had for a fraction of the thousands of dollars now charged for a part season. In those days, a revolutionary fly featuring hair, not only for the body, but for the hackle as well. Still a firm favourite with many fly fishers its appeal stems from the rough nondescript appearance which well imitates an emerging dun.

Hook: #12/14/16 Mustad 94840
Thread: Brown
Tail: Tuft of hare guard hair
Body: Hare's fur from base of ear
Ribbing: Fine gold thread
Hackle: Hare guard hair (well teased out) or dark brown cock

Greenwell's Glory

A famous fly — a general purpose artificial — said to have been devised by Canon Greenwell, an English clergyman of the mid 19th century and tied for him by James Wright, a well-known fly dresser of the times. If we still have trout fishing in the year 2099 I feel quite sure that this fly will still hold pride of place in some space traveller's flybox. Small, olive-coloured, with dull grey wings, it well imitates a number of our *Deleatidium* sub imagos or duns.

Hook: #14/16/18
Thread: Yellow or brown
Tail: Coch-y-bondhu or furnace cock hackle fibres
Body: Primrose silk thread (well waxed)
Ribbing: Fine gold wire

Wings: Hen blackbird or starling
Hackle: Coch-y-bondhu or Furnace cock hackle

Houghton's Ruby

Devised by William Lunn, legendary river keeper of the river Test, in its heyday the finest chalk stream in England, this dry fly is an excellent spinner pattern and imitates very nicely the spinner of *Deleatidium vernale*, our common small brown mayfly.

Hook: #14/16/18
Thread: Crimson
Tail: Ginger cock fibres
Body: Ginger hackle stalk dyed red
Wing: Blue dun cock hackle tips tied spent
Hackle: Dark red cock

Humpy

An American deer hair pattern now widely used in most trout fishing countries. The name is derived from the deer hair hump over the body. A fast water fly, no doubt taken by the trout for a grasshopper or similar insect. Body colour is a matter of choice but my fishing friends all seem to favour green. It is a great fish finder in the broken water of back country streams.

Hook: #10/12/14/16
Thread: Green or whatever colour you prefer
Body: Green or yellow floss
Overbody: Deer hair
Wing, Tail   Deer hair
Hackle: Grizzle and Brown cock

Tying method: Tie in a bunch of hair along the hook shank using tips for tails. Tie in another bunch with tips pointing to the eye and bind both bunches together to form the body and wrap well with tying thread. Bring most of the tail fibres back over the body and tie in at the throat. This forms the 'hump'. Pull all forward fibres back and tie erect to form a single wing effect. Tie in two or three hackles, secure and cement.

Joe's Hopper

I first saw this fly used by an American angling friend and that was more than 20 years ago. Familiar with traditional flies I was surprised at the cavalier way in which he fished it. He simply flicked and dragged it about taking trout from the most unlikely places. Floating or sunk, even if some trout only chased it, it certainly intrigued most and fooled some of them. Obviously designed to imitate a grasshopper or adult caddis it is well worth trying during high summer under or near overgrown stream banks.

Hook:	#10/12/14 Mustad 9672
Thread:	Black
Tail:	Short tuft red wool
Body:	Yellow Polywing yarn
Ribbing:	Brown cock hackle (palmered)
Wing:	Hen pheasant wing quill slips (tied close to body)
Hackle:	Grizzle/Brown cock mixed

Tying method: Tie in wool tag, yarn and body hackle. Cut tag to length later. Form substantial body and wind hackle (smaller than throat hackle) palmer-style to the throat. Tie in wings (back to back to stand flat and tied to lie against the body). These should protrude slightly behind tail or tag. Tie in hackles and wind at least three turns, mixing. Form a neat head and cement. Cut wings at an acute upward angle, scissor points to hook eye. Cut tag length equal to hook gape. Smear wings with varnish.

Kakahi Queen

One of the best-known New Zealand trout flies and attributed to Basil Humphrey of Kakahi. Despite some friendly difference between Keith Draper and myself as to the natural model for this pattern I have to stick to my guns and say the mayfly is *Coloburiscus humeralis* (see also Nymph Patterns). Nor can I accept Bryn Hammond's contention in his excellent book *The New Zealand Encyclopaedia of Fly Fishing*, that Humphrey may have tied it to represent a number of mayfly duns. One has only to note the elegant, bright yellow leading edge wing strips of 'humeralis' to come to the conclusion that, when Humphrey had the nous to tie in bright dyed yellow partridge feathers on the forward edge of his fly, he was very familiar with this particular natural. So what! It catches lots of trout and that's what matters.

Hook:	#12/14 Mustad 94840
Thread:	Brown
Tail:	Brown or dark ginger cock
Body:	Well marked, stripped peacock herl
Wings:	Grey Mallard with dyed yellow partridge strip (forward edge)
Hackle:	Brown or Dark Ginger cock (a variation is to omit the difficult bi-coloured wings and tie in an additional bright yellow hackle).

Mole Fly

One of the few patterns sporting forward wings the Mole Fly is best known as a back country river artificial. What the trout take it for I have no idea but it does take trout. I have yet to see a mayfly with wings in this awkward position so perhaps it is just as well these big fish have generally catholic tastes.

Hook: #12/14 Mustad 94840
Thread: Brown
Tail: Ginger cock
Ribbing: Fine gold thread
Body: Yellow floss silk ribbed
             with Ginger cock hackle
             (tied palmer)
Wings: Hen pheasant wing quill
             slips
Hackle: Ginger cock

Mot Marvel

This marvellous little scrap duped more selective feeding trout last season than any other. Used with some skill and fine nylon it is almost guaranteed to take trout feeding in the surface film when the passion fruit hopper is on the wing. You may notice trout feeding below the surface on nymphs and every couple of minutes breaking the surface to take some near invisible morsel. In fruit growing areas this is quite likely to be the passion fruit hopper, a small delta-winged pest but a welcome addition to the trout's menu. The artificial is not over robust, but if it is well chewed after landing a couple of big ones, what the heck! Fishes better in the surface film so rub floatant lightly into the body before using. Use as fine a nylon tippet as possible. Season December, January, February.

Hook: #16 Mustad 94840
Thread: Brown
Body: Chestnut Brown opossum
             fur
Wing: Cock pheasant green rump
Hackle: Brown cock hackle

Tying method: To prepare the wing, strip flue from pheasant feather and trim, leaving a well marked delta-shaped tip. measure for size against the hook shank. Complete the trimming, leaving a few central fibres for tying in at the hook bend (keep well to the rear). Dub the thread with opossum fur and form a plump body, securing the thread behind eye. Hold the quill part and bring the delta wing over the body and secure. Tie in the hackle and wind two turns only. Finish with a neat head and cement.

Red Tipped Governor

Another trout fly popular with New Zealand fly fishers. One of the angler's great standby's when all seems lost. Probably taken for a beetle it is at its best in the faster parts of the stream. Many swear it is the red tag that attracts the trout and I have been sometimes tempted to tie some R.T.G's without the tag to find out. But not as yet. It seems fly fishers are as conservative as whisky drinkers. Why bother with home brew when you have a bottle of Glenfiddich?

Hook: #12/14/16
Thread: Black
Tail or
Tag: Red floss
Body: Bronze peacock herl
Wings: Hen pheasant wing quill
             slips
Hackle: Furnace or foxy ginger

Twilight Beauty

For once a trout fly that really lives up to its name. A beauty it is — at a guess, probably more New Zealand trout have been caught on this dry fly than any other. If not, it certainly qualifies for the top ten. Why some trout flies repeatedly catch trout while others, to our eyes, seemingly just as attractive are non-starters is an ongoing mystery. Is it the chunky thorax of the Twilight, the seductive chocolate-coloured body or the near black wings that lift this fly into the master class? Whatever, it is a fly that can be used with confidence, and I suppose when it comes down to brass tacks it is the 'confidence fly', rarely off the leader, that brings in the most fish.

Hook:	#10/12/14
Thread:	Brown
Tail:	Grey or Dark Brown cock
Body:	Dark brown floss silk or black thread
Wing:	Dark grey or mallard dyed blue/black
Hackle:	Dark Brown cock

NYMPHS

Two types of nymphs are of interest to the fly fisher — the mayfly nymph, no doubt the most important, followed by the dragonfly and damselfly nymphs. Mayfly nymph body shapes vary considerably from the tubular to the squat. Three patterns are given covering a wide range of nymphs. The most common, the mayfly nymph species of the *Deleatidium* type, are invariably brown, ranging from burnt amber to burnt sienna in colour although there are many in between shades. Generally small, and of flattened form, there is little advantage in slavishly copying this characteristic. More important is to emphasise the middle range of colours and the dark, sometimes near black, wing pads. Most useful for this purpose are fibres from the tail of the cock pheasant.

Pheasant Tail (New Zealand)

Thread:	Black or brown/waxed
Hook:	#14/16 Mustad 94840
Tails:	Pheasant Tail fibres
Ribbing:	Fine bright copper wire
Body:	Pheasant Tail fibres (bunch of four or five strands)
Wing case:	Pheasant Tail fibres

Tying method: Prepare lead underbody as required. The small hook size allows little weight but this is in order as it is not a nymph usually fished deep. In summer conditions, especially with shallow lying fish, the least splash when delivering the nymph the better, so unweighted nymphs are used. Using the pheasant tail fibre tips as short tails tie these in. Tail length no longer than the hook shank. Tie in ribbing then take the fibres to thorax area and secure. Bring up the ribbing with no more than three turns and secure. Continue with the herl fibres to form a plump thorax, return thread to behind thorax, securing the fibres ready for the wing case. Take thread (OVER THE THORAX) and leave behind hook eye. Bring the herl (this portion of the bi-coloured herl is now dark brown) over the thorax and after tying a small neat head, finish with two or three half hitches. Or, if you are fussy, a whip finish.

Darter nymphs

Named because they are rapid swimmers, the most common are the *Nesameletus* species. They are essentially tubular with mottled body markings and legs and with feather-like tails. Wing pads are not particularly emphasised. Paddle-like gills with the tails are obviously good swimming aids. I have developed two patterns over the years — the Grey and the Blue Darter — the latter now almost completely superceding the former. Both owe their origins to the Hare and Copper pattern. Apart from refinements the blue and grey darters are basically the same.

Grey and Blue Darters

Hook:	#12/14/16 Mustad 9762
Thread:	Black (Blue Darter) Brown (Grey Darter)
Weight:	Fine lead wire
Tails:	Hare fur guard hair (short tuft)

Ribbing: Fine gold wire (Blue
               Darter) Fine varnished
               copper (Grey Darter)
Body: Hare fur (sandy)
Thorax: Hare fur (dark blue
               underfur mixed with guard
               hair)
Wing
case: Iridescent blue Mallard
               wing feather (Blue Darter)
               Grey Mallard wing feather
               (Grey Darter)

Tying method: Normally tied with some weight although under high summer conditions this is omitted. A short tuft of hare guard fur at the hook bend starts off this nymph. Tie in the ribbing and after applying ski wax to the thread, dub with grey and fawn hare fur to form tapered body. Wind to the thorax area, secure, follow with ribbing, dub blue fur and wind to form a very substantial thorax (ensure there is a quantity of long black-tipped guard hairs). With thread at rear of the thorax tie in the mallard strip (be generous in width) and, after taking the thread to behind eye (OVER THE THORAX), follow with a mallard strip over the thorax and secure with a few turns. Make a stout but neat head and cement. When dry pick out some fur and a few guard hairs from the lateral thorax area to simulate legs and break up the tight outline. This gives a fuzzy haloed effect to the nymph.

Kakahi Queen Nymph

Here is an imitation of a 'one-off' nymph. Whereas there are different species of some nymphs this one is on its own. The *Colorburiscus humeralis* or spiny-gilled mayfly nymph is very distinctive and because it is reasonably common (especially in faster flowing streams) it is well worth imitating. A very chunky nymph, its overall colour is chocolate and

the prickly looking spiny gills above the abdomen are a prominent feature.

Hook: #12/14/16 Mustad 94840
Thread: Dark brown
Weight: Early season three turns
               fine lead. Omit in summer.
Tails: Brown hen hackle (short
               tuft)
Abdomen: Bronze peacock herl
               (heavily flued)
Thorax: Burgundy (or rich brown)
               floss silk
Wing
Case: Burgundy (or rich brown)
               floss silk
Legs: Brown hen hackle

Tying method: Weight if required. Tie in short tails, floss silk and peacock herl. Return the thread and floss silk to the thorax area. Twist herl and wrap to the thorax. Take the thread to behind the hook eye, follow with floss silk forming a plump thorax, securing the floss behind it. Take the thread (OVER THORAX) to behind the hook eye and tie in a short hen hackle but do not wind. Bring the floss over the thorax, take thread back (OVER THORAX) and repeat this manoeuvre until the thorax is well covered with the wing case. Finish with the thread behind the eye and wind the hackle, sloping it back and down. Half hitch or whip finish and cement.

Dragonfly and Damselfly Nymphs

These are still or near-still water insects and unless washed out of these areas by flood they are not normally associated with faster stream trout food. Essentially lake or backwater insects, dragonfly nymphs are chubby creatures whereas the damselfly nymph is slender.

Dragonfly nymph

Hook:	#14 Mustad 9672
Thread:	Light brown
Tail:	Pheasant Tail fibres. Three and well split.
Ribbing:	Fine gold wire
Body:	Green Polywing yarn
Legs:	Ginger cock hackle (small)
Eyes:	4/6kg Nylon mono

Tying method: Tie in tails (very short), ribbing and body yarn at the hook bend. Wind yarn to behind the hook eye forming a slender body but thickening to the eye, and secure the thread. Bring up the ribbing in five or six turns and secure. Tie in a very short bright hackle and leave. Cut nylon to point and push through the yarn near the head, cut leaving short stubs on either side. Then burn ends to form eye blobs close to the yarn. These will have burnt brown, the right colour. Wind the hackle only a couple of turns and leave proud. Form a substantial head with thread and cement.

STONEFLY NYMPHS

Stoneflies, common on the swifter, gravelled section of the river, are well worth imitating, especially after a fresh or flood which forces these otherwise tenacious insects from their stream bed sanctuary. Referring to Chapter 3 the reader will be familiar with the basic form of the stonefly. From the tiny 'needle stoneflies' to the relatively massive 'green specie' the angler is advised to choose a medium-size imitation, something around the #12 Mustad 9672 hook size. The fly box should contain two patterns — The brown stonefly and the green. The chief characteristics of stoneflies are (a) long body, (b) ribbed abdomen, (c) substantial wingcase and (d) two strong tails.

Brown Stonefly

Hook:	#12 Mustad 9672
Thread:	Brown waxed
Weight:	Fine lead wire
Tails:	Two fibres brown goose biots
Ribbing:	Brown varnished copper wire
Abdomen:	Brown Turkey wing fibres
Thorax:	Red/brown opposum fur
Wing Case:	Cock pheasant tail fibres

Tying method: Anoint the hook shank with stiffish nail varnish and wrap with five or six turns of wire. Overwrap from eye to hook bend with thread and tie in biots, splitting with one turn of thread. Tie in copper wire and four or five turkey herls. Wind these to behind the thorax area, secure the thread, then follow with three well-spaced turns of copper wire ribbing and again secure the thread. Dub the thread with ski wax and, after plucking opposum and hare fur, twist onto the thread to form a very plump thorax. Return the thread to the rear of thorax and tie in pheasant tail fibres with two turns before bringing the thread to behind the hook eye. Bring the fibres over the thorax to form the wing case. Secure well with at least four turns of thread, cut away surplus fibres and finish the head with further turns. Cement and pluck out hare guard fibres with a stiletto.

Green Stonefly

Hook:	#12 Mustad 9672
Thread:	Brown
Weight:	Fine lead wire
Tails:	Two buff peacock wing quill biots
Ribbing:	#20 fine gold thread
Abdomen:	Olive Polywing material (thinned)
Thorax:	Sandy hare fur with guard hairs

Wing
Case: Shiny green mallard duck
             wing feather

Tying method: As for Brown Stonefly.

BEETLES

Although they come in many different forms, beetles are one of the easiest patterns to tie and ideal for the beginner. The Manuka beetle is a favourite trout food and this together with an imitation of a black beetle should see the fly fisher through the season. The body form is usually plump and this should be emphasised in the artificial.

Green Beetle

Hook: #12/14 Mustad 3666
Thread: Black
Weight: Bare shank summer/lead
             wire early season or deep
             fish
Wing
Case: Green peacock eye herl or
             any bright green dyed
             feather)
Body   Brown acrylic wool (crisp
             fibre)

Tying method: Wind the lead wire base and secure (if required). The shorter hook shank will determine the turns. Tie in the herl or wing fibres at the hook bend, together with the body material. Cut away the surplus wool and form a plump body finishing behind the hook eye. Secure well. Bring the herl or wing fibres over the top of the body, using at least six herls or a wide slice of wing fibre. After securing the wing case and removing the surplus, form a substantial head with thread and cement. A common fault in tying beetles is having too thin a body and too skimpy a wing case. If in doubt err on the side of too much rather than too little in beetle materials. Tease out the wool fibres to suggest legs and soften the outline.

Black Beetle

Hook: #12/14 Mustad 3666
Thread: Brown
Weight: As for green beetle
Wing
Case: Black duck quill feather
             with green sheen
Body: Black acrylic wool (crisp
             fibre)

Tying method: As for the Green beetle.

CADDIS FLIES

A very important trout food, caddis fly imitations have received far less attention than mayfly nymphs. Yet caddis flies are invariably found when trout stomach autopsies are carried out. I think it is fair to say that, apart from selectively feeding trout, if a trout will take a mayfly nymph he will certainly take a caddis fly imitation. Of the common types of caddis fly two are of importance to the fly fisher — the cased and uncased (free swimming) variety. The form of the former is very distinct, the insect secreted in its horn-shaped cell. Few successful imitations have been devised but the following will take trout under all but heavy water conditions. It is very deadly if cast delicately during low water to observed trout.

Horn-cased Caddis

Hook: #14/16 Mustad 3666 or –18
             Mustad 37160 Caddis
Thread: Black
Underbo-
dy: Primrose or cream floss
             silk.

Body: Quill torn from brown hen
           hackle
Head: Peacock herl

Tying method: Tie in floss silk, take thread to the hook bend and follow with floss. Tie in the quill. Take the floss to keep well clear of the hook eye, forming a slender tapered body. Secure. Wind the quill slightly, overlapping to the end of the floss and tie in two strands of herl. Wind this to form a bushy collar.

Green Caddis

Hook: #16 Mustad 37160 Caddis
Thread: Black or brown
Weight: Fine lead wire as required
Tail: Ginger hen or sandy hare
            fur tips
Body: Olive green polywing yarn
Dubbing: Pinch of sandy hare fur

Tying method: Tie in a tuft of tail fibres at the extreme bend of hook. Tie in polywing yarn and a short piece of thread ready for dubbing. Wind the yarn, forming a tapered body and secure. Dub the thread with sandy hare fur (sparse) and wind to near the head. Form a substantial head and cement.

Grey or Woolly Caddis

Hook: #16 Mustad 37160 Caddis
Thread: Black
Weight: Fine lead wire (normally
            used)
Tail: Ginger hen or sandy hare
            fur
Body: Hare fur (grey/blue
            underfur)
Ribbing: Fine varnished copper wire
Thorax
and Head: Black floss silk
Legs: Ginger hen hackle

Tying method: Tie in a tuft of tail fibres at the extreme bend of hook. Tie in wire. Dub the thread heavily with hare fur, wind to near the hook eye, secure and follow with ribbing (wide spacing). Tie in floss silk at the thorax area, wind to well clear the hook eye. Tie in hen hackle, wind two turns only, secure and fold the hackle back and under. Continue with black floss to form a substantial head and cement.

OTHER TROUT STREAM INSECT IMITATIONS

Dobsonfly or Creeper

Fully described in Chapter 3, the fully grown larva of the dobsonfly is one of the largest of our aquatic insects. But, during higher river flows, many immature specimens are washed down. An imitation of a fully grown creeper is likely to send all but the largest of trout speeding for cover. Tied on a #14 or #16 caddis hook they are very acceptable to trout and especially if weighted and fished near the stream bed. When disturbed or at risk the larva invariably curls so the Mustad 37610 Caddis hook is ideal.

Hook: #12/14 Mustad 37610 Caddis
Thread: Black waxed
Weight: Fine lead wire
Body: Grey/blue hare underfur
Overbody: Bronze peacock herl
Ribbing: Black thread
Head: Black thread

Tying method: Wrap lead, secure with thread (remember to varnish the hook shank) and, at the hook bend, tie in a piece of black thread followed by three strands of herl. Dub tying thread heavily with hare fur and wind to near the head. Secure. Stretch peacock herl over the body and secure. Rib with four or five turns of black thread pinching the herl to the body. Use the remaining black thread to form a thorax/head section. Tie off with three half hitches and cement well.

Midge Pupa (Goddard)

Most successful during late evening rise. Midge pupa move rapidly in their final emergence state. Imparting movement to imitation or slight current 'drag' is often sufficient to trigger trout into action.

Hook: Mustad 94840 #12/14/16
Head: Tiny shaped ball of ethafoam enclosed in fine white mesh. Pantyhose.
Thread: Brown
Body: Blue opposum fur
Thorax: Bronze peacock herl
Ribbing: Fine gold thread
Tail: White fluorescent wool

Suspender Midge (Goddard) Mark II

Hook: Mustad 94840 #12/14/16
Thread: Brown
Tail: White nylon filaments or white wool strand
Body: Green floss
Thorax: Brown or dyed turkey herl

Waterboatman

Fished to cruising fish in backwaters or along the edge of slow-flowing reaches, this little imitation more than earns its keep during the summer months. My original pattern, although eminently successful, used the olive-green wing quill from the kea, the expired bird having been given to me by a park keeper friend. After more experimentation I discovered an ideal and readily available material for the wing case — after tying, colour the wing case green with a marker pen and lightly smear the back with nail varnish.

Thread: Black or brown
Hook: #16 Mustad 3666

Body: Green/Primrose Polywing yarn
Wing
Case: Mallard duck flank feather. Black/white stippled.

Tying method: A very simple tie, similar to that of the beetle imitation. Take tying thread to the hook bend and tie in a 1 cm wide doubled strip of mallard. Tease out the green and primrose yarn and blend. Tie in and wind, forming a plump body and leaving ample space behind the head. Bring mallard strip over body and secure, making sure the wing case spreads well down the sides. Use marker pen, varnish (a smear only) and tie off the head. When this is dry, turn the fly over and, with a sharp scalpel, slice the underbody until the yarn fuzzes out underneath. This, as with the thorax plucking, breaks the sharp body outline and makes the fly much more interesting to the trout.

WET FLIES

Brown Squirrel

A simple wet that fishes well after a fresh or flood. The time is right when the water is the colour of Lion Brown. Then the trout are 'on fin', eyes peeled for any sort of food. The Brown Squirrel swinging across their bows and heading shorewards is a very tempting target. If any further recomendation is required a short while after typing this I tied a Brown Squirrel, walked down the river and fished the clearing shallows. I fancy that nice sea-run trout will taste delicious for tomorrow's dinner.

Hook: #10/12 Mustad 9762
Thread   Brown
Weight: Fine lead wire (optional in summer)

Body:	Red/Brown Opossum mixed with olive seals fur
Ribbing:	Fine gold thread
Wing:	Brown Squirrel tail

Tying tips: Use only wide-spaced turns with ribbing. When tying in the wing make the first thread turn slack, otherwise the hair will flair. Succeeding turns should get progressively tighter.

Invicta

My introduction to this wet fly was on a lonely Yorkshire reservoir. The fishing had been mediocre and I was on the point of packing it in, but a chance meeting with the local policeman fishing nearby changed my fortune. His basket was half full of half-pounders with one or two double that weight (all good fish by English standards) and, being a kindly man, he offered me the pattern he was using, the Invicta. Since then it has proved a consistent trout catcher.

Hook:	#10/12/14
Thread:	Black
Tail:	Golden pheasant yellow crest
Body:	Yellow seals fur
Ribbing:	Fine gold thread
Hackle (palmered):	Red cock
Hackle (throat):	Blue jay
Wing:	Hen pheasant tail slips (alternative, grouse wing quill slips)

Muddler Minnow

Little introduction is necessary for this American creation. In fast water it has proved itself a champion and, as a wet fly in quieter waters and in the smaller sizes, it can be very deadly, especially in the summer evenings. Deer hair spinning technique is required and the beginner is advised to practice on a thread-wrapped hook before trying the Muddler. The last trout I hooked on this odd-looking artificial was on the Buller River last season. I saw the big brown appear from nowhere, chasing the fly at breakneck speed. At the last moment he turned away and started a slow curve back upstream. Shaking with disappointment I hurled the muddler back after him and got the shock of my life when he grabbed it. Even then he got off in the end. Never mind. It wasn't the Muddler's fault!

Hook:	#8/10/12 Mustad 9672
Thread:	Brown
Tail:	Speckled brown turkey or speckled brown hen
Body:	Flat gold tinsel
Underwing:	Brown squirrel hair
Wing:	Speckled brown turkey or speckled brown hen
Head:	Deer hair

Purple Grouse

Observe any knowledgable wet fly fisher and it is an Orvis graphite to a punctured wader that one of his flies will be a Purple Grouse. A most reliable wet, one to use with confidence. I certainly do and if teamed with a Brown Squirrel, and I have no success then, even with a change of flies, I fear a fishless day. Unfortunately grouse wing quill slips are rather soft and mangle easily. Better to tie in are speckled brown hen quill wing slips. They are more durable and do not seem to affect its catch rate.

Hook:	#12/14 Mustad 9666
Thread:	Black
Weight:	Fine lead wire (omit for summer use)
Tail:	Black hen hackle fibres
Body:	Purple floss silk
Ribbing:	Fine gold wire

Wing: Grouse wing quill slips or
               Speckled Brown hen

Waterhen Bloa

A pattern favoured by the North of
England fly fishers, its appeal to trout is
universal no doubt due to its resemblance
to a drowned or waterlogged mayfly dun.
The soft hackle, when washed by
currents and eddies, flickers seductively
and must give the appearance of a
struggling insect. A non fussy fly it is
simple to tie. It is a its best when trout
are feeding in the surface film and
difficult to catch with conventional
patterns.

Hook: #16 Mustad 3666
Thread: Primrose or Yellow
Body: Blue fur (mole, rabbit,
               hare underfur or a slow
               cat)
Hackle: Waterhen underwing
               feather (spoon shaped
               and glossy)

LURES

Mrs Simpson

Possibly the best known of all the North
Island central lake lures. There are more
contenders for creator's crown that there
are hangers-on at the Governor General's
tea party. Suffice to say no one really
cares after all these years, least of all the
trout. One thing is certain. It has
remained as a 'top lure' for more years
than many of us care to remember and
looks like continuing into the 90s. A fly
of this stature deserves attention.

Hook: #2 to 8
Tail: Black squirrel
Body: Red or yellow wool
Flanks: Cock pheasant (green
               rump)

Rabbit Fly

Once again a lure that is highly
recommended by Keith Draper. Its
origins are somewhat obscure but it has
stood the test of time and no doubt owes
its success to the original idea of using a
piece of rabbit skin as a substitute for the
traditional wing. Mr Draper, no doubt
with tongue in cheek, hints at a further
improvement — a piece of black cat skin
— but hastens to add that wild cats are
a nuisance. All the same, if you own one
and live in the Taupo area?

Hook: #2 to 8
Tag: Red or Yellow dyed cock
               whisks
Body: Wool or chenille, colour
               to suit
Ribbing: Oval tinsel
Hackle: Red or Yellow cock (day)
               Black or Claret (night)
Wing: Strip of rabbit pelt (ends
               tapered)

Red Setter

In his *Trout Flies of New Zealand*, Keith
Draper credits Geoff Sanderson as its
creator. He also says it is one of the best
for taking lake-run trout and having
fished with lures in the Taupo area for so
many years I am sure Mr Draper knows
his stuff.

Hook: #2 to 10
Tail: Brown squirrel tail
Body: Orange Chenille
Hackle: 'Usually tied in with two
               large ginger hackles, one
               at the head, the other
               tied in halfway along the
               body. In the smaller sizes
               one hackle can be used
               while on the extra large
               hooks three or even four
               are sometimes tied in.'

8

The Right Tackle

It is a brave man who pontificates on the ideal sort of tackle for trout fishing. The selection of rods, reels, lines and accessories available today makes the choice much harder than in the past. But then, who are we to say that Walton didn't agonise over the pick of hazel, ash, lancewood or greenheart for his rods, or that Halford, deity of modern dry fly fishing, didnt ponder on the merits of horsehair leaders as against silkworm gut. The selection of trout fishing gear is amazing and it is no wonder that the newcomer to the sport feels like a flea in a dogbox.

So, because we have all been at the starting point, perhaps we should consider the beginner. Basically there is little difference in the range of tackle necessary to fish large rivers or lakes rather than small streams. Items such as

rod, reel, fly line, nylon leaders, spools and trout flies are essential wherever you are. Other items such as landing net, fishing bag or vest, are comforts only and in themselves will bring few extra trout to the bank.

And so to the choice of a suitable rod. A glance at the vast array in the sports stores is enough to perplex any beginner which makes the help of an experienced fly angler invaluable. Within limits, a rod that is suitable for both small and medium-sized streams is probably the best buy but, before we consider this, let us look at rod materials. Split bamboo or cane is easily recognised by its hexagonal cross section. Light, tough and sensititve. A rod of this material, if from a reputable maker, will deliver a trout fly with accuracy and 'feel' that neither fibreglass or carbon fibre can offer. Why is first-

79

quality split cane expensive? Time! Here is a brief account of the making of such a rod:

First take a length of Tonkin bamboo of excellent quality and without excessive nodes or knuckles. Cut to length and bake the cane to a choice temper. Split the cane into splits or slivers, six to a joint piece (12 in all for a two-piece), taper each strip of cane, shaving two sides only and leaving the porcelain hard skin on the third side to an exact equilateral triangle. Glue six of these together making sure the nodes are spaced apart and, hey presto, we have the hexagonal tip or butt rod piece. Repeat for the tip. The skill and time required to produce these rods is reflected in the cost and having built them I do not begrudge the maker's price. However, unless you are a Lotto winner or have backed a ten to one runner, split cane is best left for the connoisseurs.

Next down the price list comes carbon fibre, or as it is sometimes mistakenly known, graphite, this is a space-age material used wherever strength and lightness are premium qualities, as in the manufacture of jet turbine aircraft blades. When the exquisitely fine threads of carbon are stretched, impregnated with resins and baked, the result is a stiffish yet flexible, pre-stressed, strong, lightweight, fine diameter wand that offers little air resistance, and gives high line speed. This in turn allows greater line control, a decided advantage to the angler. Naturally for all this sophistication there is a price to pay and the buyer will be lucky to have change from $NZ200.

But what lovely rods they are! I can only urge the new chum to consider the cost as an investment spread over many years. But remember — car doors and boot lids do not distinguish between carbon fibre rods and broom handles so make sure your rod has a suitable case and is well insured. Graeme Marshall will flog me for this but recently he committed

the sin, after a hectic late evening on the Motueka, of leaving his best rod out of the tube. His hatchback car door did the damage. On a more recent occasion whilst fishing the Mohaka with J.G. this genial gentleman fell down a bank rock hole and smashed his C.F. Imagine his chagrin when on returning to the car we found his second C.F. chopped off at the tip by the dreaded hatchback door. So even the best fall short.

But even with normal use this wonder stuff is not infallible. I well recall an incident when fishing the Waimarino with Frank Harwood, the well-known Turangi guide. It was a day when not only Frank's temper exploded but the rod as well. He was attached to an angry two-kilogram rainbow at the time when, for no apparent reason, the rod shattered just below the two-piece rerrule. But trouper that he is, Frank played and landed the fish with the smashed splints rattling around like castanets. Fortunately such cases are rare and, providing it is not abused, a carbon fibre rod will repay its purchase price handsomely.

A third contender for the angler's favour is fibreglass, a material which revolutionised rod making. It has the major advantage of being less expensive than either split cane or carbon fibre but, being of larger diameter and less stiff, a glass rod will expend more energy in straightening the line loop, ergo, energy wasted. For all that, in a price-for-performance contest a good quality fibregrass rod is hard to beat. And another plus — whereas a broken fibreglass rod means only a few tears, with split cane or carbon fibre, you'll be considering harikiri.

Now retired and resting on my studio cum workshop wall is a 2.7-metre No. 8 lineweight Fenwick fibreglass rod. It is scarred and sun-blotched, the ring wrapping is worse for wear and the cork handle chipped and scored. I need only to take it from its case occasionally to be transported back to Fiordland where, for many years, it was a well-proven friend, delivering flies with length and accuracy and standing up to heavyweight, rod-busting browns and rainbows. On the other side of the wall is one of its triumphs, a mounted 4.5-kilogram-plus rainbow trout. So you don't need to stage a bank hold-up to own a good rod.

Far more important than the material or style of rod is the ability to wield it. An extra 100 grams lifted over a period of six hours makes the difference between pleasure and purgatory. A rod to suit the occasion can make life much easier for the beginner. For smaller stream fishing, with its myriad of obstacles and streamside hurdles, for obvious reasons, I would not recommend the use of an expensive split can rod. Either a carbon fibre or fibreglass rod would be quite suitable, providing the former was not too stiff and the latter of good quality. Contrary to the belief that on a small stream you need a small rod, I find the extra length of a 2.7 metre (9 ft) rod gives far more casting control and, as is often the case when fishing a narrow stretch between high banks, it keeps the line clear of cocksfoot on the back cast. In choosing a longer rod, try to select one with a soft action. This will enable you to use the special small stream casts necessary in confined spaces (see chapter nine on flycasting). Another advantage of the longer rod is that if it is not too light it can double quite nicely as a lake rod where length in casting is important. A longer rod also gives the angler an advantage in handling big trout in confined areas. Some small streams can contain big trout. Last season, in January, John Goddard and I fished some of the West Coast spring creeks including one or two no more than a good jump across. But of the number of trout hooked landed and lost none were under two kilograms.

The old 2.7-metre (9 ft) in this case, had the measure of John's backpack 2.4-metre (8 ft) Orvis. Both were carbon rods.

Other items to consider apply to any fly rod. My personal preference in rod rings are the 'snake' variety, except for the butt guide ring which should be of medium size (ball point pen diameter), hard synthetic, with the tip ring chromeplated. Most rods sold today come with a screw reel seat. Older type rods may have sliding reel rings fitted and the reel can then be positioned to suit, but there is little purpose in this as the nearer the reel is to the butt the better. Choose screw reel seats with the locking nuts to the rear. Don't worry if your selected rod doesn't run to a hook keeper. With leaders now being generally longer than the rod, the second or sometimes third rod ring up is suitable. A final reminder: Be sure to purchase a suitable rod case. neglect this at your peril!

The Easy Way to Thread Flyline

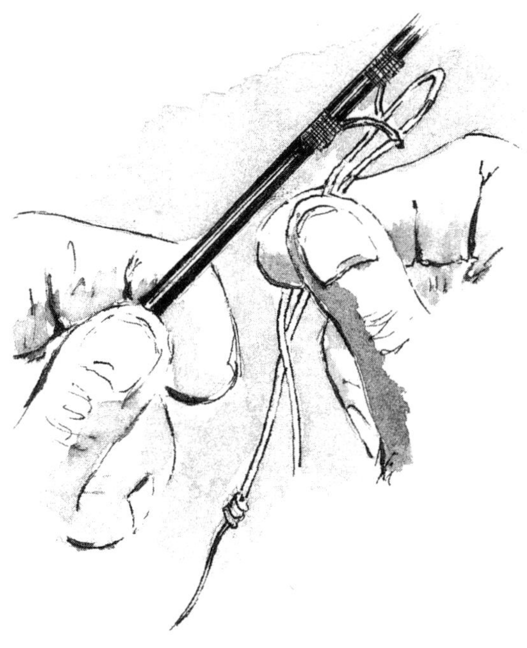

The next essential item is a reel. Many consider it only as a means of line storage, but it is not just a safety deposit box but more of a cheque account — putting some in and taking some out. It should do this reliably and complement the rod not only in size and weight but in durability.

Reels come in many designs but my advice is to go for simplicity. In small stream fishing, most trout are played, landed or lost, well within the length of the fly line, with the appearance of backing a rare event. But on larger rivers or lakes a more substantial reel capable of storing a heavier fly line (plus 50/100m metres) backing is needed. Generally though, the reel need only be lightweight and single action. After all why carry more weight than you need. One luxury feature are interchangeable spools with a line change, say from a floater to a sink tip, without having to pack a second reel.

Good reels carry an extra pawl and spring. Make sure the reel line guide opening is kind to a fly line. A rough reel strut is the surest way to destroy an expensive fly line. One angling writer recommends removing the bottom strut entirely so that in the process of stripping line off the reel at the usual angle any wearing is eliminated. But it's a brave man that can take a hacksaw and file to a new and perhaps expensive reel. My reel is now more than 40 years old and, although it has had two handle replacements and the spool flange is so polished you can see to shave by it, it is as reliable as the day I bought it. These royal reels were expensive then, and still are, but they are well worth it.

You might be able to struggle along with some less than ideal items of tackle but the correct choice of fly line is vital. It must match the casting capabilities of the rod. When rod and fly line are balanced and the caster proficient, the result is known as 'sweet' action, a joy to watch and even better to apply. From angler to fly the energy is transmitted via rod, line, leader and tippet in the smoothest possible way and the fly or nymph delivered neatly and delicately. That process is essential for smaller stream fishing and equally so for short distance casting on lakes. Today, apart from the renaissance of oil-impregnated braided fly lines, most lines are coated in thermoplastic resins and some are impregnated with millions of microscopic bubbles of gas. Not only does a line have to be fairly light per unit length, it has to be as tough as old Harry, having to travel at 160 kph one second and then at the same speed in the opposite direction.

Fortunately, because of a code developed by the Association of Fishing Tackle Manufacturers (AFTM), matching rod and line is almost painless. Above the rod grip will be a number, say #6. Simply choose a fly line coded DT6F, meaning a double taper line of which the first nine metres of taper and belly weigh between 152 and 160 grains and which floats. Nine metres is recognised as the average casting distance for most anglers under normal conditions. Replace the F with an S and you have an identical line except it will sink, a feature useful in lure or wet fly fishing. For small stream fishing a light line is essential and should be rated between a 5 weight and No 6 weight line and floating. Lines with the weight concentrated at the tip, prefixed WF, for distance casting, are obviously unnecessary, except when fishing lakes or wide rivers. Here, a line size of between #7 and #10 would be the choice.

There are now more styles and sizes of fly lines than trout in your favourite stretch and it makes sense for a beginner to seek help before buying one. Fly line prices vary considerably as does the wearing quality so you 'pays your money and takes your pick!' But take note — although a top price line will bring long service, you can buy two cheaper lines for the same price. More food for thought is that when a floating line eventually cracks and starts to sink it becomes an ideal sinking wet fly line. Level lines are much cheaper but, unless one is a diehard wet fly angler, they are clumsy on the smaller streams. A double taper line can be reversed when one end becomes worn or cracked, giving twice the life. That brings us back to the DT-F coded line. A 27-metre floating line will not fill a fly reel spool and some form of backing is necessary. This is usually a spool of braided nylon or dacron wound on top of the fly line to fill the reel. Then the line with backing is removed and reversed to give the correct level of reel spool fill. A crafty move is to grit your teeth, cut the fly line in half, attach it to the backing and store the other half for future use. A half line gives a 13.7-metre line cast, easily long enough for the average stream.

Talking of backing reminds me of an incident that occurred a few years ago on the Mataura River near Wyndham. It was a lovely evening with trout rising everywhere. One in particular, his brown bronze back frequently breaking the surface, was dimpling just under the bank, feasting on the squadrons of spinners floating downstream. Mataura trout can be infuriatingly selective but after about 100 casts (dare I say 200) he decided on my little Dark Red Spinner. Well hooked, the fish took off seawards stripping the fly line out in double quick time, with the backing close behind. When I had only a few turns of backing left, he leapt in the distance, a silvery gladiator arcing back into the water. I held tight to the reel handle, rod at full strain, hooped and trembling. A few turns, another haul of the rod. Thank God he was giving way! More turns and more slow hauls back with the rod. The very stuff of fly fishing for big trout! Was it too much to expect a trophy fish? It must

have been, because, after five minutes, despite all that reel winding and rod bending he seemed just as far away as ever and it was then I realised that the last few turns of backing were slipping on the reel spool! Ever tried to tie a knot with one hand? In the gathering gloom? My 'trophy' fish turned out to be well conditioned but under two kilograms. No doubt later, he and his mates had a laugh at my expense.

We now arrive at something much less expensive — nylon monofilament and in particular the leader or final link before the fly. Tailormade or roll your own? Whichever, the leader should be tapered, starting at a diameter not much less than the fly line tip with fine nylon at the business end. You can buy knotless or solid leaders, which avoid the knot nuisance on windy days, or different strength spools of mono and tie your own. Braided leaders which start with a flexible woven nylon section and finish with the conventional monofilament tippet are expensive and, nail my hid to the mast, I prophesy they will join the dinosaurs. Is the home made leader something to be ashamed of these days?

Leader strength depends on the breaking strength of the fine tippet or point and are rated on an X scale. For instance an OX leader has a tip diameter of .011, a butt diameter of .021 and a breaking strength of 4.5 kilograms. Near the other end of the scale, 4X has comparative figures of .007-.021, 2.26 kilograms and would be most suitable for small stream fishing. Unfortunately with the frequent retying of flies to tippet we gradually lose the fine point but this is easily rectified by tying on another short section from a spare spool of level 5X, 4X, or 3X nylon monofilament. The construction of knotted leaders and methods of attaching leader to fly line, including knots, are described in the Appendix.

We can now turn to the delightful process of dressing up. However, despite the good advice to keep accessories to a minimum the average fly angler finishes up with what looks like a jumble sale and I am afraid I am no exception. One can almost discern the gleam in the assistant's eyes as he watches the approach of an angler into his shop. He watches with amusement as the customer casually inspects some new angling device or takes a surreptitious glance at a rod's price tag. He smiles as he sees the gradual surrender, then, with straight face, compliments the relieved angler on his choice. Tackle shops are the angler's Aladdin's Cave and he or she who leaves one with a full purse must be bullet-proof. Few indeed! Well, why not? Experience alone will slim down the accessories so, in the meantime, have a spending spree.

To wade or not to wade? Wading a stream, river or lake in summer in refreshing cool water is one of life's delights. Gym shoes and shorts are the order of the day. Try it in early spring mountain water and not only your legs will turn blue! That reminds me of the famous angler William Scrope who, in 1843, in his *Days and Nights of Salmon Fishing in the Tweed* wrote:

Avoid standing on rocking stones, for obvious reasons; and never go into the water deeper than the fifth button of your waistcoat; even this does not always agree with tender constitutions in frosty weather. As you are likely not to take a just estimate of the cold in the excitement of the sport, should you be of a delicate temperament, and be wading in the month of February, when it may chance to freeze very hard, pull down your stockings, and examine your legs. Should they be black, or even purple, it might, perhaps, be as well to get on dry land; but if they are only rubicund, you may continue to enjoy the water, if it so pleases you.

They don't make 'em like that nowadays. Isn't he charming? I can't resist another quote:

If you are not much of a triton, (dictionary here) you may use fisherman's boots, and keep yourself dry, it is all a matter of taste. When you are wading through the rapids, step on quickly and boldly, and do not gaze down on the stream after the fashion of Narcissus; for running waves will not reflect your beauty, but only make your head giddy. If you stop for a moment, place your legs abreast of each other; should you fancy a straddle, with one of them in advance, the water will operate on both, trip you up, and carry you out to sea.

'If you fancy a straddle! No thank you, William.'

The standard New Zealand wader is the rubber thigh boot. Lightweight for the first kilometre, then a cross to bear if the weather is warm. Also treacherous unless fitted with the felt soles or steel heel cleats. Some foreign lightweight chest and thigh waders are available. The higher priced ones are of reasonable quality, the cheaper ones, next to useless and prone to leaking. For all but spring and late autumn fishing there is no better wading gear than a pair of nylon tramping boots fitted with steel heel cleats. The half-shod boot allows a firm grip on a slippery stream bed and the soft corrugated sole allows a quiet stalk on a stony beach. American lightweight waterproof fabric wading stockings are ideal but expensive, but they are the 'creme de creme' of wading gear in spring and autumn and if you can impregnate a visiting American with enough Glenfiddich during his stay you might just persuade him to leave behind his gorgeous wading boots.

The use of landing nets is a source of argument between some anglers. Pro-netters are convinced that the day you leave the net behind is the day you hook the fish of a lifetime and where it is all but impossible to land it without one. Anti-netters argue that a skilful angler should be able to land fish anywhere and in any case nets are a damned nuisance. There is some truth in that, having landed enough large trout in very difficult places, I must side with the netters if only on the strength that a net allows a trout to be captured and returned with the minimum of stress (for the fish, not the angler). In these enlightened days every angler worth his or her salt must be concerned with conserving, within reason, our treasured trout. I recommend a well-made, easily-collapsible, triangular net plus a canvas sheath. Avoid plastic sheaths like the plague because if you forget to clean the net after a fish, the smell will soon remind you.

I remember my first fishing bag, homemade from canvas by a doting aunt.

How proud was the 12-year-old delving into the two pockets for the cigarette tin for one of the half-dozen treasured flies! And how many times from the big pocket I proudly produced a 200-gram trout. That bag is still up on the workshop wall, a reminder of golden days. Now it's a fishing vest with more pockets than a magician's jacket. And, despite good intentions, they all get filled. A well-made vest incorporates a spacious back pocket for carrying a lightweight meal and occasionally a flour-bagged three-pounder (1.4 kilograms) for the cook. A chest wool pad is useful for used flies, and will, in no time at all, take on the appearance of a porcupine. Mine is now so well used it is nearly bald.

While the rod, reel and line are accepted as major items, it is the bits and pieces that are dear to the angler's heart.

A sure place for trout

If not essential, they make life a little easier and strangely enough give confidence in their own right. Take fly floatant for instance. Some anglers swear by an atomised silicone spray whereas I wouldn't be caught without my little, original tin of mucilin. No it hasn't lasted me 30 years. I buy the plastic ones, melt the ointment and refill my old friend. Such are the idiosyncrasies of the angler. The fact that its purpose is only to grease the fly line doesn't bother me at all and getting two for one would have my Scottish grandfather proud.

If there is one little luxury I indulge in it is retractable clippers, similar to nail clippers and attached through a nylon cord to a spring-loaded drum. This little gadget pins on to the fishing vest or shirt and is very handy for clipping off surplus nylon from knots. Like all goodies they do not come cheap and I remember clearly the loss of my last pair. It was while gazing fondly at a bevy of rising trout below a bridge over the Motueka that my friend and I saw something flickering through them. 'See that!', said Dave. 'Funny!', said I, then felt for the clippers. Missing, and by some quirk of current they could be seen lying in a rock cleft a couple of metres deep. Skin diving stuff and they are still there. I pay my respects each time I pass. Now I almost rivet the clippers to the vest.

At one time I used to carry a fine stone hook sharpener until the same friend produced a tiny diamond-coated nail file. The jeweller's stone cost the earth, weighed far too much, and it took quite some time for me to swallow my pride and buy one of those $3 files from the local chemist. Tied on to a fine cord it's perfect for the job and the old stone still gathers dust in the workshop.

Although it is not absolutely essential (an old tin would do the job), most anglers indulge in a suitable fly box. This not only provides a home for trout flies but also allows him or her to modestly display the collection to long-suffering friends. Whatever type of box is chosen it should be small and light. If plastic is your choice make sure it is of the unbreakable type and, if foam-lined, ensure it has saw-tooth strips for the hooks. Flat foam inserts are undesirable for either wet or dry flies. If the purse allows, or a present is in the offing, there is no better box than a Wheately with a half dozen or so flip-lid compartments for your dry flies. Expensive, robust, lightweight and worth it. Christmas present?

If the greatest pleasure is in hooking trout, surely the worst experience is removing a firmly embedded hook — from your anatomy. The obvious answer is to use barbless hooks which I guarantee will fail no more than the barbed variety. But unless barbless are introduced early to the beginner it is the devil's own job to convert him or her. Here is where a pair of fine-nosed pliers prove invaluable. You can either use them to press down the barb out of harm's way or, if you insist on barbed hooks, the pliers are indispensable in removing a hook from the fish's jaws with the minimum of damage. Artery forceps are ideal as hook removers. So perhaps on your next visit to your doctor?

Finally, as the girl says to her mum, something I can't do without — Polaroid spectacles. On more than one occasion I have returned many kilometres for forgotten Polaroids which are without doubt the most important of fly fishing aids. Some prefer grey-tinted lenses while others plum for the amber tint. Certainly on bright days the yellow tint draws in more light and seem to pick up more trout, but who can promise a full fishing day of sunshine! Sound advice is to purchase a cord keeper at the same time.

9

Fly Casting

If the newcomer to fly fishing were to rub the lamp and be granted a single wish, I should urge him or her to wish for a benevolent relative who is not only an expert fly caster but one who has that rare ability to instruct competently and painlessly. I wish I had had one. These paragons are scarce indeed and most people have to do as I did — stand in a paddock, rod in one hand, book in the other. Since then, after 50 years of muddling about, making mistakes, correcting them, making more, and noting how experts do it, I now manage to throw a reasonable line.

So often the beginner watches a competent caster do his stuff, and, as a result, gets a bout of stage fright. And if that doesn't put him off, his first attempts often do. But let him or her remember this — fly casting looks easy. AND IT IS!

There is nothing special about fly casting skills. They are no different from any other sport skills such as swinging a golf club, wielding a cricket bat, or to make a simpler analogy, riding a bicycle. There is no magic wand that creates an instant fly caster and some basic techniques must be learned, but in the end it comes down to balance, timing, and a soupcon of dexterity. Sorry, I omitted two other ingredients — purpose and determination, but these are prerequisites to learning any skill.

But there are exceptions. Recently I offered to teach three boys how to fly cast. Each was given a fibreglass rod. The first in line, the smallest, after I held his arm and went through the motions of casting, showed some promise. After ten minutes' tuition he was sending out a reasonable if wobbly cast. The next lad, a bit bigger, after I'd grasped his arm and given him the rhythm, gave me a surprise. I sensed his confidence, took my arm away and without any problem at all he continued with casting that would have done most of us proud. The oldest and strongest youth proved the most difficult. Despite desperate attempts he never mastered the rudiments so I had him exchange rods with the middle lad. It made no difference to either boy, one still thrashing and the other continuing to send out an effortless 15 metres.

The objective of the following advice is not to make the tyro into a top-class fly caster in six easy lessons but to turn out a competent caster in a relatively short space of time. Mistakes will be made but sooner or later will come that moment when, out of a hundred trial casts, the beginner will KNOW he has made a perfect one. It may be some time before he makes another but again he will KNOW. The next good cast will come even sooner and it is this recognition of the true, almost effortless cast that marks the first major step.

The first question is — where to practise? On the lawn or over water? I think the former but not for too long. There is nothing like the real thing to encourage the beginner. Fly casting means lifting a length of nylon monofilament attached to a rather thick line, off or near the water surface, throwing it into the air behind you, pausing until the line and leader has straightened, then, without excessive force, throwing it in the forward direction. Gripping the rod comfortably is essential to good fly casting. The thumb, the strongest digit, is normally stretched forward directly on top of the rod grip, in line with the rod — − −. If you find it more comfortable to splay the thumb a little, be my guest, just be happy with the grip. Relaxation is the key word. Beginners are often too tense.

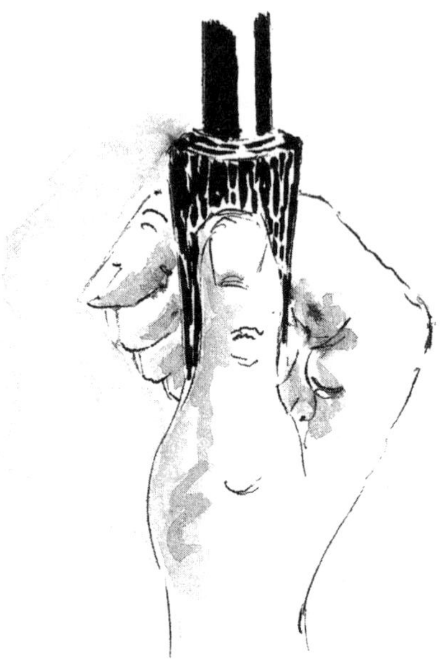

Grip

Start by picking up the rod (as described in Chapter 8, your rod and line rating should be compatible). Thread the line and leader, and on the end, tie a ten-millimetre piece of wool. Pull out seven metres of line, lay this out forward from the rod tip, and grasp the rod grip firmly. Hold the rod horizontally just above waist height. Relax. Place the left foot slightly forward (if right handed) or right foot (if otherwise), pinch the line to the rod with the forefinger, take a deep breath and, smoothly but quickly, pull the rod upright. But — and this is very important — before you attempt this first cast I beg you to remember and never forget these following words: Never, never, never bring the rod butt back any further than your ear! I promise that if you follow this advice, in no time at all you will be able to cast a fly proficiently. Disregard this and your line will forever fall around your ears!

Don't be frightened to use plenty of power with that first back cast. The idea is to throw the line back with enough force to load or 'stress' the rod. If you have taken my advice and STOPPED THE ROD AT YOUR EAR the line will be where it should be, up in the air and beginning to straighten out behind you − − −. Don't hesitate to have a look. Watch how the line is lifted and unfolds in a 'U turn' to straighten. At this point, whether you like it or not, the rod butt will have drifted slightly to the rear. Not much I hope. Now, with the rod loaded, use that firm grip together with the thumb to push the rod forward, this time bringing it half way between your ear and the horizontal. Don't develop the bad habit of over-using the wrist. The overall action is similar to driving a nail into wood with a hammer. You will almost certainly find a tendency to raise your casting arm up and away from your shoulders. Resist this. The elbow should be tucked in near the hip and the forearm pushing 90 percent of the power, the wrist giving the remaining thrust. A slight hinging of the wrist is sufficient.

If this is the 'perfect cast' the line and leader will have performed another 'U' turn and, on the way forward, will have unfolded into a straight line from the rod tip − − − . Again, have a look upwards and watch this little miracle. Then when you feel you have done enough work, drop the rod tip to waist level again − − −

The line should now be where it started and you can repeat the performance but, IF YOU LET THE ROD GO BEHIND YOUR EAR, the line will collapse either in front of you, behind you, or wrapping you up. Don't panic! Just remember to keep the rod nearly vertical during your next effort on the way back. If successful, this will have results that will surprise you. It is the secret of successful casting. Rod too far back, poor forward cast; rod nearly vertical, good forward cast. To recap! Start with a smooth but powerful haul. Rod vertical. No more. Pause to let the fly line straighten. Power stroke

Overhead Cast

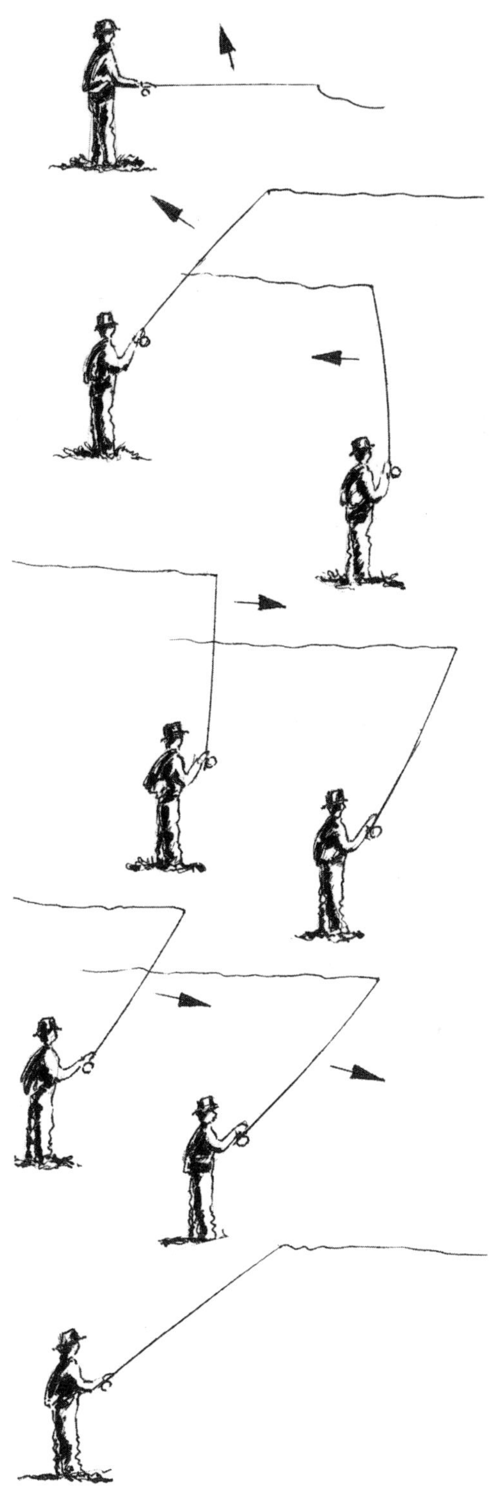

forward stopping before horizontal. Lower rod tip. Practise! A 10 metre cast is ample for a beginner.

Once you are reasonably satisfied and throwing eight good casts out of ten it is time for a trip to the river or lake and, instead of the bit of wool you can tie on a fly. Why not? As yet you may not be a competent caster but fly casting is fly fishing, and catching trout is what it's all about. But, don't expect too much at this point. There is much more to catching trout than being able to cast a fly. Concentrate on sending that line out ten, 15 metres, without effort, improving on the timing and balance until, like riding that bicycle, it comes so naturally that you wonder what the fuss was all about.

No doubt you are wondering how, under actual fishing conditions, we can lay the line out on the water before we carry on with our practice casting. No problem! When you are ready and comfortable, pull about five metres out from the rod tip and strip off the same length from the reel leaving this coiled on the ground. Now instead of pinching the line to the rod with your casting hand, hold the line firmly in the other. As before, bring the rod upright to create the back cast but keep the rod high on the forward stroke. When the line has straightened in the forward direction, pause, and create another back cast. Watching the action will immediately show you how your timing is progressing. The important thing is that split second pause at the end of either the forward or backward stroke. Practice at keeping about five metres airborne. This is where a little of that perseverance and determination pays off. Once you can manage this stage, which is known as false casting, you can try for some more distance.

Start again with the line now held gently and after a few casts, when you have developed a rhythm, on the forward stroke, let a short length of line slip through your fingers and hold firm again. The loose line will be pulled through the rod rings by the force of the extended line, which is now that much longer. Repeat this action, then on a forward stroke bring the rod down nearly horizontal and let go of the line. You will see it snap up tight between the rod grip and the first ring. This is known as 'shooting the line', a trick that will eventually allow you to place the fly gently on the water. Providing you keep the line 'aerialised' with short strokes and keep strip feeding line on the back cast and letting it go on the forward stroke, the only limit to the length of line you can cast is determined by the weight of the extended line and the power of the rod. Under normal fly fishing conditions it is unlikely you will need to cast further than ten or fifteen metres of line and leader and in fact seven metres should be quite enough for the beginner to handle. As competence grows you will cast well over 15 metres of line and leader but, apart from lake fishing, distance casting is rarely necessary. Far better to stalk the trout to within reasonable casting distance, a skill described in Chapter 10.

Assuming that the beginner can now manage to cast at a fly line without self-strangulation one or two finer points can now be mentioned. This advice concerns the presentation of the fly and is given now for one reason. The objective is to catch a trout on the fly and if we can do this while improving our casting so much the better. Obviously we have to be on the stream side and my advice is to pick a medium-sized river, say with an average width of ten to twenty metres. Choose a pool with a longish riffle at the head, nice wavy water about a half metre deep. If there is a boulder or two breaking up the water pattern so much the better. Stand on the gravel beach making sure you have no trees or bushes to the rear and set up shop. Don't wade in but allow enough casting distance so that the fly will reach the edge of the 'curly' water. Using a dry fly you will be diagonally facing upstream. If righthanded, you will be standing on the true right bank or vice versa, if lefthanded, (true right bank means the bank on the right facing downstream). After false casting and a few short true ones to get the feel of things, extend the line by further false casting until you think the fly will settle where you want it — about seven metres upstream. Aim for a point one metre above the water surface then shoot the line loop.

Unless you allow this extra metre the fly will probably hit the water too hard, at best sinking the fly, at worst, putting paid to a favourite story for many a year — a trout on the fly on the first outing. But regardless of the outcome this first time will be a real experience. There will come the time when instead of the fly floating back downstream, it will suddenly disappear, and, if your timing is right, you'll have the magical thrill that forever hooks a fly fisher — the first trout on the fly.

Unfortunately, we cannot always choose the battleground. More often than not we are hemmed in by willows, broom or gorse, and with a big hungry trout rising, we need more than the basic forward cast. Trees are a beginner's curse although, with experience, casting into awkward places can produce the best of fishing. In these tight corners the remedy lies in adapting the forward cast to dodge the tree. This is achieved by simply using the upright forward cast but in a horizontal position, as clear of the water as is comfortable. Known as the underhand or sideways cast it not only keeps the line and leader clear of overhanging branches but also makes the waving rod tip so much more difficult for the trout to see. Mastering this cast is

worth a pound of double-winged dry flies when fishing small streams.

The beginner can be forgiven for thinking the objective is to throw a straight line at all times. The ability to do so is important but once you can do this, never do it again. An exaggeration surely but there is a reason behind it. Unless fishing very still water the action of even slight currents can cause the nylon leader to 'drag', this in turn pulling the fly and revealing it as a fraud. A few curves in the line compensate for this. Trout are not partial to nylon monofilament and even more horrified to see the line. Even fine nylon over the trout's back is sometimes enough to frighten him and the obvious answer is to let him see the fly first using what is known as a curve cast or 'Shepherd's Crook'. Learning this cast requires a little practice.

By using a normal overhead cast to the fish, as the line is just straightening forward, raise the rod tip, thus checking the line; the leader and part of the line should curve to the left. This underpowers the cast at the last moment by allowing more line to shoot than necessary, and this loss of final energy will curve the leader to the right. Use the normal overhead cast but just as the line straightens on the forward, check the line by raising the rod tip. This should curve the leader tip to the left. Conversely, at the last moment, shooting a little extra line will cause loss of energy and the leader tip should curve to the right. This cast is especially handy under summer, low water conditions when trout are exceptionally spooky. In the meantime, if this cast has not been mastered the beginner should endeavour to cast from a position nearly opposite the trout and to a point upstream and to the angler's side of the fish.

Most useful is the roll cast. I use it in many situations where the overhead or side cast is impossible. Say you are

Ideal Fly Presentation

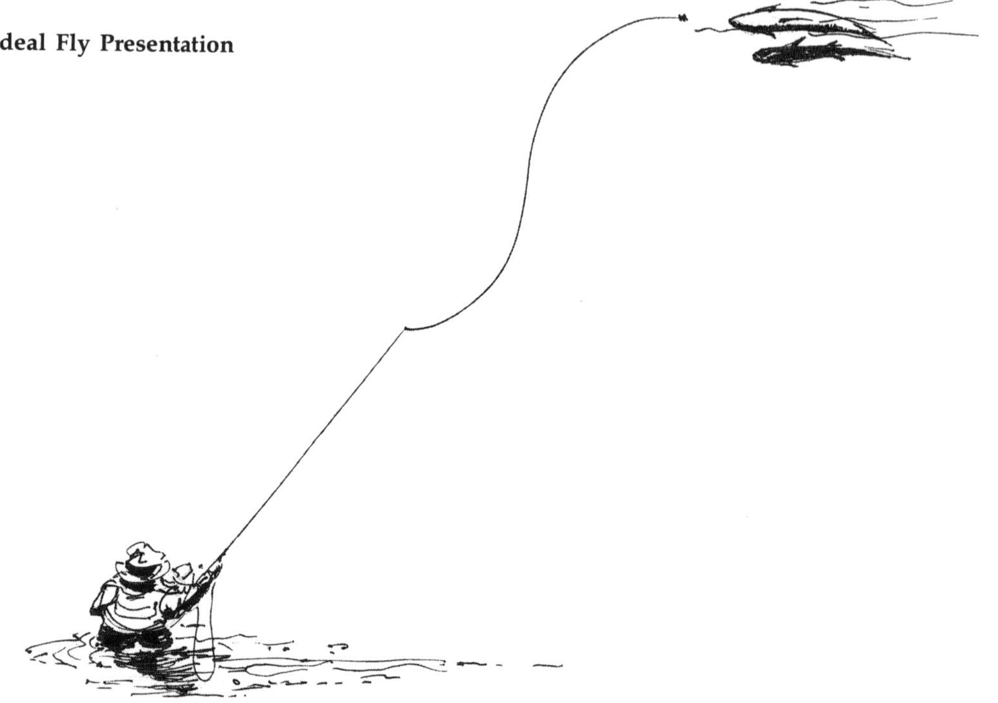

tucked into a high bank or with tall trees directly behind you. Do you watch the trout tucking into his dinner within casting distance and wish him well or do you learn to execute the roll cast? Here's how. Best practice on the lawn first. Lay out the line forward with your overhead cast, usual length. Now, with a very smooth but determined pull, raise the rod to the vertical. Imagine the fly at the end as a plane taking off, slowly, a bit faster, faster, faster, then at full speed curving into the sky. At this point, when the belly of the line reaches you, let the rod drift back just a little behind your head and, with a powerful punch forward, bring the rod tip back down to the horizontal.

If this cast is done reasonably well, the line will form a large loop just in front of you and unroll like a cartwheel back to where it started. It is important not to allow any part of the line to pass behind you when executing this cast. The roll cast is very popular with nymph fisherman, searching rapids or featureless stretches of water and who require the

nymph to be submerged as long as possible. A good roll caster is a delight to watch and if the beginner can observe such an angler he or she will learn much.

There will come a time when the righthanded beginner, now proficient with the overhead cast, will be forced, perhaps because of bluffs, to walk up the true left bank of the river. A very desirable trout is rising steadily close to this bank. You can see the problem. Even if the bushes on the bank let you get the overhead cast in the air, your forward cast will be over the bank edge and liable to be snagged. There are two ways to overcome this difficulty — one not easy but the other diabolical. The easier one first. This is the backhand cast which is really an overhead cast but instead of bringing the rod up to your casting side ear on the back cast stroke, you alter the retrieve angle, bringing it alongside the line hand ear — that is across your face. The obvious but almost unthinkable alternative is to learn to cast equally well with either hand, a feat reserved for

The Roll Cast

jugglers. Honesty forbids me advising the beginner for I have found that my own efforts at ambidexterity are guaranteed to produce much hilarity from my fishing friends. If I have any skill in this direction it can be put down to casting with two similar rods and lines. By some quirk of human behaviour one hand will always mimic the other and surprisingly, with a little practice the left hand (in my case) sends that line out pretty well. The problem starts when I try the left hand on its own! I'll never be much good at it but this little trick has given me enough confidence to try it when the occasion demands.

Something that does bother the beginner is line control and by this I mean, in dry fly fishing, taking up the slack as the current returns the fly. And, in wet fly fishing, 'mending' or flipping the line belly upstream to allow a longer drift. Upstream dry or nymph fishing requires the line to be cast with just enough slack line to prevent instant 'drag'. A 'dragging' or 'skating' fly is the anathema of the dry fly fisherman so the game is to recover the slack fly line at the same speed as the current, letting the fly float naturally. This can be done by 'palming the line' in figure of eight coils, a skill requiring some practice, or simply by recovering the line by smooth pulls and holding the larger coils. The former method is ideal for lake fishing where long casts are made and the compact coils are 'shot' forward in the next cast, but for stream or river fishing just drawing the line in three or four coils with the line hand and feeding them back out during false casting is just as efficient.

Shooting a line is not reserved for pretty girls. In angling parlance it means having a few coils of fly line held in reserve and, at the exact moment when the full power of the rod is forward, the line is released and pulled by the aerialised line 'shoots' through the rings.

Shooting just the right amount of line to allow the fly to not only reach the target but to settle gently is the essence of fly fishing.

It would be rather nice if we could cast to every rising trout by casting upstream, thus being out of his sight but all fish are not so obliging. Maybe he's stationed just upstream of a jumble of branch debris or near the top of an unwadeable pool with trees or bushes, making an upstream cast impossible. Fortunately, there is a way of casting a dry fly downstream and this is commonly known as the 'parachute cast'. I call it the 'desperation' cast because it is a once only chance. From a safe distance above the trout, an overhead or side cast is made in a downstream direction but when the fly, still in the air, some distance upstream of the fish, the rod tip is checked then lowered. This causes the leader and fly to collapse on the surface and float downstream. The trout, according to many angling stories, only has to open his mouth to take the fly but more often than not, at the exact moment the fly reaches him, it is pulled back. The ensuing 'drag' and 'v wakes' then make sure that this is one trout that you are not going to catch!

So, as we near the end of this chapter on fly casting, it remains only to provide some final hints:

1. When it comes to practising it is important to relax and not worry if progress isn't as fast as expected. Unnoticed, you will have improved.

2. Keep practising the basic overhead cast. Watch the line, see it straighten behind before commencing the forward cast. Recognise that fly casting is simply a matter of timing, not strength.

3. Don't try for long casts at first. A five-metre cast well thrown is better than a 15-metre cast that ends up around your ears.

4. When casting, try and keep the rod tip in the same plane forward as the back cast. This will form a small loop in the line cast with much greater accuracy.

5. Only when the basic overhead cast has been mastered should you attempt other casting techniques. The overhead will be used during 90 percent of your fishing so it is the most important.

6. If the beginner is having a problem it is likely to be from neglecting to heed this advice: 'A good forward cast is entirely dependent on a good back cast'. And you will never achieve that if you take the rod back behind your ear!

7. Finally, here is a tip that has helped scores of beginners: Imagine a small, hard, potato stuck on the rod tip. Bring the rod to the vertical. Then, still visualising the potato, use enough force to fling it off and forward. Simple, effective. Good luck!

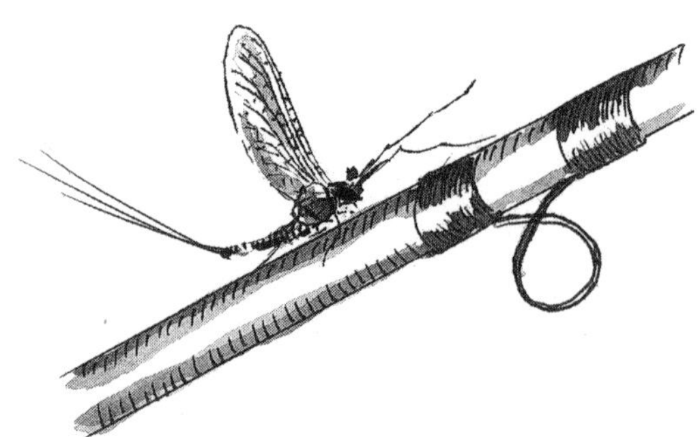

10

Streamcraft

The most important factor in trout fishing? Having fun catching trout? What about when we can't catch them? Still fun when they are uncooperative? Not quite, but even on days when no matter what we try the trout ignore us, there is always something to learn. This is because every time we venture out with the rod, trout present us with a challenge. Our canny quarry has a knack of bringing the most sophisticated of fly fishers down to earth, all part of the learning process which, if we care to admit it, never ends. To be a successful fly fisher takes more than owning fine fishing tackle. Agreed, the novice will have his or her day of days when trout, normally shy, will suddenly throw caution to the winds and take anything thrown at them however crudely. But not often. It is the angler with at least some degree of streamcraft under the belt that enjoys the full share of success.

Streamcraft can be defined as the ability to weigh up every trout situation encountered on a stream river or lake — by checking parameters such as distance and available cover, obstacles, wind, casting space, noting shadow, estimating current strengths, feed lines or drift, anticipating trout movement and finally deciding on the best line of approach. These skills have to be gained through experience but for the beginner there are basic rules which can be followed.

It is a well-known fact that trout must face upstream. Must they? It is by no means uncommon for trout to be facing the other way! In spring last year, fishing the La Fontaine, I came across a good example. Two good fish had already been returned and I was in a majestic mood as we approached the next willow-lined pool. From behind a handy bush I could see two beautiful trout lying midstream directly under a narrow feed line and both were feeding as though insects were going out of fashion. Now was the time to ask me for a fiver. I mean it is not every day you come across, not one, but two 'sitters' within easy casting distance. Eyes firmly fixed on the nearer of the two, I prepared to cast when, on looking down to check the fly, I saw, lying under my own bank, in a little back eddy, the biggest trout I had seen for many a moon. He was facing downstream and looking directly up at me. For a minute we gazed into each other's eyes, he no doubt highly delighted to be well warned, while I tried to pretend I'd never seen him. He left, of course, reminding me that even after so many years I have still much to learn. 'Cock of the North' today — feather duster tomorrow!

When fishing a river or stream for the first time, my first action, after setting up the rod, is to rest awhile and consider where I would lie if I were a trout. While we can never enter a trout's mind it is not too difficult to picture his needs. Food. Find a choice area where aquatic insects are likely to concentrate. Comfort. Somewhere preferably out of fast rough water, a run with enough depth to provide cover yet near enough to the surface to rise to any passing insect without too much effort. Refuge. On large rivers space itself is a form of shelter and trout may be spread across the river bed, but on small streams a trout will nearly always be stationed alongside or not too far away from a bolt hole. Wherever the current is concentrated, the depth moderate, and with a refuge handy that is where the angler can expect a trout.

Streamcraft means not only learning the ways of the trout and his habitat but building up a store of knowledge and, at any point in time, being able to recover it from the computer bank. An example of this occurred when I was fishing with my son on the Mataura near Garston. Walking a little way from the river we discovered an isolated scour hole gouged out by a winter flood. No bigger than a back porch and at least 20 metres from the river it seemed an unlikely home for a trout but we always inspect every prospect. A cautious peep through a leafy willow stump revealed a large brown trout, a survivor of a previous flood, cruising slowly around the green depths. But he was too cautious for us so we wished him well and moved on. It was in the following season, fishing in the same area, that Norm reminded me of the trout. Sure enough he was still there and this time, not so crafty, he took a deep sinking nymph and finished up in a trout casserole.

One important aspect that some fly anglers seem to disregard is the effect of temperature and barometric pressure conditions on the activity and location of trout. Should they change, the whole pattern of trout lies in a river can change and quite rapidly. For instance during summer, when water levels are low and temperatures high, trout will normally seek out an area where oxygen content is higher such as at the influx of a cooler feeder stream, below a waterfall, or in rapids, providing there is sufficient water cover. This is why, in the cooler evenings, with lower water temperatures, trout will venture out onto the broad shallow flats, normally deserted during the day. During the heat of the day I often forego fishing open water and concentrate solely on the willow-lined edge of the river where trout seek shade and where, despite the often frustrating casting conditions, one can enjoy some exciting sport.

The effect of barometric pressure on trout has always been cause for debate and some weird and wonderful theories

Selective trout water but well worth the effort. La Fontaine.

A long way from home but a welcome from an Oamaru rainbow.

Veteran flyfisherman returns a chunky Motueka brown.

Dry, nymph, wet, lure, spinner, worm, all are tried on the lovely Motueka River but the flyman usually comes off best.

Best approach here is upstream along left run, left hand tail of upper pool against overhanging willows then up the right hand bank run.

have been forthcoming. One thing anglers seem to agree upon is that when pressures are low, trout become torpid, so much so that some fishermen are reluctant to fish in those conditions. While I wouldn't go so far as to stay home I have to admit that I'm none too optimistic when the bottom has dropped out of the glass. Some speculate that the weight of atmosphere on the surface upsets the oxygen content of the water which in turn affects the trout. Others maintain trout go off the feed because the trout's air bladder, susceptible to minute pressure changes, inflates, and putting pressure on the stomach makes them disinclined to feed. When thunder rolls around the hills it may be a good time for lunch but if the storm is short-lived then you may have cause for rejoicing.

On the Hamilton Burn, a main headwater of the Aparima River, I had occasion to take shelter quickly when the heavens broke loose and a spectacular display of forked lightning etched itself against the dark thunder clouds. Prior to the torrential downpour the fish had been particularly dour and those that poked their noses at the fly none too keen. I was unfortunate in my choice of shelter under sparse willows because I had to share it with a long dead ewe so it was a case of drench or stench. Upstream in the long pool the rain pelted the surface like machine gun bullets. Visibility was no more than 20 metres. When the rain suddenly stopped, the water was still peppered but this time with trout rises. Whatever triggered them off I can only guess but there was certainly a massive hatch of Deleatidium nymphs. By the time the fourth or fifth trout, all around the two-kilogram mark, had been landed and all but one returned, my cup had overflowed. It was one occasion when I was thankful I had taken barometric pressure with a grain of salt.

To wade or not to wade? I know more than one fly fisherman who would no more wade than turn down a prize in Lotto. While I can't agree with the anti-waders there is no doubt that wading is overdone by many fly fishers especially when with a little strategy it can be avoided. How I wish I had listened to my own advice when I spotted that once-in-a-lifetime trout in the Worsley River in Fiordland. It was in autumn, not too far below St. Catherine Falls. The sun had nearly gone over the bush horizon but it was such a magical evening that even a tramp back in the dark seemed worth the extra time spent in wonderland. A big trout was rising steadily, just clear of the sheer rock wall shadow, the wobbly rings drifting downstream like punctuation marks and, although many years have now past, I still get goose pimples thinking about him. He looked enormous in the suns' last rays as he moved steadily up the feed line taking everything that floated down. The chance of a lifetime and I blew it by wading in too close. No sooner had my gym shoes touched the surface than the rises ceased. The big trout turned quietly and swam leisurely towards me on an inspection tour while I froze and promised to be a good boy for evermore. Just one more chance! He tortured me a little more by drawing up alongside for a better look then just to show what real trout are made of, he shot upstream at better than 30 knots. The irony of it was that I really didn't need to have waded at all. Just too anxious to get a better cast!

If wading is essential extreme care should be taken. Move slowly without creating any water disturbance, and never move nearer to the trout than absolutely necessary. Only the other day I approached a very nice Motueka trout lying upstream in a nice pocket. A feeding fish, one I was confident would take the fly. He was undisturbed and all I had to do was to pop a dry in front of him. But no! I just had to creep a metre nearer and that was that. He slipped quietly away to midstream and stayed there, inviting me to waste my time.

Of course, wading is necessary from time to time and in cooler weather a good pair of waders or wading boots and stockings makes for comfort. In summer, a pair of gym shoes are 'de rigueur' and makes for a quiet approach across a gravel beach, but in colder or tramping conditions, a pair of stout boots is the order of the day and if they are nylon tramping boots with steel cleats on the heels only, so much the better. Rubber waders, without felt soles or cleats, can be treacherous even when new and worse when the tread is worn. For the chance of a pair of custom-made American wading boots it is quite in order to walk on broken glass.

Fly fishing means concentration and if you are forever tottering about and wondering when the next ducking is going to come it is time to consider seriously investing in something better. After scorning the use of a wading staff for most of my fishing career, and having had more than my fair share of duckings, with one or two that have nearly terminated me, I am now thoroughly converted. A short length of bamboo, light yet strong, and attached by a short cord gives unbelievable confidence and reduces those embarrassing visits to the insurance company.

With modern tackle, strong yet supple rods, and reliable nylon there are few excuses for losing a well-hooked fish. It is rare for a trout to be lost through failure of the nylon, a faulty knot or a blunt hook is a more likely cause. When fishing for big back country trout or on the larger lowland rivers a 3x, or sometimes a 2x, tippet is warranted but on smaller down country rivers or streams, finer nylon will give much better results. On rivers like the Motueka or the Mataura, where trout are unusually fussy, I use 6x tippets which, providing the fish is not keel-hauled, hold trout up to 1.4 kilograms without too much heart strain.

Many fish are lost either through the angler not inspecting the area beforehand for possible snags or through sheer panic. Breakages usually occur during the first mad dash or by initially striking too hard. If this first run can be controlled and the hook purchase is good there is little excuse for losing a hooked trout. Speeding trout that turn quickly, forcing a slack line, are the angler's nightmare. This is where the practice of playing a trout from the reel becomes unstuck. Overseas videos may show the intrepid fly fisherman with rod to high heavens turning a hooked trout this way and that while he pirouettes around the pool. But the average New Zealand trout are bigger than their foreign brethren and unless one is prepared to run a marathon with the fish, playing it from the hand-held line makes the process much safer and much more comfortable.

Sometimes it doesn't matter what you do or what precautions you take. Some trout are going to give you a hard time and we had better get used to it! Last season on the Rai I paid court to a couple of good-sized rainbows in a short but deep pool. Stem to stern the two fish lay almost under a flood-thrown willow trunk, the lower fish lying just upstream of a great log straddling the pool tail. The downstream pool was much larger with plenty of playing space but in the middle were two big submerged tree stumps, hazards which I duly noted. As expected, when the bottom rainbow felt the nymph hook he spun in his own length and shot downstream, over the log sill, and proceeded to give the usual fireworks display we expect from a good rainbow.

Another view of ideal stalking water. Again note 'glare' and the need to use the willow reflection.

Twice I held him from running up the far side of the stumps but I underestimated his strength on the third occasion. With a short burst he was there, behind the stumps, and still full of zip. Trying to pull him back downstream seemed to annoy him even more. Suddenly he sped midstream towards me, past the top of the stumps, which, of course, meant he had done the full circle. He disappeared into the pool depths with the fly line (a brand-new one I hasten to add) and wrapped it tightly around the underwater timber. It was so deep you couldn't see the bottom so wading was out of the question. On other (fortunately rare) similar occasions I have stripped to the nuddy but I'm now too old for that caper. I balanced my way across the pool tail log to the other side, went the full length of the fly line downstream, crossed my fingers and started to pull. I finally recovered the line and half the leader and learned that when you think you know it all there is always someone or, in this case a rainbow, to take you down a peg.

Streamcraft (really just a handy name for riverside tactics) depends on the ability to observe, as apart from 'seeing', and to use the information at the right time and in the right place. A favourite stream soon becomes so familiar that many trout can be given names — I know one or two shrewd beauties in my local river I have christened but the names are unprintable. The true test comes when fishing strange water where even the most confident of anglers can often feel a little subdued. A small stream you can come to grips with fairly easy but, on larger rivers with few features or on lakes with a vista of seemingly empty water, one has to work hard. Whether it is stream, river, or lake, the fly fisher's first priority is to stand back and study the local conditions, even before the rod is put up. The choice of fishing area should be made carefully taking into consideration the type of water, the likelihood of it containing enough sizable trout, bank cover or lack of it, and how the prevailing weather conditions will

Easy on this type of pool to spend half the day fighting with the willows. Learning to roll cast pays dividends on such water.

affect your chances. Don't think you are wasting valuable time exploring the stretch upstream or the next bay along the lake edge. Remember it is all going into the streamcraft computer ready to use in future.

Having decided on a starting point the next consideration is to choose the best method of catching the trout. Dry, wet or nymph, lure? On a larger river, where rough water makes it difficult to spot trout the choice is either a large dry fly bobbed down the stream edge or into likely pockets or a weighted nymph also fished blind but with the aid of a small wool sighter tied on the leader. If fishing this type of water with the nymph one should concentrate on the slack water edge of the pool eye. On the return trip downstream why not fish a wet fly down

and across. After much concentration on the way upstream there is something almost euphoric in the wet fly casting rhythm with every wide sweep promising a surprise pull. Wherever you fish, whatever the method, move slowly, noting as you wade or walk, features however small — weed beds, sheltering boulders, overhanging trees, shallow sandy areas or rocky streambed clefts, feed lines, airborne insects, sheltered sections, side stream inlets, the opposite bank possibilities, wading conditions, stream bed strata, stone undersides for nymph types, future access points and backwaters. For things fishy, the fly fisher has the best memory in the world. Doctor's appointments and putting out the milk bottles we tend to forget!

11

Finicky Trout

Name me one fly fisherman that hasn't returned from a streamside visit with his carbon fibre between his legs and I'll post you my 1746 copy of 'The Complete Angler'. After an ego trip with the trout in full retreat it is easy to forget the occasions when for all the good we do we might as well fish with a fried egg. How often have we managed to fool enough trout to raise a smug smile on the hike back to the car? How often have we rejoiced when, after the first sporadic sightings of the odd mayfly, they appear in squadrons, then in droves and we shake and tremble and can't believe it is finally happening, and how often, after many refusals to our well presented fly, are we brought well and truly down to earth!.

The question of why a trout will feed on only one particular insect when others are readily available has plagued fly anglers for many generations. From experience we know that trout are unpredictable creatures, one day feeding as though the shop is going to close down, the next day on a weight watcher's diet. We can only guess the real answer but it seems to me that trout are little different from other wild creatures, being totally dependent on nature's largess — the abundance or scarcity of trout food insects. A square metre of stream bed can and usually does contain hundreds of aquatic insects that a trout, given the opportunity, can feed on. But if the trout is hard to catch so are his would-be victims. Trout stream insects have developed their own wiles to thwart the ever-waiting trout.

Take mayfly nymphs for instance. It is not common to see them on or about the stream bed. Some species do expose themselves but they are well equipped with strong, hooked claws, with such a purchase that to try and remove them forcibly is to kill them. But under the stones there is a hive of activity, industry beyond our ken, where many insects have a licence to kill, others are bent on escaping, but all with absolutely no intention of being swept away by chance. If the trout had a mind he would call himself patient, willing to wait for that magic moment when the first raindrop pricks his roof. He must then tremble a little, especially after a dry spell when his stomach is sticking to his ribs. Instinct tells him that soon those tiny but tasty morsels now so secure under the stones, will also tremble as they feel the first subtle force of a rising river. One can almost imagine an alerted trout tying on his bib in anticipation and, as the most juvenile and weaker insects are washed down, he becomes indeed the trencherman of the river. No selectivity here. It's bangers and spuds day and the devil take the hindmost. Hardly any need to shake a fin, when there is a constant stream of insects, many of which will take the final trip to his stomach.

A whole range of trout food insects is available to him — from mayfly nymphs to Neuroptera larva (toe biters), from caddis larva to stonefly nymphs, and many, many more. But his feeding will not be confined to the stream bed. For some unexplained reason, during rising river levels, near-mature mayfly nymphs start to move and, although the water may be coloured, a prolonged hatch of flies may occur. In early spring, when these levels are up and down like the Barclay index, fishing a dry fly can sometimes be more rewarding than in summer's shrunken pools. In these high water conditions trout will feast on washed-down insects and if a trout can be seen feeding well below the surface a

weighted nymph is an obvious choice. During this smorgasbord time trout are relatively easy to catch, for not only are they fully occupied with feeding but the stained or coloured water helps to conceal the angler. Even the most sophisticated of fly fishers revel in such occasions and the beginner, if he has done his sums, should feel the weight of more than one trout for his efforts.

Fortunately these halcyon days are not frequent for if trout were always obliging our ranks would thin quickly as we went in search of a better challenge. We needn't worry on that score. As long as we have clean, cool water we will have an abundance of aquatic insects for the trout, and we anglers will continue to scratch our heads and wonder why, on too many occasions, we can't catch him. The puzzle starts when, sooner or later (usually sooner), we come across trout that are feeding ravenously yet they completely ignore our best efforts. These fish are not a special breed but trout that for the time being are feeding on one and one only type of insect. They are known in fishing circles, as 'selective trout'.

These picky fish are often credited with a high degree of intelligence, perhaps, I suspect, because being so far up the biological pecking order we humans can't accept defeat. The answer is really very simple. And so natural. The trout, like any other creature including humans (although with the arms race and 20-megaton bombs you have to wonder if we should be included) have one aim and that is to survive. Survival to the trout means not only avoiding enemies but taking in more energy than he expends. For energy read insects — he will instinctively balance his efforts to catch them against their food value. We tend to think that a hungry fish will be easier to catch. It stands to reason, we say, but a trout may well regard the odd journey across a strong current as not worth the caddis cake. But put the fly or nymph across his nose and it's an All Black jersey to a last years *Listener* that he'll take it.

Under normal conditions, for most of the day, trout food insects drift sporadically downstream, some dislodged, some deliberately migrating to new pastures. A pretty humdrum day for the trout. But then, along the river, triggered by water levels, light values and water and air temperatures, there comes the mass movement of mature nymphs. No-one is certain why the phenomenon occurs but to witness it is an event in the flyfisher's calendar. Once again the trout perks up his fins and lays the table. A few rises occur in the sill of the pool followed shortly by an odd rise along the willowed edge. Soon the pool is covered in watery rings and the angler, in mind's eye, is already netting or beaching fish after fish. In the water column another struggle for survival is taking place — the dark-backed nymphs fighting to break through the surface tension and burst into free flight. As in every community there are weaklings and countless thousands of half-hatched mayflies, easy prey, are helplessly pressed up against that terrible window. With the tiniest of sips, and with minimum effort, these insect cripples are drawn down a watery vortex created by the trout, leaving only a mourning dimple. A keen observer can tell by the 'humping' riseform and the absence of any adult mayfly that the trout are feeding on aborted nymphs but after 20 minutes of disillusionment the burning question is: what kind?

You may recall mention of the common Deleatidium type nymphs which inhabit most of our rivers and streams, generally in large numbers and it is more than probable that the trout will be feeding on them. Not the smooth slick nymph of the stream bed but now a small dark grey, bedraggled insect with wings half-developed and waterlogged. The only way to confirm this is to wade in among the rising fish and take a sample with a fine net. Or if you do manage to fool a sizable trout, one promised for the cook, kill it and perform a stomach autopsy. It takes a strong willed angler to perform the first option and even firmer resolve for the latter when the light is fading fast and every trout in the river is rising. Picture the trout. The food is coming down fast and furious, in different forms, hatching nymphs, aborted adults, mature nymphs, wriggling in the surface film and emerging into adult mayflies, and fully-formed winged adults taking off from the surface. But, almost all of the same species.

Now comes an even greater question. From the above selection the trout may be feeding on one particular insect phase or the lot for that matter, so which imitation do we choose — nymph, emerger pattern or an imitation of the adult? Picture the trout again. He neither knows nor cares how long the bonanza is going to last but with all his mates tucking in he will make quite sure he isn't at the back of the queue. Trout are strongly territorial and even during hatch periods will keep close to their normal feeding station, moving upstream a little, then drifting down, but very little sideways. Economy of movement again.

It is now easy to see that, even if we offer a good imitation, our casting has to be very good indeed to land the fly in the right place at the right time. If we can see the fish this does not present a problem but on most rivers the big hatch comes just before dark and all we have as targets are trout rises. We cast just above the rise but is he there? Upstream, downstream or in my lady's chamber? This is where many fly fishers, including myself, waste valuable time casting to this rise, then that, then back to the first one, 'and that one looks promising', until, fed up with unsuccessful random casting, we are sorely tempted (but not quite) to break the rod into pencil lengths. One possible solution is to picture what is happening underwater and try to figure out why that 'selective' trout doesn't select yours!

In fact, if it appears to the trout as just another unfortunate titbit and if it is in the right place at the right time, he most probably will take it. If you are fishing a small dry fly and it floats over his nose you have a chance. If you are fishing a nymph and it almost brushes his mouth, again you're in with a chance. But among the myriads of insects drifting to, over and past him, a fly fished 'dead drift' stands out much less than one that looks alive. Tie on a small black or grey soft-hackled wet fly or emerger pattern and cast it as quickly as you can just upstream, directly in line with the rise, and draw the fly slowly and smoothly across his bows. He may not take it the first time or the second or on the twentieth cast, but keep onto the same rising fish. Fish correctly and with imagination. It shouldn't be too long before you get a surprise.

While I have still a lot to learn about selective trout, years of fishing the famous Mataura River taught me a great deal. It is a wonderful river, well stocked over its 112-kilometre course. The upper reaches, around Parawa and Garston, provide excellent daytime fishing, but it is in the lower middle reaches, notably in the Matuara and Wyndham areas, that draw fly fishers from all over the world to test their skills during the evening rise. The pools are generally long and placid, the water neither clear nor dirty, mostly a ghostly grey in the deeper runs, especially in summer when masses of fine drifting algae make fish spotting difficult. Willows abound and where they are will be found some of any river's best fishing. Stalking these ultra-cautious fish under a high sun can be either rewarding or frustrating, depending on the angler's skills. One of my favourite pools lies just below Wyndham near Clarke's Island is a classic case, — long, smooth, willows on one side, a fairly high grassy bank on the other. During the daytime the trout are well spread and in the lower reaches, are lying deep. But the top half of the pool shallows along the bank side and by lowering oneself into the water over the high bank, it is possible to do a heron's stalk to big trout, fossicking in the shallows. Using traditional flies for these selectively feeding fish generally sends them scooting for cover. But an imitation waterboatman (See Chap. 7) cast gently upstream to these big cruising browns makes for exciting fishing.

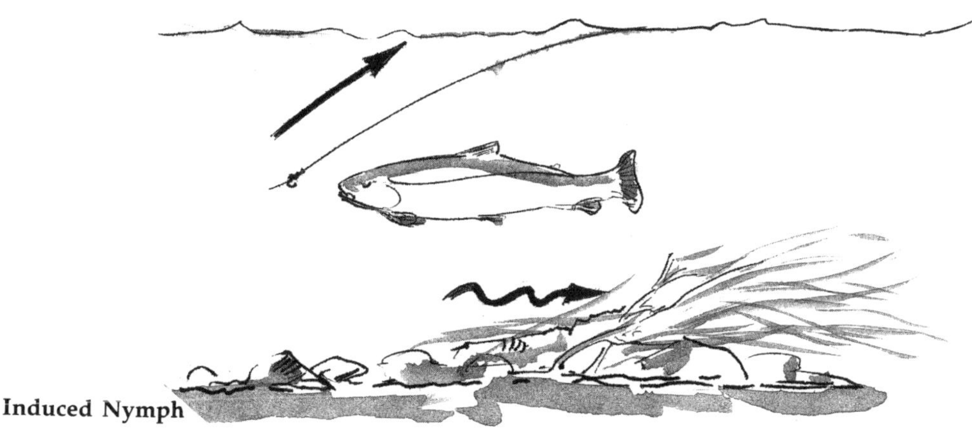

Induced Nymph

Then, when my heart pounds and my knees turn to jelly, how I wish for the steely nerves of the master fisherman. First the little dimple, the trout invisible in reflected light; then, much, much too near, the sight of a heart-thumping brown. Crouched like a question mark into the crusty bank it is time for prayers and sometimes they are answered. Sometimes (may there be more of them) I am undetected and given the chance to try a botch of a cast, barely the length of the leader. Sometimes, instead of a great bow wave heading deep, there is a gentle stirring before all hell breaks loose and my knees become even wobblier. And sometimes, instead of that stomach-churning twang as the nylon parts, there is the thrilling pull of a big wild trout which hasn't the slightest intention of letting your have it your own way. But it happens — sometimes. And all the failures, all the heart wrenches, all the 'why does it always happen to me' times, are quickly forgotten and all is well with the world. If the sight of a big Mataura brown gladdens the heart it is even more satisfying to see him, even if a bit groggy, sliding back home.

Daytime episodes like this are stimulating enough for any angler but it is when the 'mad Mataura rise' starts that the fun really begins. In the Deep South during summer months the sun doesn't set until after 9 pm and dusk lasts until near midnight. It is in the long glassy glides that the first rises appear, sporadic at first, then with increasing tempo until, with a rise to every square metre, you would swear it was raining. In the gathering gloom there is no need for concealment. The angler stands at the river's edge, ensures good casting clearance behind, and lays siege to the nearest trout rise. No need to cast very far, as the evening feast progresses a five metre cast will cover many trout rises and it is this very proximity that inevitably

unnerves the fly fisher. A refusal after five minutes does no real harm but, as it becomes too dark to see the fly and great trout are gulping 'god knows what' within a rod length and absolutely ignoring anything and everything, it's not hard to understand why fly fishers lose patience. I know, I've been there and done that. But one evening I did the unthinkable. Waded in amongst them with a fine net and in the car headlights discovered the source of activity — midge pupa, in great numbers, tiny wee critters, some green, some red, with little feathery antennae, so tiny that a 20 hook size or smaller would be needed to imitate them. No wonder a small dry or #16 nymph didn't work.

A few evenings later, after tying some creditable midge pupa imitations, I returned to the fray, same place, same time, and when the rise got into full swing I presented the trout with my secret weapon. It was so secret they didn't bother with it. After a half hour's casting practice off came the new recipe and on went the old, a #18 soft hackled fly, simply made with a waterhen undercover feather and dark mole's fur. While I never really win this age-old battle with selective trout, the autopsy performed on one of the big trout landed that night taught me something. The fish had been taking midge pupa but had just as many emerging nymphs inside him. And I'm sure it was by inducing some semblance of motion into the artificial that gave me that little edge.

Since then I have fished many different rivers and streams for selective trout with more or less the same results and it took a talented English angler to show me a new trick. And not only on the Mataura but on my more recently adopted river, the Motueka. In many ways the Mataura and the Motueka are similar, with many slow flowing pools and a great variation in water types, from tidal near

Motueka, to the fine gravel reaches and pools of the upper reaches. It was on John Goddard's 1987 visit that, after fishing many rivers and lakes between Southland and Nelson, we spent his final week or so on the Motueka. It is common knowledge that Motueka trout are no fools and can be equally as selective as their Southland cousins, so I was quietly confident that they wouldn't let me down. In short they were to give John a hard time! But I might have known that he would have something up his sleeve. That something was the Goddard Suspender Midge Pupa, an imitation he created to overcome the problem of midge-feeding trout.

Midge pupa rise to the surface preparatory to hatching, then move rapidly before breaking through the film. By using a tiny ball of polystrene enclosed in nylon mesh (pantyhose) near the head, the fly was allowed to float vertically upstream of the rise and then was drawn smoothly along the surface. One of my favourite memories of his visit is looking upstream to where John was standing on a large, smooth, sculptured rock. The sun had just set behind Mount Arthur and the Motueka in the sun's reflected glow was a river of gold, and the slow-moving feed line in the long pool was dotted with rises. While I persevered with my tiny wet fly, his curved rod was frequently bent, silhouetted against the evening sky. The serenity of the night was broken only the murmur of the water and the whining of John's reel. Although I did hook fish using those odd-looking pupa imitations, I could never match John's success, probably because I lacked his skilled technique.

My friend didn't have it all his own way, though. On a small West Coast spring creek it was my turn to lead the field. It had been raining for the past few days (surprise!) and even the dependable La Fontaine had muddy boots. From a previous tour I remembered a small stream rising from a spring and running through farmland to join a large rough river. If that wasn't in good order it would have to be an afternoon of tying flies or catching up on our paperback reading. Fortunately it was clear but very full and fast, making if difficult to control a fly — clearly a case for a decent-sized nymph. I was into my fourth fish before John joined me and took notice of my bright, red wool sighter some two metres up the leader. The fish were very difficult to see but, every now and again, by casting well upstream into good fish lies and quickly recovering slack, the sighter would slide under and the Blue Darter nymph would be firmly attached to a good-sized trout. Exciting stuff on a little stream! This shows that is is not only the fly but also the fishing technique that is important.

One of the most neglected aspect of fly fishing is that of fishing caddis imitations. From the chapter describing natural insects the reader will be familiar with the various forms of caddis fly but may be unaware that, when the mature pupa is hatching, the trout become highly selective. Daytime hatches are sometimes difficult to detect because they seem to occur in broken water such as riffles and 'drop offs'. That this should be is a mystery but maybe it is because the ruffled, choppy surface minimises the surface tension, making it easier to break through the film. However, despite the enthusiasm that trout display when taking these emerging insects, the rise in fast curly water is generally hard to see. It takes the form of a tiny splash, easy to miss in the various swirls and ripples, especially from any distance. But once you've found your target you can be assured of some fine sport using a soft hackled wet fly, a hopper pattern, or a squirrel hair caddis.

It is during the late evening that caddis hatches make for some memorable occasions. Usually the first indication is when the small splashes are seen against the darker, far bank, and it is then time to change the fly. The fly can be larger, as big as a #12 and the leader tippet strength increased. A wise move, for during semi-darkness large trout move from safe holes and take the best stations outstream. As it is normally dark by the time the caddis are about a small torch is essential.

I always compare night fishing for trout with sea fishing in that you are always surprised at the catch. As you slowly retrieve the fly all the senses are concentrated on the rod tip, honed by the sound of great sucks and slurps out in the darkness and nerves are quickened as the splash of a big trout shatters the stillness. One never knows if that sudden pull is a small fish or one that will take you stumbling down to the lower pool. And for some reason, trout hooked at night always seem much bigger than they really are, a bonus for those of us who seem to miss out on the really big ones. Whether it is fishing for finicky trout with dry, nymph, hackled wet, or caddis there is always one guarantee: when the day arrives for you to hang up the rod, the mystery of how to catch selective trout will still be around.

12

Fishing the Little Streams

Few trout anglers have cut their teeth on four-pounders (1.8 kilograms). Most of us started off with something much less than half a pound or even less but what excitement that was. Nothing over the ensuing years can quite equal the electric thrill of that first trout. It will forever be a noble fish, a strong, courageous, heroic fighter, a fish that continues to grow with the years. It will also probably have been caught on that king of the compost heap, the worm, and even more likely to have been fished out of a small stream.

Fishing the little streams, the angler will be pushing his luck to hook a four-pounder (1.8 kilogram). Even a three-pounder (1.36 kilogram) gives cause for a little celebration. This is not to say small streams don't contain the odd super trout. In a previous book I wrote about Norm, a 14-year-old who had the good fortune to be in the right place at the right time on a little stream you could jump across and landed a brown over ten pounds (4.5 kilograms). Only last season I was fortunate to net a seven pounder (3.17 kilogram) from a little tributary of the upper Mataura, a little spring-fed creek that many anglers pass without a thought. Big trout caught in these waters are remembered long after larger ones taken from bigger rivers. But back to the real world — the average size of trout in the little streams is much smaller but then again a wild two-pounder (about one kilogram), well muscled and angry, is no mean opponent. Especially when he knows his immediate habitat intimately, down to the last piece of trailing weed or sunken debris.

Success on a small stream is directly proportionate to the angler's knowledge of it. It takes many excursions to build up mental pictures of its twists and turns, the special 'trouty' pools, the willow corners that shelter the best trout, and other more subtle features. For instance, the knowing angler will note the time of day one pool is in sunshine and another in shade. He or she will have marked the position of many fish seen but missed on previous visits, learned that a particularly good fish can only be approached from a new direction, discovered a leafy tunnel through the brambles that gives a chance at that crafty four-pounder (1.8 kilograms). On a small stream he can be near certain that a good fish, once resident in a hard-to-reach corner, blessed with shelter and a healthy feed line, will seldom move away. The stability of its inhabitants is another of a small stream's assets.

During the periods when these miniature rivers are running normally or slightly above, when the water flows the colour of sherry, when pushing through the willows means an unrehearsed shower and the stream is bubbling with vitality, the trout can be most obliging and even a novice should feel the weight of a two-pounder. But when the cocksfoot is high and the heat shimmers over the paddocks, when the cool water around the knees is a pleasant relief, and what were dancing rapids are now shrunken pools, then the little streams are a challenge. And then the trout have a remarkable ability to cut the angler down to size.

I ought to know, I have been whittled away more times than I care to remember. Take our last trip to a princess of a small stream, typical of thousands of other from the Bay of Plenty to the Bluff. The sun was already high by the time we reached the bridge. From it, upstream, and along the willow-lined stream edge we could see three good fish cruising slowly along and through the bright green weed beds. It is, or should be, common knowledge that bridge trout are the most difficult to catch having been pestered by hundreds of hopefuls. Another fact is that they are absolutely irresistible so with a low rod and high hopes I waded quietly along the edge, calf deep in weeds and silt. Crystal-clear, still water, the nylon, fine as it was, cracked the mirror surface and as each trout sidled away another would lure me on, until, with the next step I went through the mudpan and up to the unmentionables! I never really expect to hook these ultra-shy fish so there must be a masochistic streak in some of us.

On small streams it is rare to find clear banks and the angler must frequently enter the stream. This of course means extreme caution when approaching a trout and, unless the angler is hemmed in by willows or high banks, all casting should be horizontal. Despite the assurance that a short rod is more suitable I find the extra length of a nine-footer (2.7 kilograms) an advantage in keeping the fly high above the bank behind and much better for roll casting when in a tight corner and a little extra distance is required. It hardly bears mention that for summer fishing the best wading gear is shorts and gym shoes although, where banks are infested with bramble, a pair of light khaki longs saves the legs. Not so long ago, suffering from an honourable knee injury after falling in the river (not infrequent these days), I had a bedside visit from a doctor/angler who reproached me for foolhardiness. He was wearing shorts and his legs looked like they had been through a wool-scouring plant. 'Oh that', he said offhandedly, 'That's from pushing through the blackberry!'

By careful observation one comes to know the types of trout food insects to expect. These cover a wide range both in variety, seasons and in times of emergence. Mayfly and caddis fly species usually predominate but at certain times of the year other trout food types may appear. For instance, during mid to late summer a considerable number of hawthorn or blossom flies may be blown onto the stream and the angler who has experience this bonanza will not forget it. On these occasions trout seem to lose all sense of caution, almost dashing across pools and riffles to snatch the obviously nourishing morsels. A reasonable imitation of the blossom fly is Love's Lure, a fly of black hackle and peacock herl body and wing. During December and January swarms of green and brown beetles make life happier for the trout which are then not difficult to catch.

I recall an evening in a Southland fishing lodge. Our fishing party was playing scrabble with pleasant music from the radio. Someone casually mentioned it had started to rain and eventually the drumming on the window claimed attention. Hundreds of brown beetles were hurling themselves at the chinks in the curtain and despite a shouted warning someone opened the door. We spent the next ten minutes sweeping with brush and shovel hundreds of the little beasties into a large bucket.

A common insect in small streams is the dobsonfly larva, an odd looking creature with what appears to be short lateral tentacles, a large black head and relatively large foreleg pincers. They turn up regularly during trout autopsies but commercial imitations seem scarce and here the fly tier has the advantage. Other seasonal tasty bits are damsel or dragonfly larva especially where shallow weedy backwaters occur but again, the fly fisher will probably need to make his or her own.

The most prolific insect in backwaters

A study in shadows. Knee bending is prerequisite on the little stream in the Nelson Province.

is the waterboatman, doomed to rise to the surface for air with regularity. This feature makes him a prime candidate for dinner when cruising trout are about and if the fly fisher is on the ball the trout becomes the victim. There is no point in casting a waterboatmen imitation to a cruising fish — in still shallow water trout are allergic to nylon leaders however fine. But by noting the trout's almost regular circuit the imitation can be laid ready and waiting. A bit sneaky but all's fair in love and water.

If the angler has the nerve of a Pot Black runner-up on the final ball and, at that split second before the trout swims over the fly, he or she can gently move it without alarm, it is a fair bet that the trout will suck it in. Last season my young friend Dion had considerable success fly fishing with a maggot. Not as bad as it seems. He discovered on his small stream, after opening up a trout, that the stomach was full of large maggots, or as the English aristocrats used to call them 'gentles'. The donor, a sheep carcass some way upstream. On his next visit Dion's fly box contained one or two imitations made from worsted cream wool wrapped around a hook. How simple can you get! It is often the basic, no nonsense items that produce the best results and this proved the case when this very astute young angler tested his creation. Not every stream has an obliging ewe or wether but this story does illustrate the need to be observant and ready to adapt to the situation accordingly.

There are times when there are no clues as to what the trout are feeding on, more commong than not. This is where some local knowledge can prove invaluable but without that it is a safe bet to try the Pheasant Tail representing a pattern covering a variety of the likely nymph food. Failing that, a small Blue Darter or a Hare and Copper may fit the bill but on small streams it is wise to keep to the smaller sizes, say #14 or #16 hooks. That is unless the river is above normal when a #12 may be more suitable. Another good imitation for little streams is the Wooly Caddis, an imitation of the free-swimming net-building caddis that makes up a fair quota of the trout's daily diet. A simple body dressing of grey hare fur, black silk head and tied on a small caddis type hook is usually sufficient to deceive the trout. The mayfly nymph most likely to be encountered on small streams is one of the Leptophlebidae species or the 'small brown nymphs'. These vary little in size but the adult range in general colour from dark brown to fawn or smoky grey. An all-round imitation for the adult mayfly is one of brown opposum fur with gold tinsel rib and a very dark brown hackle. Providing good quality hackles are used, again, simple but effective. In recent years the Passion Fruit Hopper, a small delta-winged insect, has made an appearance in trout stomach autopsies and mention of this is made in an earlier chapter. During mid and later summer, providing the imitation is fished using fine nylon (even down to 6x), it is one of the best.

There are many occasions when I wish someone would teach me how to catch summertime trout, canny enough to spot a cap badge at a hundred paces. There are days when, despite all the care in the world and all the skill you can muster, trout of the little streams thumb their snouts at you. On these days you simply persevere. There is a little stream I fish in Marlborough with some pools, one in particular, so beautiful it almost takes your breath away. Well it really is two pools but all that separates them is a great log, barely under the surface and spanning the stream. A great beech shades the far bank with native shrubs filling in the gaps while the piece de resistance is a nodding clump of gold toi toi where the big log emerges. The near

Mataura River. The end of a perfect day.

John Goddard, famous English angler hangs onto a lively rainbow on the Locky River near Queenstown.

Lake Hawea, southern gem. A procession of parading trout.

Lower Lake Mavora where a power boat ban preserves its tranquil charm. Upper lake just beyond tussocks, middle picture.

A flyfisherman's stream, the Otapiri in Southland. Not big fish but very wary indeed. Note the 'feedline' down pool centre.

bank, the fishing side approach, is steep and covered in blackberry so the only way to reach casting distance is to wade up the edge along a very narrow ledge, a journey made all the more dicey when your eye is on a big rainbow cruising around some massive sunken tree roots.

There I was, hunched up on my little perch like a garden gnome with this (must have been 1.8 kilograms) rainbow within a rod length. I waited for him to swim behind one of the sunken logs and, after a couple of botched miniature roll casts, managed to toss out a small Blue Darter. The water was so clear I could see the nymph slowly sinking on my side of the log. Then the trout appeared, a magnificent sight, so majestic, master of his domain swimming slowly towards the little lure. I held by breath as he came up to it and I tensed ready to strike at the flash of his jaws. He stopped for a split second then in a supercharged burst

streaked downstream and out of the pool!

Now that trout never saw me, so what nearly scared him out of his scaly skin? It is unlikely that he was terrified of the nymph, and why a piece of almost transparent nylon should give him the willies is a mystery. It is not a unique happening and it does suggest that trout, despite having little brain matter, have some instinctive memory base and that on some previous occasion that trout associated either the artificial or the nylon, or both, with a bad time. One of his two friends in the upper pool, where the current runs fast and deep, wasn't so fussy and took the same nymph with gusto. The hooked rainbow then threaded his way into the underwater branches and that was the only obliging trout I found that day. Others shied away even with the most careful approach and those that permitted a cast would shoot upstream a short distance, tempting any novice to have another foolish attempt.

It is not all gloom and doom on small streams during low water conditions. There are days when trout will almost beg to be caught by a skilful angler. On those 'lack of fish' days (not poor days, because on a trout stream, with rod in hand, there is no such thing) you will generally find that the trout have been inactive because of a temporary dearth of trout food insects. It seems reasonable to suppose that when a trout is concerned with feeding, his self-preservation instincts are not so sharp and make him less critical of the angler's fly. Under these conditions approaching a feeding trout is always much easier and even a poor cast will not necessarily send him scooting for cover.

There are as many types of small streams as there are breeds at the Crufts Dog Show. But whether it's a limestone lowland river, a West Coast spring-fed stream, a King Country tributary or a Canterbury creek, each has one common denominator when it comes to successful fishing. The ability to stalk trout. The anger who has served an apprenticeship on a small stream is well armed to tackle larger rivers and lakes which, although less intimate, still respond better to a careful and studied approach. Take for instance my home stream, the Motueka. Hardly a small stream yet neither is it a big river. The trout behave like small stream trout though, with a reputation for being very wary and unforgiving, anyone who has fished this river will no doubt agree. To give some idea of the need for stealth perhaps an account of my last few hours of last season will suffice.

I'd come across the almost hidden access to this lovely pool by accident a few days before when I crossed an upstream rapid and, from the opposite bank (don't all far banks look more promising?), noted a steep bluff and a pocket of bush. That is where I would search for a track. Returning a few days

later I found a trail leading through almost impassable scrub bracken and bramble to a high bushclad terrace overlooking a deep slow-flowing pool, studded with large rocks. It was mid morning, a sunny day with little wind, the fantails already busy in the riverside trees and swallows almost flicking the river for unseen insects.

In a deep bankside hole near the tail of the pool two fish were busy, one almost bracketed by large sunken rocks, the other on a Cooks Tour around the still water of a secondary pool. Using the terrace trees as cover I made downstream of both fish and spent the next ten minutes watching them. Satisfied I'd gleaned enough information for action I set up the rod, made sure the leader was at least three metres plus and the tippet 6x, I attached a hopper and after stalking within easy casting distance of the lower fish, laid the fly out in ambush. Around he came, deeper than I thought, and when he ignored the hopper I didn't pester him but changed to a small, quick-sinking black nymph. A zephyr crinkled the surface and for a few seconds the bottom was unclear. Then I saw the trout, almost stationary around where the nymph should be. Instinct said 'Strike' and at the firm pull a fine Motueka three-pounder (1.4 kilograms) was tearing the line from the reel. For instinct read experience. There was only split seconds in it but although I had no confirmation that the trout had taken the nymph the instant I realised the trout had paused the line was tightend.

One of two for the smoker the fish was autopsied and the stomach was found to contain countless (I estimate 500) midge pupae. Typical for still water and the #16 black nymph was evidently a sufficiently good imitation. The rock pocket fish was still feeding and, although I was sure he was taking small black nymphs below the surface, those swirly rises spelt 'hopper'.

Not a brilliant deduction but no mayfly or caddis were about and hoppers were still, but only just, in season. This trout was extremely active with a fast circuit of perhaps a 10-metre oval so placing the fly proved a problem. I solved it by sending the fly, at the end of a 10-metre throw, into the middle of his beat. At that distance I had no idea where he would rise next so when a ring appeared near the fly I struck and he was gone — the penalty for striking a fish when he has taken a natural and not the artificial.

In the main body of the pool, where rock formations sculptured by countless floods shelter some of the best trout in the river, three large browns were feeding on the surface. For a few minutes I enjoyed the luxury of watching them, noting their movements, particularly the one tucked against the rock face below me. Reaching him from stream level wasn't as easy as I expected and the best I could do was to stand on a little rock ledge some distance below. Perhaps it was my precarious position and the possibility of a ducking in deep water that put me off. On the first cast the trout obliged with a classic rise to the hopper and for a second I felt his weight. Then he was gone. Although some distance away the other two fish stopped rising and one, the nearest, gradually sank out of sight. While I have never subscribed to the idea of telepathy I have seen, on many occasions, when one of a line of feeding fish is disturbed in quiet water, they will all stop rising.

The zephyr had now strengthened to a fair sea breeze making it doubly difficult to see fish especially in the ripply water of the pool throat. It seemed a good time for lunch so, while enjoying a sandwich, cake and coffee, I watched the river. Of one thing I am sure — watch a river long enough and you will see a trout. A large brown came to the surface followed soon by another and both appeared to be feeding. When still another joined them I accepted the invitation and offered the lower fish the hopper as a dessert. He took it straight away, I tightened, too smartly and the 6x parted. Never mind, two to go. For some reason known only to God and impulsive anglers, I changed to a #14 Blue Darter which was immediately snapped up and when that fish, all of 1.4 kilograms dived deep, he ran the nylon along a rock edge and that too parted. Now the wind changed into top gear and churned little back waves up the pool but the fish kept near the surface, swimming this way and that, out of sight then back again.

The sky was now grey and rain was in sight and what began as a beautiful day was now turning dreary. Heavy rain followed by a flood would make this my last day for the season and that trout became eminently desirable. I tossed the nymph upstream but it landed to one side. Hampered by the wind I tried again. It landed on the other side. Here goes, I thought, and hurled it hard to wherever it would go. Then, like a dream, I saw the trout slip at least a metre to one side which was good enough for me. I tightened, felt him solid for a second, then away he went, deep. Suddenly he leapt clear of the water. Praise be to St Peter, he was still on and at one stage did a tail hopping exercise in classic style. Finally I slipped the net under him — a beautiful trout of more than 1.4 kilograms lay before me. I already had one and here was his twin. I thought of all the many trout I had returned during the year, thought of how nice the two of them would be after smoking, then whacked him on the head. This is trout fishing. Neither cruel nor sentimental. The angler may sleep well if he harvests without killing unnecessarily. And it did rain, and the river did flood, and I was pleased that I landed such a grand fish on the last day of the season. And he tasted delicious!

Back Country Fishing

13

One of the treats (if not the best) available to New Zealand anglers is the chance to fish back country rivers, streams and lakes. If reaching them is sometimes difficult, think of the scores of overseas fishermen who travel around the world to enjoy them.

Contrary to popular belief, wilderness trout are not always easy to catch, especially later in the season when, despite their remoteness, many anglers have had a go at them. Even if these supertrout are not always cooperative, it is a wonderful experience to be in the back of beyond, with the unique aroma of the rain forest, the sweet sad song of the warblers, the sound of the river, clean and fresh, the joy of feeling at one with nature. But, however pleasant it may be in the wildwoods, the angler will always have one eye open for trout and in these waters, they will most likely be big ones. Obviously there must be small fish to propagate the breed but I hardly ever see one. Perhaps it is the type of water but even in the easily scanned long green pools they seem scarce. Maybe it's not so strange. A little trout sharing a pool with a fish maybe 20 times his size, he could well make himself scarce. Another reason may be that we are too preoccupied searching for large fish.

The enjoyable anticipation of a back country expedition is something special but as the day approaches the worry starts. Will the weather be kind? Has anyone been in recently and if so will the fish be spooky? Will I take in a bit of extra tucker, just in case? Can't make up my mind whether to take in wading boots or paddle around in gymshoes. Maybe we'd better not go to the top hut. Must remember the spare pair of Polaroids. Remember last trip when you forgot the salt. I wonder if the wood will be dry? Better take in the little primus. Bread — Harry will never remember. Put in an extra loaf. Forget Johnnie Walker's miracle cure for emergencies? No danger here. Last time we all took a bottle. But no bread! What about weight? To heck with it — throw in another spongy pud. They're calling for you at five. Is that daylight through the curtains? Thank God — just the moon. I'll try counting two-kilogram trout.

And so it goes, that bitter sweet love-hate period building up to what turns out, for better or worse, a memory to be cherished. These days a helicopter is a common means of transport to the back country, providing you have the cash. It is no secret that in the past I spearheaded anti-helicopter campaigns where these have tried to operate wilderness fishing trips into National Parks and I beg no forgiveness for this. I have also flown in on these marvellous machines to enjoy back country fishing but *not* in rivers in the Parks.

But there can be a catch with helicopters. I hosted a well-known overseas angler and, together with Dion our young companion, we flew into a remote valley, the obliging pilot landing us to sample the odd stream on the way in. Hyped up after a workout on a couple of big browns we waved farewell to the pilot for a couple of days, laid claim to three bunks in a tramping hut and, after discovering what we had forgotten, settled down for a great fishing trip. The morning dawned clear, the river in good order and God in his heaven smiled down on the three tiny figures wading and rockhopping up the beautiful mountain stream. Blue green pools, lacey aprons of white water, lazy currents swirling around giant boulders, bleached long dead branch debris spanning rock caverns and where, in the turquoise water, big browns challenged.

'Age before beauty!' said our young friend 'You go', 'You go' 'No, you go!' Unable to stand any more of this shilly-shallying and being a man of decision, I cast a large nymph at a trout, watched him chew it for a second or two, then struck. That was the last I saw of him before, much to the delight of my companions, the big fish snapped the 3x tippet on his way back home. That's another requirement for a back country trip — a thick skin against heckling mates. But we didn't spend too much time fishing the lower pools. The previous day well upstream my overseas friend had seen more than one trophy-class fish and we spent most of the morning tramping. After a kilometre or so it became apparent that fish were becoming increasingly scarce and, as we rounded a bushclad bend, the reason became clear. Perched on the river flat upstream was a helicopter! So much for our remote fishing! Following the occupants upstream a waste of time — back country trout don't need telling twice to run for cover. So you might say we had a dismal day. There's a penalty for you. If things get tough, there is no car to hop into and shoot off somewhere else. As it happened the hut wasn't too far from the main river so we did manage some sport the next day but it just goes to show. Never count your big trout until they are caught.

Fishing for big fish is pretty much the same anywhere except that you sometimes need to control the jitters. Apart from this providing you don't do anything silly, back country trout can be most obliging and the only thing to do once he is hooked is to hold on and pray. The worse part of the deal is when a fish spins around and speeds towards you creating a pile of dreaded slack line. In which case the solution is to take off

The Eglinton. Bright, sparkling, dashing rainbows and particular browns. Note the East Branch entering on the left of picture.

backwards as fast as possible. The axiom, 'Always keep a tight line' is never more true.

A rod with some backbone helps a lot. Before I was seduced by carbon fibre I fished for many years with a Fenwick fibre glass for a #8 line. Today I might find it cumbersome to cast but many is the time, with big rainbows tearing towards some terrible snag, I have been thankful for its power. As long as the rod is stout or steely enough and can cast a decent line it doesn't matter what it's made of. When the wind blows down a narrow mountain valley it really blows and you can be thankful for a heavier fly line. An extra reel in case of emergency doesn't go amiss and if it sports a slow sink tip line, a luxury, so much the better.

Before a back country trip many anglers agonise on which flies to pack and usually err on the heavy side, with 100 or so dry flies and as many nymphs, very few of which will ever get wet. If you can learn what these mountain dwellers expect in the way of food the list is small indeed. It is a lucky fly fisher who coincides his visit with anything more than a brief hatch of mayfly during the day. In the evening it is a different matter, especially later in the season when caddis hatch in prolific numbers and it seems almost a shame to catch trout. More likely the trout will be on the lookout for passing insects but these nowhere near the surface. Unless he is prepared to use a nymph the angler may have slim pickings. These should be weighted with three or four turns of lead wire under the dressing and preferably tied, with fur for body material. This waterlogs easily allowing the nymph to sink to the trout's level as quickly as possible before 'drag' results.

Few patterns can beat the popular Hare and Cooper or, my Grey or Blue Darters, these well tried and tested. If one does come across a finicky trout then ring the changes with a weighted Pheasant Tail or a green stonefly imitation. Whatever time of the year champion trout are always receptive to a green beetle imitation and an experienced angler usually packs a few into his fly box. In the dry fly stakes it is hard to beat a Kakahi Queen or a Twilight Beauty and when the cicada is chirping a deer-hair imitation of this insect doesn't go amiss, — a Humpy type dry is quite suitable. Although flies on small size hooks would be just as successful the advice is to keep to 10s or 12s. Little hooks hold very well but who needs one straightening out during the first blinding run of a three-kilogram nylon buster?

A good parka is essential on any tramping trip. After a frosty night with the morning clear and cloudless, it is easy to imagine sweating up some rocky gorge and leave the sweater behind. Don't be fooled. Back country weather can change very rapidly and the small extra weight of sweater, a change of underclothes and lightweight trousers may well save some discomfort, and in the extreme, your life. Similarly the simple addition of a box of matches. On a recent trip with two companions I crossed the river a half hour behind them and about halfway, in the deepest part, slipped and went under. The weather, so pleasant when we set off, now turned to rain and it was very cool. Is there anything more miserable than standing about in wet clothes even after wringing out? By the time my mates arrived back I was in a poor way, shivering, with my skin putty coloured. With the dismal prospect of a three-kilometre tramp in wet clothes I presented a sorry sight. Fortunately a cigarette lighter was produced and, after lighting a fire, I was a much happier and warmer man despite the burn holes in my vest and underpants. I mention this

at the risk of ridicule because who better to advise than a sufferer? My camera didn't come out of it so well. It cost me over $200 for the repairs.

If one of the party is a hunter as well as a fisherman so much the better. Only an average shot myself I am fortunate in being the father of a very good hunter who rarely fails to return with game. On one of our fishing/hunting trips I left him lying on his back glassing the bushline for deer while I fished a lovely piece of water below a steep scrub-covered terrace. Here were two good rainbows, both feeding, and before long I was into the nearest. Hoping to show off I looked for Norm but he had disappeared. Just as I was landing the trout a loud explosion made me leap and nearly drop the rod. Then, a little way downstream, from out of the scrub, over the bank and into the river toppled a fallow stag. Norm's face appeared from the manuka, a wide grin on his face. 'Any luck?' he shouted.

It was on the same trip that an international incident nearly occurred. Sharing the hut with Norm and I were an overseas visitor and his New Zealand friend. Maybe they were ignorant of the fly only regulation but one morning from our bushline perch we could see two people and something sparkling in the sunshine as they walked up the river's edge. 'That's a spinner!' said Norm. It certainly could have been and, when we returned in the late afternoon, an inspection of the scrub behind the hut revealed a spinning rod and reel. With no actual proof they had used it, the situation was difficult but I said enough for the culprits to get the message. The following morning, still dark, after a breakfast by candlelight, I gathered the dishes, washed them, and having missed what appeared to be a mug full of water, flung the contents outside. Late that afternoon I was confronted by an angry tourist. 'Was it you who threw my teeth out?' he demanded. In view of my comments on sportsmanship the previous day there didn't seem much point in protesting my innocence!

After searching for brown-backed smaller trout in down country streams with their mixture of darker gravels, spotting back country trout is a delight. While forgetting to bring a pair of good Polaroid spectacles is not the end of the world it would come very near to it. These trout-spotting aids must equal nylon and eyed hooks in importance and you would be wise to always carry a spare pair. While on this subject I wonder how many flyfishers, who have to interchange prescription glasses with Polaroids every time they have to tie a fly are aware of special anglers' spectacles. Of American design they have two lens sets, the upper normal Polaroid (either in amber or smoke) and a small lower set which offer a variety of magnification. Over the years these have proved a boon and if the reader with an eyesight problem cannot find a pair in New Zealand I strongly recommend a letter to an American friend.

Unless in deeper, choppy water, large trout are not difficult to discover but this doesn't allow a careless approach. Back country pools don't always have handy tree-lined banks for cover. Sometimes the only way to cover fish is by casting from a high bank or rock outcrop, and in that position it is essential to cast horizontally, keeping the rod tip as low as possible, and naturally exposing as little of your torso as possible.

While using the dry fly is considered the finest way to take these big trout, when you have either spent a goodly sum of money on transport, or sweated blood to reach a distant stream, sticking to that method alone may result in a blank day.

Every angler's dream. The Crow — Karamea tributary.

You may be lucky, of course, and find the trout busy on a prolific hatch of mayfly, caddis, or, rarely, stonefly. But quite likely, surface insects will be few, with the trout's dark shape at the bottom of a jade green pool. This is where the weighted nymph or some other suitable imitation can make all the difference between a blank day and one to celebrate. In these situations, being careful not to line the fish, the nymph should be cast as far from the side and upstream as possible above the trout's station giving the nymph maximum time to sink. If an approach from the side is at all possible the nymph will drop to his level quicker with little advance nylon to warn him. In fast currents fish lying really deep present a problem and, unless you are desperate and have time to spare, it is best to pass them by. There is one way to reach them, however, and that is by using not one but two weighted nymphs which not only get them down to the bargain basement quicker but double your chances. I can't say I am a fan of this method. Why not three? Four? Why not forget them!

If you are going ever going to land a trophy trout of 4.5 kilograms or more chances are it will be on some back country water. The best time to find one is early in the season before too many other anglers have appeared on the scene. Even if one of the big fish is seen, it is usually in a diabolically difficult situation such as at the bottom of a gorge.

I once came across one of these heavyweights in a pool in Fiordland. I'd seen the trout on a previous trip and this time, accompanied by my American friend Hank, I was eager to rediscover the big rainbow. Gertrude, as I had christened her. The fish was still there, sole resident of a mysterious jade green pool studded with massive sun-bleached boulders and fringed with tree fern, toi toi and forest beech. Gertrude wasn't shy — she blatantly displayed her Junoesque proportions, slipping this way and that in the fast curly currents or taking an occasional tour of the pool, checking for intruders. As we approached the pool I motioned to Hank to keep low, then, through the lattice of fern, introduced him to Gertrude. He bristled with excitement. 'Gees,' was all he could muster. I ushered him down a mossy side creek to emerge below the pool. Overhanging beech made casting difficult and the two giant boulders guarding the pool added to the problem. The fast currents flowing between the rocks made 'drag' almost inevitable and, as one would expect from large trout, Gertrude would give a botched cast no quarter, the slightest error sending her beyond reach into some underwater cavern.

Hank was a veteran fly fisherman but as he prepared to cast I noticed his hands were shaking. It was a long cast up into that narrow gorge. 'Remember to shoot plenty of line,' I urged but his nymph fell well short. His next cast was better, the nymph landing abreast but well to one side of Gertrude. She turned half-heartedly but then kept station. Hank's third cast rolled out nicely with just enough slack to let the nymph dally awhile. We held our breath as Gertrude slid over, eyeballed the Hare and Copper, drifted back with it for a second or so, then ignored it. The suspense was unbearable.

'My God, Norm', gasped Hank, 'that's some fish!'

'Take it easy Hank', I cautioned, 'Give her a rest'.

And so we did, passing minutes that seemed like hours watching the antics of two blue ducks. It was then that I thought of the Cicada — big, attractive, surely a tempting target for Gertrude.

'Stick this one on Hank,' I said, passing on a #10 Cicada.

Hank's eyebrows raised a notch or two when he saw the rough-looking fly, but with touching faith he tied it on without hesitation. Gertrude had even more faith in it for on the next cast she had it. Who got the biggest surprise — Hank or Gertrude — when the hook was set is hard to say. I remember who acted first. With a blistering, line hissing run, she left Hank openmouthed and staring at the line and backing now fast disappearing from a near smoking reel.

'Move!', I shouted.

Galvanised, and with an agility born of desperation, Hank set off in hot pursuit, scrambling over great rock and log jumbles like a young goat and frantically trying to recover lost line. Meanwhile, having passed a perspiring Hank and standing on a small bluff overlooking the upper pool, I could see Gertrude, all stops out, diving and dashing all over the place. Hank appeared around the corner, rod doubled, grimly determined. Suddenly Gertrude went into reverse, hightailing it downstream. Off we went again, chasing that robust lady through the green pools, down foamy white water, over and around dreaded, submerged log jams, until at last, we arrived at the final battleground. Here in an idyllic bush setting Hank gave no quarter. Gallant fish that she was, Gertrude found the relentless pressure of the dynamic carbon fibre more than a match. Searing, heart-stopping runs were

now reduced to short dogged pulls and finally the weary champion was drawn up onto the small sandy beach.

Silently, and in shared admiration, we gazed down at he superb trout, without speaking I wet my net, slipped an exhausted Gertrude in it and weighed her. Hank gasped. 'Double figures at last', he exclaimed proudly. Then with the net in the gentle current he coaxed Gertrude from the meshes. He nursed her, the great magenta flanks upright, large spotted tail waving slowly in anticipation. Perhaps it was imagination, but as she slipped back home over the beautiful gravel mosaic. I fancy she cast, over her dorsal fin, a reproachful if thankful eye, back at Hank. On the tramp back to camp, the battle was relived, Gertrude a lifetime memory for Hank. It was later, by the camp fire that Hank gave credit where it was due. 'Norm', he said, in his slow Southern drawl, 'that's one helluva fly!'.

Back country rivers are exciting places to hook big wild trout, no doubt about that, it is a unique experience, one the angler will remember long after his muscular physique has given way to an extended waistline and when, instead of a 20-kilogram pack, the weekly groceries make him puff. That kind of fishing is what dreams are made of.

Part 2

A Trout Stream Safari

There are so many lakes, streams and rivers in New Zealand it would be impossible to fish them all in a lifetime. For more than thirty seven years I have tried my best but when the time comes to put the rod on the wall I reckon I will have only just touched the surface.

Having spent so many years in Southland I suppose it is as good a place as anywhere to start but, before anyone can accuse me of divulging their secret fishing spot, I hasten to add that the purchase of the Southland Acclimatisation Society's excellent handbook on where to fish in Southland will provide more information than you will get from me. Anyone who has never fished in the province, noted for its well-stocked rivers and dry fly fishing will be either delighted or disappointed depending on how they strike the weather.

If only we could have the long fine periods of the North Island and the quality of the Southland angling in one package New Zealand would indeed be the Anglers' Eldorado. But, in fact, it is the rainfall that makes the angling what it is — excellent. Trout are not interested in fishing conditions but they do like food-bearing floods providing they are not too severe and, although this may please the worm fisher, for the rest it can be very frustrating. But when the sun shines Southland is one of the finest fishing areas, dare I say it, in the world.

A Southland stream

Southland, home of acre wide streets, whitebait patties and so called erotic oysters. Also a province where five pound or 2kg brown trout fail to raise the local's eyebrows. Far across the great Plain the snow capped Takatimu Mountains dominate the western skyline and looking north on a fine day the peaks of the Garvie mountains can be seen. From East, West and North flow the larger rivers, Aparima, Oreti and the lovely Mataura but the reputation of these is well matched by the scores of smaller streams less than an hours drive from Invercargill. One of these is the Waimatuku. This little river running clear when most other rivers are coloured, flows not far from Wallacetown and where, incidentally, some of Frank Bucklands 1873 trout ova were hatched. It has no single source but seem to rise in swamp country. A short stream, not wide, with a firm cobblestone bottom, it holds a good stock of trout averaging 1kg and with a fair sprinkling of fish double that weight. Clothed sporadically with gorse, fairly straight, it hardly qualifies for the troutstream of the year but with high banks overgrown with rough grasses, clear stable water flowing through and around islands of waterbuttercup and crowsfoot and liberally sprinkled with large brown trout, it is the dry fly or upstream nymph fishermans delight.

Rarely have I achieved a limit bag, and the day when this was an objective has long passed, but one morning on this delightful stream, the Gods smiled. Panic stations however when I found the polaroids missing, only to recover when they appeared tucked down a seat side and crossing the fence I ripped my trouser seat. But it was a gem of a day with blue sky and cottonbud clouds, a gentle breeze, a day to savour as I sat on the riverbank. Another little disaster when I discovered the sheep droppings underneath and the torn trousers hadn't helped. Washing ones backside in a trout stream does nothing for the spirit. Near a handy getaway gorse bush a rabbit kept an eye on me, in the swampy area a pukeko gave his sore throat imitation and a friendly horse nuzzled up to me. It was one of those lazy summer days and it almost seemed enough just being there but a lovely rise along the edge of some watercrowsfoot caught my attention. This set the adrenalin coursing, and in no time I was wading quietly up the weedbed edges hoping for the first trout of the day.

As ever, the first question that plagues the flyfisherman is 'what fly?' but with fish rising and no sign of surface naturals it didn't take an Einstein to decide on a Pheasant Tail Nymph. Whirls and boils betrayed the fish and before lunch I had netted four and lost two in the weeds. A glance into their mouths before returning confirmed they were feeding on small brown nymphs. With three fish landed and the sun at its zenith it was time for a snack. Lying back in the warm grass I recalled a beautiful summer evening near this pool when, during that magical hour, the only sounds were the hum of insects and the last of the birds chorus. The sunset was glorious, a molten golden ball slipping behind the western hills, pukeko's screeching goodnight and, dear to the heart of every angler, the plop of good trout feasting on evening caddis. It was while besieging one of these that my backcast was suddenly cut short and instead of a trout I had hooked a cock blackbird in the wing. It finally landed in a gorse bush, a mixture not to be recommended when recovering a dry fly.

The inner man satisfied I settled under the bank edge at the tail of a very fishy pool and watched four fish swirl and dimple within easy casting distance. The Waimatuku, although small is usually in a hurry to meet the sea and in moderately fast water it was difficult to decide if and when a trout had taken the nymph. But a mouth flash and a firm strike sent the lower fish downstream past my boots. The hook and nylon held and after netting, (beaches are scarce on the Waimatuku) the golden flanked fish was returned. Without moving, three more followed and were also returned. The time now 1pm. Shirtsleeves, a warm day, standing in waterbuttercup, and with trout in attendance. If this isn't utter bliss, what is?

Upstream, a gem of a pool beckoned, at a bend shouldered by a solitary willow, a deep hole alongside the roots, a long runnel below following the overhanging sedge grass and a shallowing gravel bed pool tail. These pools are made in heaven. From my crouched position tucked under the bank I could see trout everywhere, all on station, some nymphing, others occasionally picking off a surface fly. I cast my eyes upwards. Surely, all my sins must have been forgiven. The trout entered into the spirit of things, either grabbing my Pheasant Tail or for a change sipping down a small Coch-y-bondhu. Nine fish, two killed, these cached under dampened cress. The weather still lovely and fish still feeding I debated whether now was the time to finish. I had been carried along by some indefinable urge. Was it a case of 'making hay while the sun shines'? Was I subconsciously laying in a store of memory to counteract the lacklustre days sure to come?

It was then, looking upstream to the willow that I saw what must have been the grandaddy of the stream, a beauty, a trout big enough to quicken the pulse of even the most blase of anglers. No thought now of packing in. What a grand finale this was going to be, what tales to tell. He wasn't a difficult fish, a little deep but no problem. In fact he occasionally came to the surface. An obliging fish I thought and prepared to hook him maybe after a few casts. By 4pm I was still throwing things at him and in desperation, after trying a score of nymph patterns, I tied on the largest dry

fly in the box. This miniature feather duster floated directly over him and, as if he had been waiting for it all his watery life, he gulped it down. First, hook your fish. Then what?!

With a tremendous burst of speed he turned tail and before I had time to say Izaak Walton he was long gone downstream, his passage marked by little sprays of foam. Clambering up on the back I chased after him, with little hope but two pools down we met again. He was tucked into a weed bed and after running my fingers down the nylon I could feel his broad back. He didn't like that and with a flurry hopped, skipped and jumped his way out of the greenery. Off we went again, downstream, on our merry way, both of us tired. A few metres above willows that completely covered the stream I held him, straining in the fast current. This was it. Any relaxation and he would be home and free. Fine, he was only a trout and there would no doubt be many more, but that fish had become very, very desirable. He was No 10.

Gently he swung in the current, leader near breaking point. Even the lowering of the rod tip slipped him nearer the dreaded willows. It was a classic stand-off and I had just about decided to give in when I heard a voice, 'Can I help?', it said. I looked up and there was this very old angler, weatherbeaten, his skin brown and walnut wrinkled. Hardly daring to take my eyes off the fish I called back. 'Too right, any time you like!'. He was old and small but surprisingly agile, making short work of the steep bank and with skill born of experience soon had his net directly below the suspended trout. It was simply a matter of dropping the rod tip and the thrashing fish was carried safely ashore. 'A very nice fish' he said, 'Are you going to kill it?' 'Oh no', I replied, 'I think he deserves better than that', and proceeded to nurse the exhausted champion by the stream edge. My new companion's sharp blue eyes lit up with pleasure as he watched the trout sidle away. 'Beautiful fish, nice trout', he said quietly. I wondered on that beautiful day how many had felt the sharp point of **his** hook and been returned. Whatever, my cup was filled to overflowing. It had been a very good day on my little Southland stream.

Mavora Memories

The Mavora lakes, sandwiched between the Livingstone and the Thompson mountains, offer some of the finest lake fishing for brown trout in New Zealand. The turn-off to the lakes at Mararoa Station on State Highway 94 is roughly half way between Lumsden and Te Anau. Of the two lakes, South Mavora, much smaller than the North Mavora, is by far the more attractive, and it was in one of its many lakeside clearings that we parked our little two-berth caravan. With the weather forecaster offering a couple of fine days it was with high hopes we slept, lulled by the lapping of waves against the lake edge. As promised, a clear blue sky greeted us, with a chorus of bush birds adding to the welcome. While I'll always be a river or stream fisherman, lake fishing is always a nice change — and a hard challenge.

Even before 8am the notorious Mavora breeze was ruffling the lake surface creating shimmering reflections of forest edge and high mountains. Pretty to see but a nuisance when trying to spot cruising fish. But unlike its nearby big brother, the south lake is generously endowed with scored of little bush-edged and grassy coves where, sheltered from the wind, both browns and rainbows patrol the shore line. The rainbows are just that but the browns are almost as silver with amber green backs, golden fins, yellow ringed eyes with blue-black enamelled centres. It was one of these that I saw moving slowly across the dark

green weed beds and by good fortune, coming my way. The suspense of lakeside fishing can be almost unbearable — watching the trout approach the sunken nymph, the tense wait. The strike! Too soon, too late. Whatever it was, that Mavora trout wasn't having any. I lifted off those painful kneecaps, hoping that I would get a second chance. During that morning's fishing, before the breeze turned to a strong wind, I learned something — Mavora trout are hard to catch and if you hook one you're only halfway there.

The following morning at the breakfast dishes. 'There's one!', said Jean looking through the window. Showing clearly against a sandy avenue between the weed beds swam a familiar form. In quick time I was crouching at the lake edge sending out a tiny black nymph at the end of a four-metre leader with a 5x point. For a few moments I saw his dark shape cruising in the direction of the nymph then he disappeared in surface glare. Just when I'd started to worry, the tippet shot forward a fraction and instinctively I struck, rejoicing in the solid resistance. Then the line was disappearing from the reel. Providing the hook and nylon hold, playing a lake fish is a novice's delight because, as a rule, there are no snags. A small sandy cove provided an ideal place to land the fish and what a lovely trout he was — small head with pretty yellow streaks along the belly. Being the first fish of our stay, and on the orders of the chef, he received a whack on the head. With extensive weed beds it wasn't surprising to find lots of dragonflies and damselflies in the stomach. Now a bit cocksure, it took two or three bungled attempts for other trout to knock the stuffing out of me and by noon the wind was in full sail. Anyone who thinks they will catch Mavora trout willy nilly is a candidate for the King's retinue, complete with bells and pointed cap.

Away from it all in Rainbow Land. The Young River — North Otago.

Brunner. Home of the Golden Trout.

La Fontaine. The 'Kennet' of 'down under' where trout present a high challenge.

Overnight, a cold sou'wester came sneaking up the valley and we had two fishless days before the sun reappeared. This time I was up earlier and from the bush edges, in calm water, I spotted and waylaid a couple of good fish. But no rainbows. By 10am the wind was up again so in desperation we launched our three-metre Lancer inflatable and trolled a lure. Rowing an inflatable against the wind is like walking downstairs, backward, so I was very tired when I put into shore. It was while we were enjoying a welcome cup of coffee that about 20 metres offshore I saw the fish. He was at medium depth on a sandy bottom and facing into the wind drift. 'This might be a reward for all that hard work,' I said to Jean, who was optimistically unwrapping the camera.

God knows how I got the nymph out to him but when he moved out of line I set the hook. Gaping, I watched the backing follow the fly line out towards the lake centre. He never detoured, just took a straight line while I stood mesmerised by the high-pitched whine of the reel and I'd still be there if Jean hadn't shouted some unheard comment. I stumbled over beach edge litter, retrieving some line, the rod tip nodding even with a great belly of fly line between us. I retrieved more line. He borrowed it back. No sooner did I appear to have the upper hand than he would go into top gear and tear back into the green depths. Once I saw his tail smack the water and he leapt once, so far away he looked like a kipper. Then I had him in close but if I got him inshore once I must have done it a dozen times. I admired his strength and cursed his obstinacy.

'How long do you think you have been playing him?', asked Jean, close to my elbow.

'About five minutes or so'.

'Wrong, it's been over ten minutes!'

The old Winstone rod was puffing. It was tired. And so was I. Nearer, nearer, rolling, twisting, spinning, anything but giving up. I drew him into the shallow. One final effort and his head was touching the shoreline. I gasped with relief while Jean clicked away. What size? Does it matter? Let's say if we had been nearer a taxidermist I would have been sorely tempted but he was going back. We just wanted a moment to admire him. 'Here, hold him for a second,' I said, and then he was immersed again. After nursing him for a good two minutes we watched him swim slowly away. It was his world and he was going home.

Mataura Magic

No travel yarn would be complete without reference to the famous Mataura. Overrated? Never. It probably holds more trout than any other New Zealand river and as these are generally good surface feeders it is a dry fly fisher's paradise and well-known to overseas anglers. The wise ones park themselves somewhere in Southland, renting a flat or a cottage for a few weeks, and they are then certain of some good river conditions. Mataura trout wax fat on the prolific quantities of nymphs and caddis larvae, feed avidly on willow grubs in season, and during summer evenings feast at a regular banquet of emerging midge pupa. During its 112 kilometre journey from above Garston to the Fortrose estuary the river habitat changes considerably from wide, deep and slow whitebait water, where a sunken smelt or flashing spinners hook very large trout, to the long, willow-lined, calm pools of the Wyndham area, notorious for the legendary 'Mad Mataura Rise'. Above Gore the river gains a little pace and the pools are shorter with prime fishing around the Riversdale area. A little further upstream the trout of the Waikaia provide the fly fisher with his or her best challenge.

A glance at a map of the area shows a

peculiar ancient deviation in the river where it reaches Parawa and flows through the Nokomai Gorge to Riversdale instead of down its natural course to Lumsden. There it would have joined the Oreti to make a very large river indeed. But happily for the anglers, it did not. Today the twists and turns of green-tinted, willow-lined pools, and numerous sparkling gravel runs of the Nokomai gorge attract anglers from far and wide and, being close to the Central Otago region with moderate rainfall, the river is generally in good order. Clusters of summer holiday baches, mostly well built and attractive, are tucked away in odd corners and it was to one of these that we were invited by my good friend Len Prentice.

It was a beautiful November morning with misty wraiths rising from the valley floor but by 7am the far side of the gorge was bathed in sunlight and a clear blue sky accentuated the few remaining pockets of snow. 'McQuirter McQuirter McQuirter,' called the cock quail from a post outside the window while the flashing scuts of rabbits from the tiny vegetable patch told us the day was already underway. A day to expect good things to happen and, with the river in good order, the weather fine and an upstream breeze, it seemed a fair possibility. A short stroll from the cottage ended with my crawling the last few metres to spy into a large shallow backwater in the hope of seeing a trout or two. In fact there were four big ones cruising around the silty bottom, occasionally raising puffs of silt and searching the cloud for bloodworms.

Watching trout is a pleasure in itself but it's better after you have caught one or two, so rather confidently I tied on a tiny waterboatman imitation and flicked it in the path of the nearest fish. This he ignored despite what I thought were lifelike twitches. A little surprised, I

changed to a #18 Pheasant Tail for the next fish, one with a dark scar on his flank, but got the same result. After scores of casts, the fish continued to feed on the bottom, and after an hour and a change down to 6x nylon the net was still dry.

Finally I admitted defeat and moved to where the pond met the river, the deepest part of the backwater and where, in a revolving feed line, two fish occasionally lifted to pick some unidentifiable insects. The small Dad's Favourite never made it to the half way round mark before it disappeared in a rise so explosive that I couldn't have been blamed for missing the strike. But my lucky leprechaun didn't let me down. Well hooked, the unseen heavy fish bored deep and I prayed that he wouldn't find an underwater snag. Thanks to my little elf he didn't and, after putting the fine tippet far beyond the call of duty, I slipped the net under a fine hen trout weighing the better of two kilograms. For only the third time in a long angling career I saw a second trout fly in the mouth of the fish just landed. A large wet fly with a short piece of nylon attached. Pocketing this for a souvenir and, after returning the fish, I tried again with the Dad's and was shortly rewarded with a tiny sip in the feed line and the weight of another trout, this one by the feel of it larger than the last. It was, by another half a kilogram and, as I gazed in admiration at his lovely form lying in the net folds, I noticed the scar. Without doubt my earlier tormenter — what a roundabout way to catch him!

Later that day, I fished the Riverview area near Athol. Downstream from the wooden bridge, an avenue of willow trees gently guides the river through a series of tranquil pools where eventually it is joined by a small nondescript drain by the name of Quioch Creek. Generally disregarded by the angler it nevertheless holds some very big fish and I couldn't help but take a look at the last of its almost still water pools. A short careful stalk and a large brown slowly appeared from under where I crouched on the almost bare bank. He swam slowly upstream giving me a chance but the nymph caught on some cocksfoot, the resulting twitch sending the trout racing upstream. Having disturbed the pool I had little hope of finding another fish when to my surprise I spotted two, one cruising upstream, the other down. Still keeping low and being nearer to the latter I offered him the same nymph, a very dark Pheasant Tail. He kept going and passed the other trout. Both disappeared but soon repeated the slow cruising, up and down. My best chance came when both were a rod span from each other and the nymph plinked into no-man's land. Then the fun started. The smaller of the two, a fish of some two kilograms, dashed for it but he didn't move as fast as his big mate who, without any help from me, hooked himself. Big fish in a little creek can be quite an armful and inside seconds he had the creek so stirred up it was impossible to tell what was what apart from the slicing leader. A great fighter, it seemed a shame he never got away. I'm kidding!

Back at the river, I crossed and continued downstream behind a high, badly eroded stopbank, making frequent stops to peer over the top into the fast run below. But for that vantage point trout would have been impossible to detect against the rock and dark cobblestone bottom. Moving shadows betrayed them — some were in midstream, some appeared periodically from under the willows opposite but all were feeding in very fast water. It was too deep and too fast to wade so the only possible casting position was from the river side of the steep thistle-clad hummock. Using a weighted Grey Darter I hooked two, then after a hectic scramble after the racing trout, lost both of them. In each case the nylon broke at the hook.

At the top of the run lay an angler's delight — at least six nice fish working the gravel fan. But there was a problem. The only casting position was from between a high clump of young willows downstream and on my close right was a gorse bush. Underneath my posterior, the damned thistles and, for good measure, the dreaded sheep droppings. After some pitiful casting I latched onto a good one which naturally sped down shady lane and during the ensuing pursuit I slipped, falling flat on my back which literally knocked the wind out of me. Meanwhile the trout was having a great time and I could imagine him knitting the leader and the fly line around a log or two. But he didn't and I did land the fish and for the second time that day found something unusual. Never have I seen such a beautiful fish. Silver-flanked, he had no spots or even stars but a pattern of coloured whorls almost like those we used to see on psychedelic shirts and dresses or like the marbled markings of a brook trout. The trout was so beautiful I stumbled upstream with it in a wetted net and showed it to my wife Jean. Unfortunately a photograph didn't do it justice but I know we will always remember that strange Mataura trout. It was a fitting end to a lovely day.

The Lochy

The Athol and Garston areas were happy hunting grounds for the late George Ferris, author of many books on fly fishing and I was once fortunate to spend an afternoon fishing with him. Another fly fisherman of note was the late Dick Black of Athol who was renowned for his friendly advice and his skill at the fly bench. A character, some of his escapades were recorded in the journals of the prestigious *Flyfishers Club* of London.

Leaving such a good fishing area is always a wrench but, a little further north, Lake Wakatipu awaits and on the far side of this very cold but trout-filled water is a small almost unnoticed river, regarded by many anglers as a gem. This is the Lochy and on that cold blustery November day the prospect of fishing it looked rather dim. A glance through the chalet window showed a well-ruffled lake with grey cloud obscuring the mountain tops but a knock on the door and some ribald comment from Len, our guide for the day, confirmed that the trip was on. By 8 am the Hamilton Jet, complete with three well-wrapped figures, was bouncing over white tops towards Kingston and the Lochy. Once across the lake the western shores gave us a welcome shelter and shortly afterwards we glided over long swards of weed to tie up in the river mouth.

We then made a solemn pact to tramp well upriver to the Longburn hut before fishing, this with the idea of spending more time in less fished waters, but it didn't work. Passing feeding rainbows would have needed a saint's willpower. After spotting a deep-lying rainbow, John waded midstream while Len and I refereed from a high bank. It seemed strange watching John Goddard, co-author of the noted *The Fly and the Trout*, so far from his English chalk streams in the fast water of this Antipodean mountain river. But trout are trout and talented anglers can adapt to any angling conditions. As the lively rainbow lifted to take the nymph, Len and I shouted in unison, 'Now!'. John made no mistake and the hooked rainbow lived up to his species' reputation for hard fighting. After that we were good boys, keeping away from the river as we tramped up the valley.

And what a beautiful valley it is. Grassy flats with pockets of native bush shouldering the river here and there and always the high peaks as a background. A gaggle of Canada geese whistled overhead as we raided the backpack for coffee, meanwhile gazing into a deep magical corner pool to watch a couple of cruising browns. With thought of greater upstream treasures we pressed on until within sight of the hut and, where the Longburn joins the Lochy, spent some time hooking, losing and landing rainbows, almost all around the 1½ kilogram mark.

Back country huts never lose their fascination. Nestled in little clearings, surrounded by native bush, bracken and fern, they always send out welcome signals as you approach. I can imagine the same hut on a wild stormy night with tree branches crashing down and the wind howling outside while around the open log fire angler and hunter enjoy hot tea and toast and swap yarns. As usual the hut log book proved interesting. One entry showed that friends had recently enjoyed its shelter and another was a laconic request for a cat to sort out the mice, a few nails to pin down the banging tin roof, and a pair of long-legged waitresses from Queenstown.

Now in sunshine, a pair of Paradise ducks escorted us up through the upstream pools. If only they were silent birds. We were pleased when the hoarse quacking finally receded and we could concentrate on spotting trout. They were there in good number, some behind midstream boulders, some circling the turqoise pools, others hugging the grassy stream edge. Playing lively trout in such delightful surroundings with good friends must be the angler's ideal. And so we worked our way upstream to end at a pool the likes of which all anglers picture in their dreams. So beautiful one almost expected to see fairies bathing in the blue-green water, sunning on the massive midstream boulders, or fluttering above the cascading waterfalls at the head of the pool. On the opposite side a little stream bounded its way out of the beech forest to splash into the pool. Here rainbows feasted near the outlet. Below us, and close to a rock face, a very large brown idled in a gentle feed line, almost on the surface. 'Your turn', 'No — your turn!' 'You have a go'. I could stand this gentlemanly behaviour no longer and slipped downstream below the fish. He half-turned as the #12 Kakahi Queen floated over him, his jaws opened. The fly disappeared, the line tightened and for the next five minutes or so it was 'Good on ya Norm!' from the Kiwi and 'Good show!' from the Britisher. At over three kilograms that brown deserved the half roll of film that John clicked through.

Next it was Len, seasoned fly fisherman and excellent fishing guide, who put the rainbows through their paces. A downstream breeze had sprung up with increasing cloud and it was clear that the weather was changing for the worse. John performed the finale by fishing to a rainbow in the fast central tongue of the pool. His #12 Grey Wulff worked, the fish almost dashing to the surface to take it. John struck and missed it. It obliged again. Once again the fly flew back in the air. From our grandstand perch Len and I couldn't let this go. Whoops of laughter. 'Back to school, John!' 'Third time lucky John!' After another striking fiasco John examined the hook and to our surprise found the barb end of the hook pressed tightly against the shank. Another fly and that obliging trout got his comeuppance.

It was time to go. By the time we passed the hut the wind had strengthened, the darkening sky promising rain. Halfway down the valley a furious squall hit us, the pelting rain on the back of our parkas hurrying us along. Splashing along high terraces, down slippery banks, across the now rain-lashed river, heads down, we must have looked a dismal sight but in truth each of us must have been inwardly singing. We were still playing rosy-sided rainbows and big browns, remembering those green limpid pools, the sparkling riffles, and perhaps, best of all, the fun of each other's company.

More Trout Stream Travels

15

Half hour at Hawea

From the bridge, the Clutha at Albertstown always looks inviting and it seems a shame to leave it but a short distance north lies Lake Hawea. It was a beautiful day, almost cloudless, as we motored along the western shore, a slow gradient at first then, a few kilometres along, on higher ground, spectacular views. On the far side of the lake, a small dinghy splintered the mirrored images of Dingle Peak while out in the lake, fishy dimples promised sport. Below the bluffs, on golden sandy margins, trout, big ones, cruised along the lake edge. Opposite Timaru Creek about halfway along the western shore, the temptation became far too strong and we stopped to watch half a dozen cruising trout behaving according to the lakeside rules — nicely spaced in two lanes, some going

north along the lake edge, the others nearer the lake centre, swimming south.

Keen to have one sample a dry fly (it didn't matter to me which way they were going), I left the caravan in a roadside layby and strolled, not too slowly, down to the lake edge. A notice from Electrocorp warned of lake level fluctuation. At this point a clay spit ran out into the lake forming, on each side, two small shallow bays, one sandy and flat, the other pockmarked with raised yellow sediment strata. Even from that low vantage point I could see clearly three dark shapes patrolling the shoreline so the only question now was what to offer them in the way of a fly. Having had some success on Lake Hawera with a blossom fly imitation I tied this on, size #16. No sooner had it touched the water near the first fish than he streaked away for the deepest part of the lake. Landing the fly too near the fish? The next attempt saw the little fly settle at least five metres away. This one came within trembling distance. 'He's coming for it', I whispered to Jean, and poised for the strike. I needn't have bothered. That lovely trout followed the first only even faster and what should have been a day at the races was fast changing into a day mucking out the stables.

Having emptied that larder I inspected the other bay and to my delight spotted an even bigger fish working around the just-submerged ledges and caverns of the clay bed. The roving trout, sometimes with dorsal fin exposed, would circle into the deeper water, return, and fossick the shallows. Twice I watched his circuit in the calm water then, as soon as his back was turned, I laid out the line with the tiny black hackled fly cocked proud on the surface. My heart thumped as he lifted and took an unseen natural insect near the fly. Then, before I had time to wonder, another rise and this time the right one. A pause, a firm strike and he was zipping out into the deep emerald depths, the reel playing the tune we all love to hear.

While he was tearing about, a small blue van drew up close behind and an angler alighted, picked up his spinning rod and walked away along the beach. I couldn't have done that for the life in me. Curious, call it nosey if you like, but in a similar position I would have had to know the outcome. Jean meanwhile had some bad news. 'No more film in the camera!' It was 'Bally dang!' and 'What a nuisance' or words to that effect and as I held onto the trout, she climbed the hill for a new film roll. After what seemed an eternity she returned and while she played the fish with no mean skill, I changed the film. An active two kilogram lake trout needs some taming but eventually he was near the edge and the

only decision now was whether to get my dress shoes wet. They were never a good fit after that. And so we left Hawea with a happy memory of that brief encounter.

Young River

Every angler must know of one particular river which has captured his or her imagination. For many years the mention of the Young was enough to send me daydreaming of big rainbows, gorged on green bettle, big browns circling around turquoise pools, scooping in a never-ending supply of gauzy winged mayflies. Travelling along the eastern shores of Lake Wanaka, with the snow-tipped peaks of the Southern Alps turning purple in the sun's last rays, the dream was fast becoming a reality. The road between Hawea and the West Coast, if beautiful, is a lonely one and we were pleased to reach the oasis of the Makarora Camp Complex, a pleasant spot to relax. Unfortunately for us the evening was spoilt by two busloads of teenagers who, after a raucous game of volley ball, spent the rest of the night stomping to rock music from a 30-watt loudspeaker. Somewhat bleary-eyed we awakened to a splendid dawn chorus of blackbird, thrush, bellbird and tui, and as I relished the prospects of fishing my 'dream' river, dire threats to knock up the previous night's revellers quickly vanished.

A short distance north of the camp, at Brady's Creek, a rough gravel track followed by a short tramp leads to the junction of the Makarora and the Young Rivers and, if the former is not above normal, a safe gravel bed crossing. This lands you on the true left bank of the Young so with the track up the Young, on the true right it means another crossing. The crossing looked easy but when we were halfway across, the water was well up the thighs. From the wrong side Jean looked doubtful. I tried a short trail up the true right which petered out but not before I'd looked down on a very big rainbow in the first pool. 'Whadyareckon?' 'I'm game if you are!' and in we went to midstream with Jean on tiptoe. Two more steps and we were in up to the jocks and frillies. That part of the pool was still in shade and it was very cold. Gasping and soaked to the waist we scrambled out the other side, headed for the sunshine, drank coffee, and warmed our chilly bottoms on the warm boulders.

My dreams came true. There they were — an enchanted stream, crystal-clear, tinted pale green, large pools, lovely rock outcrops, curling eddies and long pebble gravel runs where rainbows find home, all enhanced by flowing through native bush. Picture postcard mountains furnished the backdrop. Even so it was some way up the trail before I suddenly stopped.

'Have a look at this one,' I urged Jean and pointed through a window in the overhanging toi toi. In the fast flickering water a large rainbow, betrayed only by his olive green back, swerved now and again to seize an insect.

'Good fish.'

'Feeding well.'

'Take a nymph.'

'Be a hell of a job to land him!'

The bank was steep and covered in all sorts of clingy vine and woody plants. A cast from the opposite beach would have been easy but the thought of another deep river crossing decided me. It was only a small pool, more of a deep bankside pocket, overhung by a large flax bush. Even the shallower water downstream was knee deep which meant a very long cast to cover him. Too far for my modest talents, I squirmed through the tangled cover and aiming for a short cast, slid over the bank edge onto a dinner plate size ledge. Cramped it may have been but it allowed a perfect casting position directly below and in line.

Hooking the fish was the easy part. It was when I set the hook that things became difficult. It was thrilling stuff as from my little podium I felt like a maestro conducting the orchestra. That is until the solo performer decided he'd been mucked about long enough and took off down the rapids. When God gave out the brains I must have been looking the other way. When a fish runs you follow him so I stepped off the tiny platform and disappeared. Emerging in the shallows I glanced up to see a laughing face. 'What a fool,' chuckled Jean. Ever the optimist, after a splutter, I recovered the line slowly but that fish and my fly were far, far away, leaving me to dry out yet once again. That hadn't been in my dreams!

Further along the sun-dappled track, other rainbows made dallying a delight and, while we enjoyed lunch sitting on sunbaked rocks, feet dipped in cool water, a bellbird entertained us. This is what makes the New Zealand angling scene unique. Where else in the world can the trout fisher enjoy such excitement amid such magnificent surroundings? Leaving Jean to sunbathe I threaded my way upstream, noting on the way another good rainbow feeding against a steep bluff. Before long I came to a series of magnificent, dramatic pools, so deep the green had turned to deep blue. Trapped in the giant boulders were massive logs, captured during what must have been awe-inspiring floods. It was only the sight of big rainbows, deep, but feeding steadily, that tempted me to negotiate the stacked forest debris littering the rock crevices. Back eddies and wayward currents made casting a nightmare but, when I was near despair, some freak drift let the nymph sink just that much deeper. It was enough to raise the nearest trout, a fish I judged to be well over two kilograms. With one hand grasping an overhanging log and at times the rock face, playing that lively rainbow over deep water provided more thrills than I had bargained for. I was thankful not to receive another dipping as I helped him out of the net. A nice fish — my handspans couldn't ring him.

After some more heart-thumping incidents, leaving me with no more than broken tippets, I made to return downstream but to my surprise spotted another angler on the far side of the deep pools. A loud shout above the noise of the river caught his attention and by hand signs I indicated I'd already fished the pools and that his chances were limited. I also signalled for him to move downstream where I hoped he would stand a good change of hooking the fish under the bluffs. After wading the river, comfortably in his neoprene suit, he joined Jean and me and told us that this was his first visit to the Young and his first fly fishing expedition. Now with some misgivings but resolved to engineer his first trout on the dry fly, I gave him a large Coch-y-bondhu with instructions on how to reach the stream fish. It was still down there, weaving in the current, tail just touching a large submarine boulder, I perched above it and waited for Grant, our new-found friend.

'Hang on,' I yelled, 'he's directly below me.' Grant cupped his ear. 'Just above the rock!' I shouted. He waved and for what seemed like a half hour settled under the far beech trees and tied on the fly. Fish don't wait forever and both Jean and I were urging him to get a move on when he eventually reappeared. 'Not too far up!', 'Not too far down!', 'Move up a little!' He began casting and I groaned. He was awful, the fly touching the water on the back cast. A few more attempts and he was into the trees. 'Keep the rod up!' I called for the umpteenth time. Amazingly, he took heed of the shouted instructions and whether because of that or the law of averages, the fly settled a metre above the fish and was taken

immediately. The shout from our bank 'STRIKE', was followed by 'BLOODY HELL!' as he felt the weight of the fish. The rainbow belted off for the Makarora. For a time it seemed Grant had a chance but at the crucial moment he slipped, jerked the rod tip, and the trout gained his freedom. Grant recovered his balance, looked forlornly at the trailing fly line then shouted across the river. 'BLOODY GREAT! BLOODY GREAT!' The makings of a fine fly fisherman.

It was late so we retraced out steps and in an hour emerged from the bush to recross the Young. Our across-river companion was there to greet us complete with jet boat. After a dry trip across the Makarora he informed us, somewhat sheepishly, that he had lost my fly in the trees and had attached one of his own. Intrigued, I asked to inspect the fly. Whatever its merits in hooking the fish it was clearly badly rusted and raised eyebrows drew his comment. 'A hard way to learn a lesson!' I didn't reply thinking back on the many silly things I had done over the course of a long fishing career. Grant may have been a new chum at fly fishing but he excelled with the Hamilton jet. Warning us to grasp the forerail he hurled the craft at the upstream gravel bar, skimmed it and roared up the Makorora. Spinning around in a flourish he delivered us near the car and with one more whirl and a wave, headed off down river in a flurry of spray. From the car I looked back at the Young and the mountains. 'Well,' said Jean, 'was the dream worth it?'

Fishing the La Fontaine

Three years ago I was invited to fish some of England's finest chalk streams among which were the Test, the Kennet and the Itchen, the last-mentioned above Winchester on private water. I also spent a never-to-be-forgotten day following Skue's footsteps on the Abbott's Barton fishery. The Surrey and Hampshire water meadows have no real counterpart in this country but some of our streams come surprisingly near to it. One such stream is the La Fontaine with its prolific weed growth and steady flow of crystal-clear water. Trout love these conditions, the weed providing not only an ever-ready supply of aquatic insects but good cover when needed. Small and overgrown as it is you have to be pretty quick to spot the stream where it runs under State Highway 6, a short distance south of Hari Hari. But not far downstream where it joins another, larger, tributary it becomes a river than many fly fishers would break a rod for.

My first experience of this delightful river was highlighted by typical West Coast hospitality. Bob and Christine Harrison were busy pulling out old fence posts on their small farm when I asked for directions. Not only were these forthcoming but also the immediate offer of a camping spot on their lawn and the use of shower and toilet. For sheer warmth and friendliness these people are hard to beat. Once settled I hurried through the paddocks for a first view of this gentle legendary stream. Placid it may have been but the colour — amost pea soup! On returning to the Harrisons with my tale of woe, Bob guessed that some upstream farmer was clearing ditches. If I was going to match wits with La Fontaine trout it seemed the first thing to do was to discover the culprit with the dragline and fish upstream from there.

The following morning dawned bright and sunny and as draglines are pretty conspicuous we soon found it, well upriver. Further up at a handy farm, we asked for and were readily granted permission to cross to the river. Down the bumpy gravel track we went, a bouncing hare leading the way and a couple of red-beaked pukeko dashing back into the adjacent creek. Parking on a nice flat area

overlooking the stream I cast a sly glance over the profuse blackberry bushes wondering if this renowned river would live up to expectations. It was beautiful, the river bed a mixture of rich green weed tresses and pockets of golden gravel against which the wavering form of a respectable trout could be easily seen. What a welcome! I soon found however that if the river welcomes you, thanks to the blackberry and 'old man's beard', getting to it presents quite a problem. Even so, after a few scratches, the trout was within range but from river level no more than a smudge against the dark runnel of weed. A weighted nymph seemed a good choice but I couldn't see the nymph, the fish disappeared and too late I realised what had happened. I tightened, felt him almost underfoot, and he was gone. I wasn't all that worried — after all, with a full day ahead on such a lovely stream, it would have taken Scrooge himself to grizzle.

Upstream a Paradise duck eyed me suspiciously from a small green-turfed peninsula. Honking monotonously, it gave wing, circled and skimmed the pool. A wise retreat downstream rewarded me with the sight of another trout, larger than the last but lying in an almost impregnable position.

This against the far bank with a log and overhanging branches just upstream. Ready to cast I was then distracted by a herd of young bambi-eyed Hereford steers followed by the Paradise duck plus his female friend. Both birds skimmed the water and two large trout dashed downstream. In general I love birds but those two honking silly Paradise ducks seemed bent on annoying me. If they were a nuisance, their neighbours, fat blue pigeons, swooping in whistling flight from the white pine and miro trees were delightful, as were the pirouetting fantails. Sneaking downstream, away from the terrible twins, I finally came across what we 'in the trade' call a 'sitter', a good trout, on an open stretch, in a feedline of quiet currents. The small Red Spinner cocked nicely just upstream of him and without hesitation he sipped it in. Glorious dry fly! No wondering about nymph takes and where is he! Cut and dried — one, two, three and into him!

I mentioned the similarity between the Itchen and the La Fontaine, but when it comes to the trout it's a different matter. No chalk stream trout could hold a candle to the sheer fight and zest of the wild fish that I was trying desperately to hold and keep out of the weed. I might as well have tried to stop a Brahman bull with a piece of string. But, after a prayer or two and a few shouts of encouragement from Jean, once again busy with the camera, the fish emerged carrying with it on the leader, a great lump of weed. With luck I landed both, held the fat bronze trout for a moment or two, then watched him wriggle away. Another fish, an even harder fighter, after being nursed for some time after netting, turned upside down in quiet water and had to be given another helping hand. Such is the pugnacious quality of La Fontaine trout.

On my fishing trips, a ducking seems almost obligatory and this day was no exception. Jean had wandered off on her solo nature study while I fished near the car. After losing a lively trout in weed again I managed to net an exceptionally good one and on the spur of the moment decided to take a photograph with the ten-second self-timer. Jamming the net handle in the bank, with the fish unhooked and comfortable, I scrambled up the bank for the camera and tripod. After setting it up and focusing on the net and pressing the button, I quickly slipped down the bank, picked out the trout, turned to the glass eye and smiled. The trout, perhaps camera shy, gave a flip and in a poor attempt to recover it I fell backwards in the waist-deep water, a

performance duly recorded for posterity.

It was hard to leave this special trout stream. I thought how nice it would be to live near its banks then reminded myself that, although my adopted river, the Motueka, may not have the charm of the La Fontaine, it is still picturesque in its own way, holds a good stock of trout, and is, generally, minus Paradise ducks!

Brunner Browns

A sign 'the only pub for miles' is certain to attract passing trade, so after sampling the amber brew, we headed across the Taramakau, a gravel, rock-strewn river in search of better pastures. A half hour later, after passing Lake Paeroa and the Crooked River, we drew into the Moana camping ground where I was delighted to find not only a friendly custodian but a very knowledgeable fly fisher. Malcolm Garrod proved to be worth his weight in Hardy's reels with detailed directions to the best of local fishing. Lake Brunner itself needed no directions, we were camped within easy walking distance of it, but on his advice we were on the lake shore early next morning before the dreaded breeze ruffled the surface. The atmosphere was still, brooding, with a low mist over the lake, calm except for the splinters caused by flighting ducks. Further along the shallow lake edge a solitary heron set a good example by working stealthily for his breakfast.

My chance came when a fin surfaced near the lake edge and gradually approached.

'He's coming nearer,' whispered Jean, as though the trout had ears.

'Come on,' I whispered, falling into the trap, 'just a bit nearer.'

This was the sort of trout hunting I enjoy — the delicious thrill of anticipation, the fly sitting temptingly on the surface, underneath, the fossicking fish. As still as the heron, I watched the trout turn to the fly, rise slightly and inspect the fly. He hesitated for only a second, back-pedalled a bit, had another look, then, in a surge of speed that would have done Ben Johnson credit, headed for the far side of the lake.

But disappointment was short-lived — another cruiser appeared and once again the adrenalin ran high. It ran even higher when yet another arrived from the other direction. Two big trout! And both within sight of the fly! Surely one must see it. Too interested in each other, neither did, and both turned away. 'Damn! Shame!' Wouldn't it rock you? You wouldn't believe it!' The lake surface crinkled, the wind was on its way and time was running out. I felt an idiot crouched on the beach with, I hoped, only Jean for an audience but against the reflection of some submerged timber debris I saw him coming and looked heavenwards. It was only a bit of blue tinsel and a black hackle wrapped around a #18 hook but this time it worked. Tiny it may have been but it stung the trout which put as much distance between us in the shortest time possible and at the end of his first run I feared for the one kilogram tippet. Trout hooked in rivers, with their attendant streamside hazards can often be missed but I hardly ever lose a lake fish on a dry fly. But they fight just as well and soon I held a trout of the most remarkable colouring — a deep amber is the only way to describe it. In the next day or so I found that without exception the trout from the Brunner watershed were all endowed with flanks of burnished gold. A railway jigger clattered along the nearby track and the jigger-jogger gave us a friendly wave. It seemed to signal the end of our fishing. Perhaps a wet fly fisher would have revelled in the now windy conditions but I gave it away, pleased to have caught a Brunner trout. And vain enough to not think that it was the village idiot I'd caught.

The Arnold

Later, when having coffee with Malcolm and his charming wife, he mentioned the Arnold River which flows from the lake to join the Grey River near Stillwater. He suggested a spot not far from the lake outlet. Dinner that evening was eaten in record time and by 7 pm, leaving Jean with a good book, I hurried down an overgrown trail to emerge onto a broad gravel beach for my first glimpse of the Arnold. Flowing deceptively slowly between willow and bushclad banks, the water tinted amber and the stream bed made up of firm dark cobblestone. With the sun long set I didn't give much for my chances of spotting a fish but three or four dark shapes close to the gravel scour edge made me more optimistic and when one of them moved my spirits soared. I contemplated which one to catch first. The lower one was in faster water and deeper but he was nearest. He wouldn't disturb the others with his wild dashes when I hooked him. A half hour later I was still waiting for that mad dash and the trout were all in exactly the same places, glued to the bottom. Just upstream a creek entered the river and, in the last little pool, I saw a rise. Carefully I approached the pool and, to my surprise, over the sandy bed swam not only one big trout but four of them. This, I rejoiced, was more my style and I planned to turn the first one caught into the river and play him there. A large semi-submerged log jutted out nearby and I would keep him well away from that. I needn't have bothered. Twenty minutes later I was beset with that terrible malady that besets fly fishers when feeding trout studiously ignore them, when fumbling fingers tie on a long procession of flies, to no avail. It was near dark and still the fish rose, sometimes with back fins clearing the surface. It was an angler's hell!

But finally, one made a mistake and I hooked him. Into the Arnold it dashed and with the help of the fast water looked sure to break the nylon. By this time I couldn't even see the rod tip but with more pressure on him than was proper I eventually brought him nearer and decided to land him at the shallow end of the gravel beach. In the event there was no problem in landing him. The hook pulled out at the last minute! It would have been nice to have given a little rue smile and said, 'Good sport and all that.' I tried but it didn't work. Muttering in the dark I retraced my steps back to the car.

'Good evening.'

'Good evening.'

'You wouldn't by any chance be going to the Moana camp, would you?'

'What a coincidence — hop in.'

'Too kind.'

'Think nothing of it — been fishing?'

'Just a bit.'

'Easy to catch are they?'

'You must be joking!'

Haupiri

Still smarting after the Arnold fiasco (I did redeem myself at a later date by using 6x nylon), and after receiving detailed directions from Malcolm, we drove along a dusty gravel road in search of one of the West Coast's lesser-known streams. After exploring various no-exit roads we arrived at a substantial bridge.

'How about that!'

'Lovely river.'

'There's a nice one.'

'Where? — yes — I see it.'

'They're all over the place!'

Definitely dry fly.

The first pool, an angler's delight — long beach one side, deep run against the bush on the other. Escaping the sun, we lunched in the shade of a miro tree overlooking the river, enjoyed the company of grey warblers and finches and watched the trout rise to drifting insects. One in particular, lying out on the shallows, was marked as a first target. Fishing your favourite stream is warm, comfortable stuff but a new stream always tickles the palate with the added spice of the unknown. In bright sunshine I approached the almost motionless trout, not from below, with the near certainty of scaring him, but from the side, crouching low. This technique, using a very short low cast, allows only the fly and a short length of nylon to drift into the trout's window. It doesn't work every time but this fish decided the sparsley hackled Brown Spinner was the real thing, gulped it down and, hooked, sped downstream for the deep water and under the bridge. More by luck than skill I recovered the backing, then the line and finally the silver-sided trout.

'Beautiful fish.'

'Nicely played.'

'Skite!'

With the lower part of the pool now thoroughly disturbed I fished the tongue of current flowing smoothly against the far, overhung bank where at least three good fish could be seen. Rising frequently they looked very appetising and I wasn't surprised when the lower one took in the fly. One run and he was free. The next one, text book cast, text book strike, and I lost that one as well! My previous euphoria now gone, together with some confidence, the cast for the last and largest of the trio was well and truly fumbled, the fly hitting him on the head. To make matters worse, after a very careful approach, the next trout seen, in perfect water, never let me make a second cast before sliding into deep water. Landing trout isn't everything, I consoled myself, at the same time wondering what I'd done to deserve such a run of bad luck. Or was it lack of skill?

An upstream pool beckoned, quite different in character from the last. No gravel beach here but a deep pool studded with large boulders and bankside rocks, the steady current between them bringing foamy flecks. A careless step sent a big brown off into deep water. In a gravel pocket at the pool tail lay two other good trout, nymphing but very deep. But even as I studied these poor prospects I saw the telltale rings. Climbing the high bank, taking care to keep well hidden, I looked into mid pool, the deepest part, where in the sudsy feed line, a bruiser of a trout helped himself to passing fare.

'Five pounds — as near as dammit'.

'Where?'

'Put your Polaroids on.'

'Ooh yes!'

'Not easy to reach.'

Nor was he — on the far side of a great boulder, with an upstream cast out of the question. Leaving Jean where she could see the trout I crept to the back of the boulder but at that level spotting the fish was impossible.

'Can you see the fish?'

'Yes, he's still there.

'Tell me if it moves.'

'Okay.'

Leaving nothing to chance I changed the tippet nylon to 3x and tied on a new fly. Standing in deep water behind the boulder, crouched almost to stream level I risked a peek. Those tantalising rings just visible on the other side. A short switch cast and the fly landed in the feed line but it sailed past untouched.

'Still there?'

'Yes — still same place.'

A moment later after the second try, three things happened. Quickly! He rose, Jean shouted, and the hook went home. After two or three determined runs for freedom the fish seemed to visit every snag in the river before he tired a little and I began to hope.

It is not often I'm distracted when playing a good fish but a commotion at the head of the pool caught my attention. There, two Paradise ducks were having a fight, a rollicking roughhouse of feathers and beaks. First on the far beach, then thrashing into the river. Eventually they separated leaving the victor honking in triumph. Meanwhile one arm and one eye had been working on my opponent until he slipped over the net ring. My luck had really changed, for the hook was attached by only a fragment of gristle and, lucky for him too as he was returned to perhaps thrill another angler — another day. It was getting late, and we had still to return via the Cobb and Co road to Moana where Malcolm greeted us.

'How did it go?'

'Pretty good — pretty river — lots of trout.'

'They're pretty spooky those Haupiri fish.'

'Now he tells me!'

'Good day though?'

'I think we deserve a "spot".'

As the sun set in a fiery glow over Lake Brunner, the three of us, Malcolm, Jean, and I, and our silent friend, Johnnie Walker, toasted the most lovely stream, the Haupiri.

16

A Few Last Casts

An Evening on the Buller

A few years ago, when travelling between Nelson and Murchison, we stopped close by the Buller River at a handy roadside layby. Sharing it was another angler preparing for the evening's fishing. We talked a little, as anglers do, of prospects. He was getting on but sprightly and, as he walked to the near pool (the river in good condition but not low), I expected him to start fishing. Instead he waded in and continued across water normally reserved for the young and active, small bow waves against his trousers. Full of surprises, he laid his rod down on the far bank and climbed a steep bushclad cliff overlooking the long pool below and disappeared into the trees. Along the cliff top the shake of the odd bush marked his progress until opposite the campsite his pale face peered down to inspect the river. This strategy marked him as an old stager and well he knew that fish in the turbulent currents were easily seen from a height. Having marked his fish he returned below, concentrated his efforts in selected pockets and runs.

A season later, we arrived at the same spot, having fished up the West Coast. It was fine but cool, the wind moderate, and downstream, but high cirrus cloud forewarned of a weather change. A sore back had plagued me for the past day or so but by some miracle, the sight of that 'trouty' water immediately cured it.

'So much for your promise to rest it,' said Jean as I slipped on the fishing vest.

'No really — it's much better — only be away for a half hour.'

It was 2 pm. 'See you about six o'clock then,' she called as I sped streamwards.

I remembered the agile senior citizen's

143

tactics and made to cross the river but a few steps in that rushing water made it out of the question. Instead I wandered upstream along the boulder-studded banks hoping to see a trout in that strange green tinted water. It's a lovely, refreshing river, the Buller, pretty with native beech and bushes in many places overhanging the stream edge. Although the pools were well spaced it was obvious that the quieter corners and back eddies could well harbour big fish. It isn't easy spotting trout, even big ones, in that fast curly water and I'd travelled a long way before my heart gave a leap as I saw a tail, waving like a small fan from the far side of a large boulder. Tricky light made it impossible to see more. A little bit more luck and I would have done for that fish. Up he came from at least a metre deep, opened his jaws to take the well-hackled dry, and the tippet dragged. That was the last I saw of him. I retired to a grassy knoll and got the shakes out of my legs. That fish was all of three kilograms. Close encounters with big fish do that to me. A kingfisher perched nearby and kept up his steady whistle. I hoped he was a good omen.

The next fish I spotted was in a substantial side stream off the main river and in shallow riffly water — an easy fish to cover. He wasn't as big as the other one but, what the heck, one half his size would be nice on the end of the line. I managed two casts for him before he slipped sideways, never to be seen again. These Buller trout, I began to realise, were no fools — perhaps it was going to be a fishless day. I didn't reckon on fickle fortune. Crunching towards me on the bouldery beach came a 4WD and as it rumbled to a halt out climbed a tall, very fit, young man, and with his short fishing vest, even shorter shorts, and Polaroids slung around his neck. After introductions Graham encouraged me to try again pointing to a particularly rough

piece of water and offered me a nymph nearly as big as a grown bully. He also tied on a chunk of darning wool about two metres up the leader. Finesse took a back seat as I flung the hairy thing into the confused current keeping a close eye on that bit of fluff. A dozen casts later, as I was beginning to have doubts, my new aquaintance shouted 'Yes!', just as I saw the fluorescent wool dart below the surface. Somewhere, down in that maelstrom, a very big brown became very annoyed as I set the hook and for the next half hour, or so it seemed, bent the rod double and set me on a near course for a heart attack.

'Great fighter!'
'Typical Buller.'
'My arms aching!'
'What do you reckon?'
'Near three.'
'What!'
'Oh, in pounds? — about six.'

'The best fishing is on the far bank,' said Graham, eyeing the river. I glanced across the tail of the pool at the swirling pattern of stones in the deceptively shallow water. 'Taken some nice fish behind those boulders,' he said temptingly.

I looked again. It was time for me to return to Jean, I thought of the tot of pre-dinner whisky and a warm jumper. It looked deep, that river crossing.

'Good fish?' I said to Graham and saw the challenge in his eyes.

'Some big fish,' he said convincingly, and with that I grabbed his collar, and he mine, and off we went.

I weigh about 64 kilograms but, as the strong current lifted me off the gravel, I felt his grip tighten on the scruff of my neck and together we emerged (am I always to suffer wet Jockeys?) on the far side. That was the easy part. Graham, a seasoned forester, used to bush whacking, pulled his way up through the steep scrub and, sure-footed, threaded

One of the best stocked rivers in New Zealand. The river not far from the Owen/Buller junction.

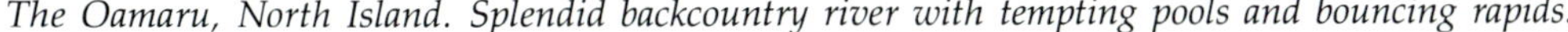

The Oamaru, North Island. Splendid backcountry river with tempting pools and bouncing rapids.

Motueka River. At the Ngatimoti Bridge the author fishes for the 'regular' Aunt Sally's.

his way along a perilous track high above the river. I followed wondering if we would meet Barry Crump coming the other way.

'Off you go!' I said, sensing his keenness. 'I'll spot for you.'

Graham didn't need urging. In a flash he disappeared down the bushclad slope to emerge just under an overhanging bluff. It was now child's play spotting fish. No sooner had I moved a short distance than I called, 'Don't move — there's one slipping down towards you!' The big trout curved into the stream edge only a few rod lengths upstream of Graham.

'About 20 feet upstream and five foot out from the bank,' I shouted, in my eagerness quite unable to measure in metres. It hardly mattered as the fish rose twice, quiet little sips that belied his weight. From that grandstand view I saw the trout lift to the deer hair humpy and Graham strike empty air. The fish swerved midstream a little and I groaned. It then settled behind a large, almost white, triangular stone and after a couple of minutes rose again. Graham, who at this level, had no chance of seeing the trout looked for directions. 'Ten feet out, cast over the big white stone!' This time he made no mistake, lifted his rod to my excited shout and the big Buller brown was on.

Stumbling back along that apology for a trail, and rounding risky precipices, I finally slid down the steep bank to join Graham, rod fully bent, still battling it out with the fish. The sun had long since set and the light was poor for a photograph but I chanced it, trying from all angles to get some light in the picture. What looked like firm support failed as a boulder suddenly gave way tipping me over, sprawling, the camera clonking on the stones. Graham spared a second to glance downstream, no doubt amazed to see me sitting in the river's edge. Dander

now fully aroused and thoroughly wet, I grabbed the camera and snapped a couple of shots as he landed the fish, a beauty, equally the size of my one and only. After unhooking the fish he held it in the current for a minute or so then released it. 'What's this?' he said and from the stream bed picked up my camera lens cover with its broken elastic strap. Lucky find.

'Wonder if there's another up there?' said Graham, peering upstream.

I looked into the darkening river crossing, said a few choice words, which had an immediate effect, and together, once again, half-carried, half-towed, I made an exhilarating Buller River crossing. By the time we reached the caravan, still dripping, it was dark, but not too dark to notice the ample measure of Johnnie Walker that Jean had poured out for us. After a late dinner-early supper, my new found friend took his leave while I related the evening's events to Jean. Still later, drowsy in my sleeping bag, I savoured the experience — that lovely Buller trout, the river crossing, the chance meeting, Graham's success. Having had more than my share of wonderful fishing days I wasn't envious. I recalled when I too had been sturdy, muscular and surefooted, wished him well, and drifted into the land of great rainbows and even bigger browns.

Motueka Browns

Long domiciled in Southland perhaps I can be forgiven for then regarding the rest of the New Zealand fishing scene as a sort of poor relation. That's how you get when you have a score of excellent rivers and streams and a few lovely lakes within two hours' drive of home. Not to mention the legendary trout of Fiordland. But not everyone can enjoy such a variety of trout streams. Many of us having to take whatever is offering, and providing there is a good chance of a trout at the end of the day, we are well satisfied. Living for the past few years near or on the banks of the Motueka River I have been fortunate, in that this charming stream is almost the sister river to the famous Mataura but, if I were forced to choose, the Mataura would get the laurels. It would also get the brickbats for its Southland environment with fine days throughout the year at a premium.

So what's so special about the Motueka? It has three fine attributes. It is one of the most picturesque lowland rivers in New Zealand, it holds ample stocks of brown trout averaging one kilogram and, with Nelson weather it is fishable for most of the season — in the lower reaches, the year round. That's the good news. The not so good is that most Motueka trout have a Master's degree in self-survival, know most anglers' flies by name and, so some fly fishermen say, are now converting Imperial and 4x into metric. It is a rare fishing guest who returns victorious. Most of them come back scratching their heads never quite sure if it was the wrong fly, poor presentation, or too thick a nylon. It takes a day or two to get on equal terms. And it's not only visitors who suffer. Local anglers, although we do get our share of sport, are often given the raspberry.

A half hour spent on nail biting, and fly changing is common on this most challenging of rivers but, when those supercilious trout make a mistake, it is an experience to cherish. Few anglers, fishing the Motueka for the first time, can resist the charm of this gentle river. The quiet pools and lighthearted rapids soon exert a peculiar fascination. The long glides, burnished gold with the setting sun, the water-sculptured rock formations guiding foam-flecked currents, the beauty of the river valley itself, must attract even the Philistine. The trout, brown only, are notoriously difficult to see in ripple and dance waters where surface reflects sky, and the fish hover just below the surface.

My first experience of the Motueka a few years back was in the Stanley Brook area and, although it appeared in an issue of *Rod and Rifle* it is worth retelling. It was a lovely sunny day. The water in the large rock pool below curled and swirled around the giant boulders. Even in sunshine it was too deep for one to see the river bed. A good trout rising in an upstream feed line held my attention and, by clambering down a great rock face, I managed to throw a fly at him. After a few casts the fish stopped rising and I wondered what I'd done wrong. Then I noticed, directly below me, a few bubbles rising to the surface, growing in intensity until a snorkel tube appeared attached to a frog-suited diver. Surprise turned to indignation. I didn't mind his using the river as well but not at the expense of a rising trout. Before he swam out of range I reached out with the rod tip and brought him up spluttering by whacking the snorkel. Hardly cricket but an angler scorned is something to be reckoned with.

Living alongside the river has its advantages. A short stroll through the boysenberry paddock brings you to the long pool where, in the evening, just out of casting reach, there is a tempting line of trout rise. But a wet caddis imitation, across and down, just on dusk, is almost sure to bring a 'pull' and if you're in luck, a well-hooked heavyweight. A riverside home also brings many friends and visitors and few forget to bring a rod. Recently, while working in the garden, I was greeted by 'Can I get this way to the river?' The stranger was walking and, when I asked him where his car was parked he told me he had flown down from New Plymouth in his own plane for a days fishing! Later I gave him a ride back to the airfield where I saw his transport — a sleek rear-winged aircraft propelled by a sizable Rolls Royce engine. He offered me a 'trip around the bay' but when he said the runway was a bit short and he had to 'give it some gun' to take off, I suddenly remembered a previous engagement.

A couple of pools upstream from home is Tibbs Bank, a low grassy shoulder with scattered clumps of young willow and old gorse. The pool is over a half a kilometre long, and apart from the poolhead rocks, the flow is slow and uninterrupted. A long beach runs along the far side, making for easy casting. But, for the careful, cautious angler, the bank is the place to catch fish. Weaving in and out the bankside rubbish, snatched by blackberry runners, poked by willows and wattle, fishing isn't easy but the rewards can be great. The trout love to lie close to the bank in kneedeep water either browsing for snails and caddis larvae or feeding nearer the surface on mayfly nymphs or, in season, willow grub or passionfruit hoppers. Between 9 am and lunchtime during summer short hatches of adult mayflies occur. They are usually Deleatidium duns, those small blue-grey floaters often imitated by the Blue Dun artificial or, if you're an American, a #16 Adams. The trout are very shy, slipping away at the slightest hint of danger, an ultra-sensitivity that never fails to amaze even experienced visitors. By far and away the best strategem with these fish is to stalk low along the bank at all times, never showing a skyline silhouette, and at the first glimpse of an upstream trout either sit or kneel for a minute or so to observe if the fish is feeding. If it is almost stationary, be warned. Despite the fact that he has not disappeared he could well have seen you and is just waiting for further advice. But all being well, the clever angler, having noted some bankside object to mark the position of the fish, can slip into the water and by working very slowly up the bank edges spot the fish again and be within casting distance. Having a friend or guide spotting and marking trout from the bank top while you quietly wade upstream is the ideal method.

I have taken many friends and visitors to fish this stretch and few have failed to hook a fish or two. But using the necessary 5x or 6x nylon with a strong Motueka trout at the end of it often produces a glum face or two. I remember one visitor (who shall remain nameless) who, used to the well-tended banks of the English chalk stream, insisted on standing at all times. But, by the end of the day after the trout had him well educated, his trouser legs were as muddy as mine. He also caught one of the best trout I had seen for some time, a beauty of nearly two kilograms. Another overseas angler, used to fishing lakes, could cast prodigious distances and land his fly with the delicacy of a feather. He could also cast a high steep line to clear troublesome willows or wattle. But when it came to sneaking a switch cast to a rising fish between two close clumps of brush he was flummoxed. Like most, he appreciated the challenge, caught fish and learned a little bit more.

Another guest had trouble with his knots, landing some good fish but losing too many with badly-tied half barrels. Flyfishers can be sensitive about knots but he didn't object when I offered to tie on the next fly. After a hundred or so casts over a particularly difficult fish he managed to hook it only to lose it when the nylon broke. On running it back through his finger he looked ruefully at the little pigtail and said, 'Well, it's nice to know even the experts make mistakes!' What he didn't know was that although I am nowhere near an expert my knots are good. I waited for him to notice that the nylon had broken at the leader knot one up from the fly, one of his own tying.

His 'Oh my God! — I'm so sorry!' wasn't needed and we had a good laugh over it.

Rising in the Golden Downs area between Nelson and Lake Rotoiti, the Motueka flows for near 100 kilometres to enter the Tasman just north of the Borough and, apart from the upper reaches and a few kilometres at Stanley Brook, is within easy reach of the traveller. It sports two minor tributaries — the Graham and the Pearse and a major one, the beautiful Wangapeka which enters the main river below Tapawera. This river contains larger trout, up to two kilograms — they are even more suspicious than their Motueka cousins — hard to believe but true. Unless the Motueka is above normal and discoloured the Pearse and Graham Rivers are best left in reserve and the angler should concentrate on the 50 kilometres between the Baton bridge and the estuary.

Some say there are too many trout in the river and that at an average of plus-one-kilogram would be enhanced by fewer trout. These pundits may be among the chosen few but, after a hard day's fishing for these sophisticated trout, I reckon the more the merrier. The remarkable thing about the Motueka is that wherever the angler decides to wet the line he or she stands a good chance of finding fish along the full length of the river. It is ideal for both the spinner and the fly fisher, although the latter is much more in evidence these days. If one method is slightly more popular than another it is fishing the artificial nymph. It may not have quite the charm of dry fly fishing but, when the river surface is bare and the trout feeding avidly below, it takes a determined angler to resist taking part in the banquet.

If there is one place on the Motueka where the river regularly displays its wares it is at the Ngatimoti bridge, roughly half way between Motueka and the upstream Baton bridge. From the Ngatimoti bridge, upstream and down, the trout parade and perform to titivate even the most jaded angler's palate. Below, a slow feed line, with lots of insect fare, means the trout are easily seen, just under the surface. As with all bridge trout they have seen the lot, from wormers to spinners to fly fishers, all of whom they tend to ignore. But they are not infallible, providing (1) you can balance on a dinner plate size rock, while at the same time execcuting a perfect roll cast to land the fly exactly half a metre upstream of the last rise, (2) strike at the right moment and still stay on the rock, (3) if you hook him, on nylon not much thicker than your hair, and can stop his first express run under the massive sunken boulders and unsling the landing net at the same time, every Good Friday or Whit Tuesday, you may land one of these charmers!

Today I managed it, not once but three times, and with an audience of three boy scouts. These delightful lads, from their annual camp, were my wards for the day, having been promised a day out with members of our fishing club. Fortune smiled on us. The day was fine and sunny, no wind, the fish were feeding on or near the surface. Fish were hooked, some lost, some landed. The boys felt the bend of the rod, netted good trout, saw two filleted and I hope, enjoyed them for their dinner. A couple of days before, while typing this manuscript, I felt the urge (although the day was dull), and dashed post haste to my favourite pool. Not a rise, gloomy skies, fish seen fading away like ghosts. Then it started to drizzle. Disappointed, I made my way through the paddock back to my 90cc Honda. Then I wondered what there was to be sad about. Here I was, a weekday, on the banks of a grand river with more pools than a dog's fleas, more trout in it than I am ever likely to catch in the rest of my lifetime, and with as much time as

I want to fish it, I reminded myself that there are no good or bad days in trout fishing — just days to savour when you are too old to cast a line, too feeble of sight to spot a trout, even from a bridge. Then, I will remember the Motueka.

Trout at Turangi

As a Southlander by adoption, it is easy to laud the angling merits of the South Island, plentiful and varied as they are, but no fishing excursion could be complete without an account of trout fishing in the North Island. Occasional visits give only a taste of its excellence but perhaps this is good. Much better to leave the table, satisfied but with room for a little more. Having enjoyed fishing in Taupo, Taranaki, the Wairarapa, Manawatu, Hawkes Bay and other provinces, I would need another book to relate the many stories I could tell. Meanwhile I have chosen, rightly or wrongly, a few tales from Taupo and Rotorua. Much has been written about these areas, indeed writing Taupo guide books has almost become a national pastime. I'll leave the mechanics to anglers more knowledgeable than I, and simply tell you some of my own experiences.

My first encounter was in the 1970s when I first visited my son, a Wildlife Officer living near Turangi. Visiting a well-loved son is always a pleasure but when he lives near good trout fishing then one can be forgiven for believing in fairies at the bottom of the garden. Some fairy! Flowing past the bottom gate was the Tongariro! Having heard fabulous tales of this river I could hardly wait to fish it but he had other ideas.

'No rush, things are a bit different here,' he grinned. 'After dinner will be soon enough.'

When in Rome, I thought, and tried to suppress what I now know as the dreaded Tongariro fever.

'Got any wets?' he asked.

'Wets!' I replied, 'After me tying a fly box full of Parsons Glory's and Mrs Simpsons.'

'Got any caddis imitations?' he persisted.

The short of it was that, after rummaging around his fly tying gear, I found some mallard wings, turkey quills, gold tinsel, and quickly produced some emerging caddis on #10 hooks. These seemed to meet with his approval and at 6.30 pm we set forth. On first sighting this famous river, I was a little disappointed. It was smaller than I had imagined (owing, as I later learnt, to the strangling of it by the then Electricity Department) but it was still thrilling to be alongside it and when Norm pointed to a couple of good-size boulders and said, 'Cast there,' I did so willingly. Two or three casts 'there' and I was attached to my first Tongariro rainbow. For a second. The fly came fluttering back.

'Whatyerdoin'?'

'Just testing them,' I mumbled, at the same time marvelling at his confident style. I made to move downstream.

'Whatyerdoin'? — there's more there!'

Now his slave for the day I made a couple more casts and the rod nearly jumped out of my hand as another rainbow grabbed the fly.

'Jeez! — you're getting rusty.'

'Blunt hook,' I returned, but I didn't bother to check it. Another cast into that swirly water and this time, an electric pull announced another rainbow, this one well hooked, and scorching back to the lake. The scramble that followed produced all I expected from my son and heir, hoots of laughter and some ribald comment but my prayers were answered as the hook held and the glittering prize lay gasping in the shallows. I got all the praise I could expect.

'Not bad,' he said grudgingly and set

off downstream. 'You'd better hurry!' he called back, 'They'll be rising!'

Hurry I did, wondering as I stumbled over the boulders, how the dickens we could fish 'wet' in one pool and 'dry' in the next. Did he have a timetable? I looked about. There were no dancing mayflies. From downstream I heard the faint call 'You'll be late' and put some curry into my stride. I caught up with him standing by a heap of boulders by a strange backwater. This was Barlow's Pool, now regrettably no more, an eerie place where the Tongariro hit a rock bluff diverting a nice circling current to form a quiet pool. The only possible place to cast from was a little boulder jetty with hardly enough room for the two of us. It was like sharing a single bed.

'Is this it?' I asked, more than a little surprised and somewhat apprehensive standing just clear of the apparently bottomless depths.

All I got in the reply was, 'Just wait — and be ready.'

As the daylight faded in our little cover, under a well-pruned willow tree, I wondered how anyone could cast in that restricted space and how many anglers' flies the branches had claimed. My musings came to a sudden halt when he said quietly, 'Whatyerwaitinfor?'

Across the pool, against the now dark cliff wall I saw a tiny splash. 'Tiddler!' I called. More splashes, sprinkled down the far feed line. Tiddler's or no I feverishly swished the line out. God knows where it landed but before I had time to recover a rod length a savage tug nearly bowled me off my perch. The hook pulled free.

'Some tiddler!' I heard him say, but I was too busy throwing another cast to reply. 'Bring it back SLOWLY,' he said quietly, in keeping with the mood.

After another few casts it was rainbow time again as a heavy fish tore the line from the reel and headed into the rapids.

How I kept that fish from bolting downstream I'll never know but eventually, by torchlight and with a skill I never fail to marvel at, Norm scooped the fish in the net. I bent to unhook it but was firmly directed back to the fishing.

'Get into them while they're feeding,' he urged, something he didn't have to say twice and belofre long another rainbow followed the first. At 9 pm the rise ceased but by this time five fish had been landed. One kept showed a stomach content of river weed. What peculiar fish these rainbows are!

The next day we fished the Otamangakau, noted for its trophy fish but, with its bare banks, I found it uninteresting. Sour grapes perhaps as I failed to interest the only two trout seen or maybe I was thinking too much about the previous night's excitement. On our return, impatient, I head for Barlow's. 'Wasting your time mate' he said. 'Won't rise before half eight — I'll be down later.'

He was right of course but it was a lovely evening with the bellbirds belling and the shining cuckoo piping his steely call. Approaching the pool, someway ahead I spotted a large shag resting on some willow roots. Feeling naughty I carefully stalked the dozy bird and when close gently pushed him off his perch with the bagged rod. Into the river he tumbled, all beak and wings, righted himself and with an indignant look sailed down through the Cattle Rustlers Pool. While I was waiting at Barlow's, an electric blue flash revealed a kingfisher and for the next few minutes I watched my fellow angler commute between river and branch, sometimes with a tiny fish for a moustache. I could just make out the time and remembered Norm's advice, 'Pays to have a couple of casts before they start.'

The line sailed across the pool, the fly landing somewhere between the edge of the backwater and the rapids. It swept through the narrow feed line. Two more casts, a determined pull and the rod hooped. In that confined space in the semi-darkness, with submerged willow roots and very deep water at my feet, it took as much courage as skill to bring the strong rainbow to the net. Soon the caddis rise was in full swing and for the next 20 minutes I thought all my Christmases had come at once. I was just playing my fourth fish when a flash of light warned me that he had arrived.

'Howyerdoing'?'

'Not too bad — just keep an eye on me and perhaps you'll learn something — you can net this fish if you like,' I added nonchalantly. And he did.

Flicking on the torch I turned to pick up my four rainbows and for a moment thought I was dreaming. There were FIVE fish, one a big, beautifully-conditioned brown. I couldn't believe it. Then I realised he had fished the Lower Birch Pool on the way down, caught the fish and in the dark slipped it in. My rainbows beside that magnificent brown looked like a string of herrings. 'You were saying?' he chuckled.

Two days on the Oamaru

It was a beautiful day with a clear blue sky, the hot midday sun tempered by a southerly breeze. Below lay the junction of three rivers. To the west the Kaipo, to the east, the Upper Mohaka; and to the south, famed for its big browns, the Oamaru. High manuka-clad terraces flank the valley floor, while in close escort, clumps of golden toi toi pilot this lovely stream to its meeting with the Kaipo and there, to give birth to the Mohaka. No alpine passes or granite buttresses to dominate, but here and there, where the river hugs the terrace, large bone-white slips stand out starkly against the soft green bush. Across the valley, on a low ridge, blending nicely into the surrounding bush, the 12-bunk

forestry hut beckoned and before long, after climbing the gut-busting hewn steps, the pack was soon off and the billy on. This was the Kaimanawa State Forest area lying 35 kilometres south-east of Taupo, part of which is set aside for recreational hunting. But it was no four-footed quarry I had come to hunt. Refreshed, I hurried down the narrow winding trail in search of those paddle-tail browns.

The first pool was typically long and narrow-gutted and brushed thickly with manuka on one side and bordered by a small, beach on the other. The pool tail fan was a mosaic of clean gravel, mid channel with a patchwork of exposed rock bed strata and the pool eye, a deep, mysterious, emerald green gem. The pool head had shallow, crinkly water, full of swirls and eddies, a perfect trout haven. Showing clearly against the stream bed lay a very large fish. Too good to be true, I thought, shaky fingers threading the line. And it was. The sparkling #12 Cochy-bondhu floated nicely over him. He ignored it. A second drift and he made a half circle to end up with his head under a stone. Had the fish spotted my approach? Was the 2x leader too thick? It was sunny — was it rod flash or a glint from my gold tooth?

I moved upstream to search the pool head and, after a minute or so, close to the far bank, the kaleidoscope of water patterns settled into a familiar grey form. The fly bobbed jauntily over him and a formidable set of jaws clamped on the fly. I struck, felt that wonderful thud and then — nothing. A quick check of the hook revealed a sharp point. Hmmm, poor start — good finish, I mused optimistically.

Below the ruffled surface, the next trout seen was so well camouflaged that I nearly missed spotting him. A sitter? From a high grassy bank I watched his feeding pattern and savoured the prospect of my first Oamaru brown. Again the little dancer was sent on its way, bested the wind and settled a rod length above him. The two met, a pause, a confident strike, solid resistance then, apart from a brief glimpse of his rapid departure downstream — again nothing.

Now more than a little perturbed I check the hook again. The point bit into a fingernail. Nothing wrong there. Somewhat less confident I moved upstream. Would it be a jinxy day? One of those unexplainably bad ones? Trout holding pools are well spaced on the Oamaru and it was quite some distance upstream before the next encounter occurred. A patch of toi toi overhung a small but deep run, I gently parted the fronds with the rod top. Tight against the edge in fast broken water, a very big trout kept station. With confidence a little frayed, I waded across a lower pool, to creep up the small gravel beach opposite for the cross cast. Surely this time. The now strong downstream wind didn't help. It was a poor cast, the fly landing somewhere below his tail. No matter. If fish can cartwheel — he did — a head to tail effort to engulf the fly. A pause to set the hook firmly in his jaws. Now for a battle, but again — nothing!

Three good fish. Sitters? All gone! It was brooding time. Time for a change. Change what? In the welcome shade of manuka, I pondered over a snack of bread, cheese, apple and raisins. It wasn't the trouts' fault. They had been most obliging. Either it was just a run of bad luck or for some reason the hooks were lacking. Then the penny dropped. Fine wire hooks — were they springing on a hard jaw? It was getting late and tempted as I was to try again, it was time to return to the hut. Wandering down the trail gave me more time to speculate on the day's events. It would have been good to land just one of those chunky browns, but, even though I had been outwitted by

three good fish, it had been a fine day. That night I snuggled into the sleeping bag, listened to the clockwork morepork, and settled on the old maxim: Poor start — good finish. I hoped so.

'The little bugger's got the chocolate!' Startled, I opened my eyes. Further shouts and stumbling, shadowy figures ran from the bunkhouse. 'There he is,' shouted someone. I dashed outside in time to see the possum heading for the bush, still hanging on to half a bar of Cadbury's. Lawrie, Wildlife Ranger, laughed as he shone the torch on the porch floor littered with the tramping pack contents. It had been dark when he had arrived back from a nearby hut and the forgotten pack, left on the porch, turned out to be a lucky dip for the enterprising marsupial. 'Better check yer false teeth,' shouted Keith, wag of the party. Visions of the furry intruder grinning back at us with Lawrie's teeth sent us into fits, but then bunks creaked as everyone settled down. It was beautiful outside and I stayed a while longer, gazing up in awe at the vast canopy of stars.

By 8 am a new sun had sent the morning mist packing. With two hunters away early and the Wildlife team on a survey up the Kaipo, I sat on the porch steps, enjoying the solitude and the scenery. It was the last day and, reflecting on my lacklustre performance, I wondered what the Oamaru, glinting in the morning sun, would offer. Swooping and darting, a pair of welcome swallows ushered me from the hut down the trail again, across the dry crunchy moss, where an old sika skull told a story. Back to my start pool of yesterday. No fish seen this time — but that tempting riffle at the pool head deserved a cast. Once again, a Cochy-y-bondhu, this time a #10 standard wire, tripped lightly down the riffle. A large neb broke the surface, became attached to the hook and an extremely indignant Oamaru brown shot downstream. A fine day, even with no fish hooked, is still a good day, but a fine day, with rod hooped and a big bonny fish at the end of a taught leader is nothing less than glorious. The reel sang, then stopped as he turned at the pool tail. Had he had the nerve to keep going, I fear the outcome would have been different, but with a snag-free pool and only his sheer strength to combat, the result was almost predictable. What beautiful fsh these Oamaru browns are, and what fighters! It was a tired trout that slipped back into the depths.

The next pool was much shallower but with a long deep run against the far bank, overhung with toi toi. A downstream breeze ruffled the surface, but even so I discovered another big brown lying almost motionless in the shade. Overhead a silver jet pencilled a vapour trail across a blue backdrop. I glanced back at the fish. Vanished! But a quick search of the stream bed revealed him lying slightly upstream. There is almost as much delight in watching a big wild trout as hooking him — but not quite! Once again the Cochy-y-bondhu went on its merry way and the hook went home. Whoosh, down the frothy rapids he ran, while, in hot pursuit, I dashed over the slippery stones. With an inborn talent for falling in, a ducking was inevitable and sitting in the river I was in no position to control the fish. Halfway down the cascades the fish jammed himself between a couple of great boulders. A tug on the leader and out he rocketed, a grey blur, streaking past my shaky legs. I looked ruefully at the flyless tippet, bid him goodbye, and made off upstream.

The next pool, long and narrow, with the slow current flowing over bedrock looked promising and, when I saw the long fishy shape clearly marked against the pale rockbed, my cup ran over. Two choices. A long snag-free cast from the one bank across the mirrored surface, or a sneaky approach from the rear. He was so still, I thought he was asleep but the fish made no bones about lifting to take the fly. The next few minutes turned the tranquil pool into bedlam, the strong fish testing the tippet to the limit. Arm-aching trout are rare, but before he finally clapped the gravel, both hands had held the rod. After thanking him for a thrilling battle I watched him swim slowly upstream and, as if in reward, a tiny swirl in the feedline betrayed yet another fish. He too fell for the tiny floater, fought with strength and vigour, but finally joined his tired predecessor, flank to flank, in mid pool. Now in utter contentment and within sight of the next pool, I lay on the sun-bleached dry moss, a potpourri of Oamaru browns flickering through my drowsy mind. A crackle of twigs in the nearby manuka and a small movement caught my eye. For a brief moment I saw the sika hind and fawn eyeing me intently before slipping away through tangled branches. Another indelible memory of the beautiful Oamaru.

Time was marching on. Already the sun, past its prime, was heading westward. Dallying no longer, I moved on, keen to reach the top of the flats and the smaller bush-lined pools. It was well worth the effort. An angler's fairyland awaited me. The river danced its way through the beech groves, slowing here and there to breast a root-lined bend. Unseen in the dappled shade, trout, equal in size to their downstream cousins, rose readily to the fly. Brown, rainbow, rainbow, brown, one per pool, fell to the rod until at last, cup now truly overflowing, I watched the last fish glide homewards. More tempting pools lay ahead, but already shadows were lengthening across the clearings and it was with a feeling of reluctance, mingled with pleasure, that I made off downstream.

It was almost dark by the time I climbed those king-sized steps up to the hut. Candles flickered and billies clanked. Friendly banter reached me. Norm, my son and heir, appeared. 'Do any good?' he asked. 'Not too bad, not too bad at all,' I replied.

Appendix (1)

Kitchen Trout

A good feature in trout fishing is that, unlike other forms of hunting, the quarry can be returned, hopefully unharmed. Knowledgeable people tell us that our fisheries are far better for the return of large trout, encouraging a gene pool of rod busters instead of those mediocre 1 kilogram fish. This philosophy fits in very well with the other aspect of troutfishing, eating them.

Smaller trout are much nicer to eat than the ones we like to brag about. A half kilogram fish makes a tasty meal for two, a 1 kilogram fish, casseroled, will provide three or more generous portions and anything bigger should be considered for smoking.

Preparing Trout

With the fish already gutted, remove the head, gill stirrup or bony arch and all fins, including the dorsal bones. Cut away the tail and slice the tail wrist from vent to the bone. Slide a fine pointed fillet knife under one row of cavity bones to the vent and repeat on the side. Try not to cut the fine lateral backbones. With fingers ease the gill end of the backbone from the skin using thumb and finger working towards the tail wrist. Then hold the backbone in one hand, and pull hard with the other. The remaining tail end will easily tear out of the wrist.

The fish is now pancaked and can be cut in half along the back line. Place each side, in turn, on a hard surface, skin down. Hold the tail end firmly, place the knife between the skin and flesh, and pressing very hard, saw towards the other end. These attractive golden boneless fillets after being given a liberal sprinkling of salt and a little pepper can now either be packaged as a gift, stored for future use or cooked.

Recipes for cooking trout can easily be found elsewhere but there is one way of preparing trout to eat that, in my opinion, will win you many friends.

Smoked Trout Pate

Head, tail and split, two 1 kilogram trout. Sprinkle liberally with salt and brown sugar and leave overnight. Hot smoke for about 20 minutes. When cold remove backbone and other obvious bones using the fingers to flake out the flesh. Do this carefully then place it briefly in a blender to fragment the flesh. This will now weigh about ¾ kilogram. In a saucepan heat a cup of water, add salt, pepper, 1½ tablespoons of mustard paste, 1 tablespoon of white vinegar and 3 tablespoons of gelatine. Stir gently until dissolved.

Have handy small tin of sweet corn, peas, capsicum, a half dozen slices of beetroot, finely chopped and any other cooked vegetables you may fancy. Place a quantity of trout in a large bowl, add two tablespoons of corn, add some liquid, add more trout, add two tablespoons of peas, then trout, then beetroot, trout, more corn, capsicum, and beetroot until all the trout and liquid is used and most of the vegetables. Quantities are not critical. Mix thoroughly then add a pottle of sour cream. With more stirring the mixture should be a stiff paste and can be spooned into saved ice cream or mousse pottles. Place in freezer. The pate is very rich in flavour and is delicious with salad or on biscuit. The above quantity should produce about 10 to 12 pottles. Serve Chilled.

Bon apetit.

Appendix (2)

Fishing on film

There used to be a time when I measured fishing quality by the number of trout landed but that phase is long gone. Releasing trout is a much better experience. Even moreso, to catch a trout and keep him forever — on film. Angling pictures are reminders of pleasant days but they must be good. Here are a few pointers to give a touch of class to your pictures.

(1) Focus. The main target. Whatever the other qualities of your picture unless it is sharp in detail it will forever haunt you. Many modern cameras have built in focussing aids while others depend on the operator. Learn to adjust the focus quickly remembering it is sometimes quicker to move a pace or two than fiddle with the controls.

(2) Composition. Try and visualise the finished picture. Look for a balance of contrasts. In general a river scene without an angler is like bacon without eggs or Torville without Dean. Long distance angling shots are usually a failure. Close ups are the thing. Top class leaping trout pictures are as scarce. When your mate lands a good fish don't rush things. Make sure there is no fussy background so that he stands out. Try to have him stay at the river's edge. Don't press the button until you have the sun or good light on his face. Encourage him to smile — after all — he should be happy! Have him rest the fish in the current until you are ready and if it is in a net so much the better. Never have an angler standing with a trout dangling from his finger. Far better he kneels, holding the fish by head and tail, fingers behind, flank towards you. Have him adjust the fish so that the lovely glint on the flank is highlighted. Press the button, thank both of them and return the fish.

(3) Scenic. Fishing is not all fish. Trout fishing usually takes us into the most delightful surroundings and pictures are hard to resist. We become trigger happy. Slow down. Choose the scene carefully and shoot only in sunshine unless you want a moody picture. Choose unusual angles remembering that some of the best shots are taken from a height. Try and include a splash of foreground colour if possible such as a vivid green mossy bank, a cluster of sand primrose or bright red fireweed. Filming through the edge of overhanging willow leaves makes a soft picture frame. Ration the sky to the upper third of the picture and remember, a large expanse of river with glare is most uninteresting. The exception is wind ruffle on a lake in sunshine but again try for height.

Knots

Until the beginner learns to tie secure knots this aspect of troutfishing is a source of worry. They are our Achilles heel, parting when we least expect it so it pays handsomely to select knots that can be trusted. There are many different kinds of knots used by anglers and this in itself is confusing. Once learnt and used with confidence it pays not to change a particular knot for another. The trout will soon tell you which are dependable.

Types of Knots

Leader to fly line, Nail or Needle Knot

This knot is used to attach the leader to the line. Other methods can be used such as tying a crude knot, or a loop in the line and leader but the nail or needle knot is much neater. Overlap the line and leader, the line end short. Place the nail or needle against line and leader at the junction and wind the butt end of leader back around line, leader, and nail/needle towards the end of line. If a needle, thread the leader butt through the eye and pull the needle and line under the leader wraps and out up the line. The fingers of one hand should be holding the long end, or tippet end of the leader while the needle is withdrawn and helping the knot wraps tighten. When

secure tighten the choking coils even more by holding the leader with one hand and with pliers pull the butt end of the leader. Surplus ends of line and leader can then be cut or clipped very close to the knot, the line end at an angle.

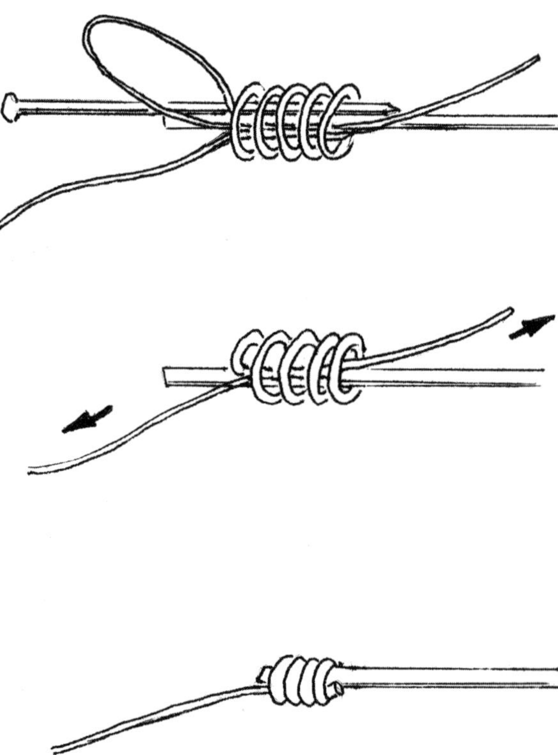

The Nail Knot

As a refinement a needle can be inserted into the flyline and brought out through the end of the line, the leader tip threaded through the needle eye and pulled to emerge out of the fly line centre. Nice but not necessary.

Nylon to nylon. Blood knot or Triple Surgeons knot.

Blood Knot

Considered by some anglers to be a devilish knot to tie, once mastered it becomes the most favoured. I can't remember learning my method, it just seems to have emerged. It works for me so here it is. Overlap the two sections of nylon (keep any two within two standard diameters) leaving approximately 7 centimetres free ends. Pinch junction with fingers and wrap five turns around thicker nylon. Change fingers. Wrap similar turns around finer nylon. With thick nylon held in one hand and fine in the other, push the twists towards the centre where a small loop will be formed. Pick thin end of nylon and thread it through the loop. Pinch this with fingers. Pick thick end of nylon and thread through loop in OPPOSITE direction. Hold the half formed knot in fingers while pulling the short ends. With a little practice you will know when to release the knot and let the continuing pull draw the knot to its final tension. Clip off the ends close to knot.

Triple Surgeons Knot.

Just as effective as the Blood Knot and probably easier to tie the Triple Surgeons Knot has the advantage when the angler is desperate to tie on another tippet in fading light. Overlap the two sections of nylon leaving approximately 5 centimetres free ends. Form a loop, gather the short end of the heavier nylon and the added nylon and take the pair three turns around the loop. Pull all four sections and the knot is complete apart from cutting the appropriate ends. Ideal for adding a dropper to a leaders by allowing a longer end to the heavier nylon.

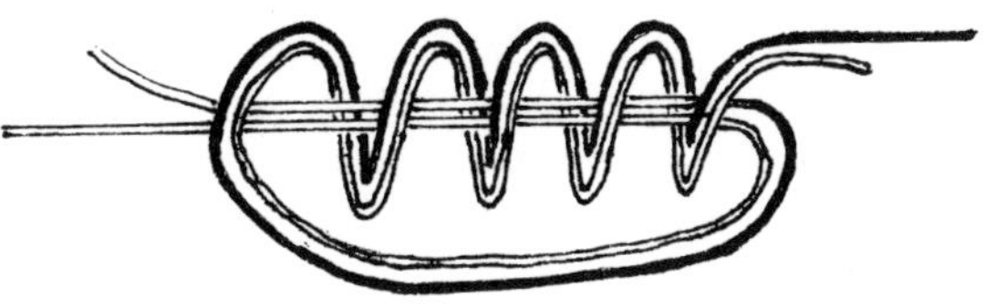

Hook to nylon

Half Barrel or Half Blood

A simple knot but tied properly a secure one. Pass the nylon through the hook eye and wrap it around the nylon stem keeping a nylon loop near the hook eye. Five turns are sufficient then pass the end of the nylon through the nylon loop next to the hook eye and slide tight. Cut away surplus nylon.

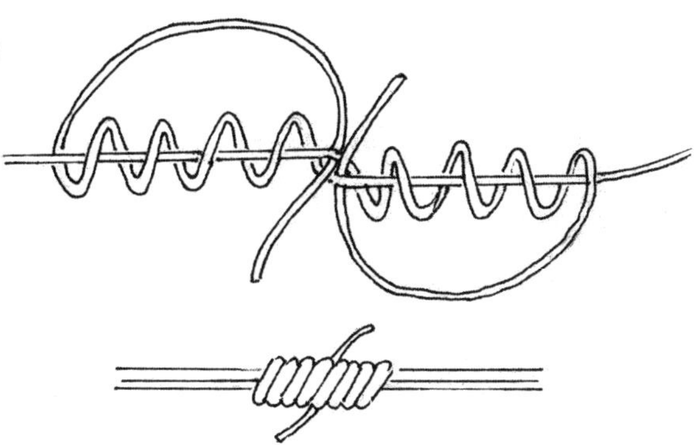

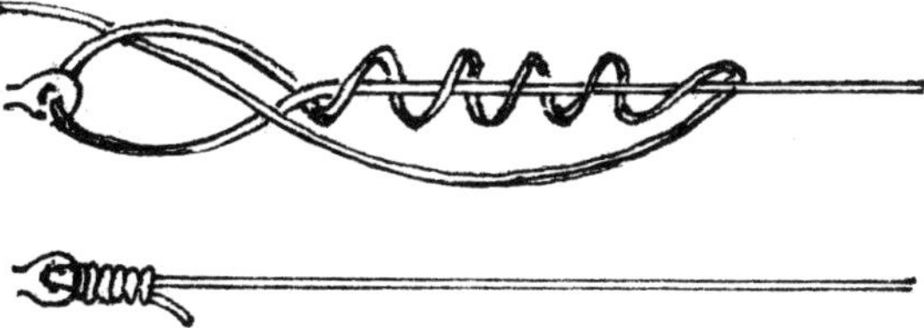

Knot strength

Depsite the many theories on knot strength, the advantage of one knot over the other, there is one way to make sure the knot can be relied on. Simply take the nylon firmly both sides of the knot and concentrate on this. Imagine an angry 2 kilogram trout on the end of the nylon and pull as hard as he would. If it breaks you are lucky. It may well have been a poor knot and you have saved a disappointment. When all is said and done, if the knot stands up to YOUR test what does it matter what kind of knot it is.

Nylon — a warning

While new brands of nylon now on the market claim high breaking strength for small diameter, there is a price to pay. These nylons are prestretched and, although they meet strength requirements, are more likely to snap with a sudden pull. Nylon monofilaments of 5 x or 6 x should be used with caution and reserved for ultra shy trout. Try it. Slowly stretch the nylon. Very strong. Now give it a very sharp tug. The minimum pull required to snap it will surprise you. After working hard to hook a wary trout, what a shame to have the nylon break. If a trophy trout, it may break your heart as well.

Leaders

Leader design is a matter of choice. One simple method is to buy a continuous tapered leader tapering to 3 x (approx 2.7 kg) and add a 100 cm length of 4 x (approx 2.4 kg) spool nylon. A general use knotted leader can be tied using monofilament nylon sections to the following formula:— Bub 0.18 (100 cm). Taper .015/.012/.010/.008 (28 cm). Tippet .006 (100cm). Total length 3.12 metre.